Epic Television Miniseries

Epic Television Miniseries

A Critical History

JOHN DE VITO *and*
FRANK TROPEA

McFarland & Company, Inc., Publishers
Jefferson, North Carolina, and London

For our parents:
David and Rose Tropea
John and Michelina De Vito

Who knew all along that
even the purest gold
passes through the fiercest fire.

All photographs are provided by Photofest

LIBRARY OF CONGRESS CATALOGUING-IN-PUBLICATION DATA

De Vito, John, 1953–
    Epic television miniseries : a critical history /
John De Vito and Frank Tropea.
       p.   cm.
    Includes bibliographical references and index.

    ISBN 978-0-7864-4149-5
    softcover : 50# alkaline paper ∞

    1. Television mini-series—United States—History and
criticism.   I. Tropea, Frank, 1949– . II. Title.
PN1992.8.F5D42   2010
791.44'75—dc22   2009043326

British Library cataloguing data are available

©2010 John De Vito and Frank Tropea. All rights reserved

*No part of this book may be reproduced or transmitted in any form
or by any means, electronic or mechanical, including photocopying
or recording, or by any information storage and retrieval system,
without permission in writing from the publisher.*

Front cover: Jeremy Irons as Charles Ryder, Diana Quick as Lady
Julia Flyte, and Anthony Andrews as Lord Sebastian Flyte in
Brideshead Revisited, 1982 (Granada Television/PBS/Photofest);
background ©2010 Shutterstock

Manufactured in the United States of America

McFarland & Company, Inc., Publishers
  Box 611, Jefferson, North Carolina 28640
    www.mcfarlandpub.com

Contents

Introduction   1

Chapter 1 • Beginnings: The Melodramatic Impulse   9
Chapter 2 • The Triumph of the Heroic Slave   30
Chapter 3 • The Extraordinary Ordinary   53
Chapter 4 • Visions, Values and the Void   81
Chapter 5 • Transitional Places   102
Chapter 6 • The Lady Is a Champ   127
Chapter 7 • Outer and *Outré* Spaces   154

Afterword: Where We Are and Where Are We Going   177
Epic Miniseries Credits   179
Chapter Notes   199
Bibliography   207
Index   211

Introduction

> *The miniseries, at its best, offers a unique televisual experience, often dealing with harrowing and difficult material structured into an often transformatory narrative. The time lapse between episodes allows occasion for the television audience to assimilate, discuss and come to terms with the difficulties of the narrative. The extended narrative time offered by serialization makes possible the in-depth exploration of characters, their motivations and development, the analysis of situations and events. But the conclusive narrative resolution of the series, also allows for evaluation and reflection.*[1]
> — Margaret Montgomerie

SIZE MATTERS. Indeed it is not going too far to say that ultimately, size is all! For a full validation of that fact, all one has to do is consider the monolithic obsession with the concept of "largeness" as it developed in the history of the epic miniseries made for American television audiences. Not only is size a factor in the strong emphasis placed on the amplification of running time (the typical miniseries of the Golden Age of the Epic Miniseries [1974–1989] ran from eight to twelve hours), size also gets factored into the equation by such distinctive tropes of the serial drama as enormous casts (often numbering well into the thousands); fullness or density of reference; lush, high-end production values; superb atmospherics of place; and, of course, the larger-than-life variety of mythic characters associated with the classic epic miniseries. Referring to the characters as mythic is especially appropriate. And it is for this reason, we shall argue, the epic miniseries can very well be viewed as the stuff of classic myth. For at its deepest level, the epic miniseries truly is a highly wrought and richly detailed myth in which the trajectory of the epic narrative follows all the classic stages of the mythical hero and heroine: from adventure to departure, initiation, a mysterious journey to the Lifeforce, transformation and, finally, apotheosis.[2]

Traditionally, the epic miniseries functioned much like some great oral epic, depending crucially upon its mythic characters and formulaic narrative structure to keep its complex, multi-leveled plot humming along at a swift, often cliffhanger-filled pace. The standard epic miniseries tended to contain one or more — usually many more — of these key ingredients: square-jawed heroes; supportive wives; shockingly beautiful, seductive mistresses and fiendish villains; liberal amounts of poverty, and even more liberal amounts of fame, fortune, intrigue and suspense; war, and most particularly World War II; torture and human suffering of every conceivable kind; seduction (of many, many different varieties), rape, murder, mayhem, and suicide; alcoholism, adultery, drug abuse and plenty of sadomasochism; mysterious appearances and mysterious disappearances; a lusty heiress or two; skeletons pulled out of closets and skeletons that should have remained locked in those closets; the Ku Klux Klan, Nazis and Communists; forced marriages, lots of bad marriages, divorce, and amnesia; naked ambition and nakedness in general; a great deal of vengeance; and an ending that generally struck an amazingly happy note no matter what may have transpired before. Some of the more memorable characters who peopled this highly addictive televisual construct and have found a way to enter our consciousness include: Tom and Rudy Jordache, Julie Prescott (*Rich Man, Poor Man*, ABC, 1976); Kunta Kinte, Kizzy, Chicken George (*Roots*, ABC, 1977); Rudi, Karl, and Inga Weiss (*Holocaust*, NBC, 1978); John Blackthorne, Lady Mariko (*Shogun*, NBC, 1980); Charles Ryder, Sebastian and Julia Flyte (*Brideshead Revisited*, PBS, 1981); Pug Henry, Aaron and Natalie Jastrow (*The Winds of War, War and Remembrance*, ABC, 1983, 1988–89); Father Ralph de Bricassart, Meggie Cleary (*The Thorn Birds*, ABC, 1983); Philip Marlow, Nurse Mills (*The Singing Detective*, PBS, 1988); Gus McCrae, Woodrow Call, Lorena Wood, Clara Allen (*Lonesome Dove*, CBS, 1989).

But what were such larger-than-life characters supposed to be all about anyway? Who were they exactly, all these towering, square-jawed heroes and beautiful heroines who dared to venture out onto that vast formulaic landscape of the epic miniseries? And what were they like, these highly adventuresome and highly mythic men and women? Well, actually, they were quite an interesting variety of extraordinary presences upon whom we will bestow such curious names as the Heroic Slave, the Adventurer, the Wife, the Whore, and, later, the Avenging Angel. Iconic stereotypes from the start, they were essentially designed for the same desired effect: to command the full attention of the American television audience, and keep that audience glued to the TV for the duration of the miniseries. And that is in fact what all five types accomplished, for the most part, and a great deal more. The early years of the epic miniseries are important, not just because they provide us with a deeper appreciation and fuller understanding of how these five types operate, but also because four of the five were introduced to audiences very early on.

The Heroic Slave

In the beginning, there was the figure of the Heroic Slave. Although this might initially strike us as a contradiction in terms, it is not. Despite the less than satisfactory circumstances of his lot in life, the Heroic Slave still possessed the attractive attributes of the traditional mythical hero: bravery, a keen intelligence, and true nobility of spirit. But heavy with disadvantage, his world was a teleological closed-off site of crushing limitation, which nonetheless could not stop him from dreaming of something beyond those limitations. Two excellent examples of such an intolerable televisual space are projected onto the American South of Kunta Kinte at the time of slavery as depicted in *Roots*, and the profoundly anti–Semitic Nazi Germany of brothers Rudi and Karl Weiss depicted in *Holocaust*.

The Adventurer

Not too long after the debut of the Heroic Slave, a second mythic figure made his debut on the epic miniseries scene — the Adventurer. Although not as legendary a type as the Heroic Slave (owing, principally, to the lofty canonical status the latter came to achieve as a result of his appearances in *Roots* and *Holocaust*), the Adventurer is, hands down, the most popular of all five types. Upon first encountering the Adventurer, we cannot help but be struck by how much more inviting a place his world is compared to the one occupied by the Heroic Slave. Because of this, we tend to view the Adventurer as the very embodiment of a character destined for a more promising future. In fact, the future seems to be offering him one exciting adventure after another. What the Heroic Slave was only permitted to dream about suddenly seemed a real possibility for the Adventurer. And much of this was usually connected to the American ideals of wide-open spaces, the connection back to the openness of Eden: the visionary equation between an Edenic pastoral and the inviting sense of an endless space always beyond the horizon. Therefore, how could we not also view the Adventurer as someone who, if he did not already have it all, was fast on his way to acquiring it all for himself? And yet, for all his admittedly appealing heroic activity, his indefatigable optimism, and his high hopes for a more promising future, the Adventurer could also strike us as something of a naïve figure, ultimately as trapped and defeated in his own way as was the Heroic Slave. For he, like his less privileged predecessor, was still a victim of the often-brutal consequences of being stuck in time and space. Two paradigmatic incarnations of this mythic type can be found in the dashing characters of John Blackthorne in *Shogun*, and in the ultimate adventurous patriarch Pug Henry in both *The Winds of War* and its even more magisterial sequel *War and Remembrance*.

The Wife and the Whore

Standing faithfully by the Heroic Slave and Adventurer (or, as was often the case, sprawled out in a state of seductive repose) were the third and fourth types: the Wife and the Whore. Of course, since the world of American television was dominated by men, it should come as no great surprise to us that women were, for the most part, closed out of all major creative decision making. As a result the figure of the female as depicted in the epic miniseries was typically imagined in the most stereotypical terms possible: in the sexist dyadic configuration of either the Wife or the Whore.

As their titles clearly indicate, the primary purpose of these two great archetypes was to provide comfort and support to the poor, beleaguered hero in any way, shape, or form she possibly could. Expectedly, the role of the Wife was by far the more reactive of the two types. Besides offering apparently inexhaustible quantities of wifely support, love, and caring, she was there for procreative purposes. Bell, the loyal wife of Kunta Kinte, and the unfaithful Rhoda, the not so loyal wife of Pug Henry, provide memorable examples of this type.

Infinitely more proactive than the Wife, the Whore functioned primarily in miniseries of this genre to provide the hero with unending quantities of recreational sex and erotic fantasy. An elegantly refined, most subtle depiction of this mythic type occurred with the memorable character of the young and beautiful Englishwoman Pamela Tudsbury in *The Winds of War* and *War and Remembrance*. First, Pamela falls in love with the very much married and very much older Pug; then, after he is successful in divorcing the increasingly irrelevant Rhoda, Pamela is redeemed when he asks her to become the next Mrs. Pug Henry. And with the simple placing of a golden ring on her finger, Pamela is at once transformed from the scandalous Whore to the respectable figure of the Wife, Madonna, and Conjugal Saint. So codified did these two types become for women, the only way an actress could individualize the mythic type was by towering above its limitations through sheer acting talent alone.

The Avenging Angel

Later, a fifth figure would join the other four mythic types in the epic miniseries pantheon. By far the most mythical of all, the Avenging Angel is distinguished by the possession of a decidedly otherworldly set of characteristics. Usually deeply enigmatic and mysterious, the type thrives in a special space of revelatory apocalypse, defying all prior notions of time and space and gender. Such an exalted position allows for the transcendence of all the requirements of formal and aesthetic closure, which always hindered the other four types. This enables the acquiring of a new perspective of totally visionary, even psychic, mystical wisdom, understanding and, ultimately, freedom. No longer held back by any limitations at all, the Avenging Angel is free in other matters as well. Some new zone of distinction seems to have opened up in which all things are suddenly possible. Often rather androgynous in nature and appearance, the Avenging Angel could be either male or female, shooting far above and beyond all the confinements of the usual gender prejudices and boundaries— although, for the most part, the type usually did take the form of the female sex. One of the first and more memorable incarnations of the type comes in the superb television adaptation of *Tales of the City* (PBS, 1994), in the magical transgendered figure of the flamboyant Anna Madrigal. Other no less memorable incarnations of the Avenging Angel include the 100-year-old Christ-like Mother Abigail in the epic TV miniseries version of Stephen King's novel *The Stand* (ABC, 1994), and the AIDS-stricken hero Prior Walter and the Angel of America in *Angels in America* (HBO, 2003).

Program Notes

Although the five mythic types give the impression of being distinctly American, the televisual landscape they inhabited did not originate in this country. It actually began in the form of the popular BBC–produced English serial radio dramas of the 1930s and 1940s, which, in turn, evolved into the BBC–produced English serial television dramas of the 1950s and 1960s. The details of this history, along with how these serial dramas were eventually "Americanized" for this nation's television audiences, will be traced in Chapter 1, "Beginnings: The Melodramatic Impulse." The terms and boundaries of our inquiry will also be established in Chapter 1. Specifically, we believe that a systematic, critical analysis of a select group of epic miniseries will allow us to demonstrate how the form was first born, thrived, fell and was ultimately resurrected and reconfigured, mainly through the auspices of cable television in general and HBO in particular. We also believe an extensive study of this select group of programs will provide us with a great deal of valuable cultural information.

We should note here how we came to select the epic miniseries we cover. Our main criterion was to focus mainly on those best received by both critics and television audiences at the time of their initial broadcast. In some cases, however, we decided to examine shows that for one reason or another have been underappreciated or simply overlooked. Chapter 1 will conclude with a close reading of the enormously popular miniseries *Rich Man, Poor Man*. The overall importance of this show cannot be overstated. Not only did it open up fertile creative ground for the realization of the first four of the mythic types, but *Rich Man, Poor Man* was also the prime reason the epic miniseries landed on the televisual map in the first place, singlehandedly ushering in the Golden Age of the Epic Miniseries.

Chapter 2, "The Triumph of the Heroic Slave," focuses on two Americanized, didactic, and enormously successful responses to the melodramatic histrionics of *Rich Man, Poor Man*. The first of these programs, *Roots*, marked the most serious attempt up to that time by American television to address the problematic issue of slavery and the catastrophic effects of the nation's continuing racial divide. Similarly, the second program, *Holocaust*, addressed anti–Semitism and the Holocaust of World War II. It is interesting to note that in each miniseries the subject matter concerns the issue of man's inhumanity to man, making it the unlikely source of the grand spectacle that drives the epic narrative onward, as does that most persistent motif of the epic miniseries— the idea of the regaining of an Edenic paradise through the means of never-ending spatial movement. Although it is true that both *Roots* and *Holocaust* were overwhelming popular successes and received universal critical acclaim, and despite their now legendary status, neither of them has been exempt from heated critical debate over the years.

Chapter 3, "The Extraordinary Ordinary," continues our critical analysis of the epic miniseries with readings of four shows that feature the dashing figure of the Adventurer as protagonist. In each of these, we are presented with a fundamentally self-centered (and even, at times, narcissistic) hero whose personal welfare is closely connected to the importance of his ability to act within the rigorous framework of historical time. In other words, the Adventurer's own identity and the course of his private destiny, as well as the destinies of others, become one and the same. As will become evident, whether the Adventurer is fully aware of it or not, the way he responds to the specific context of his unique historical positioning will often take ironic forms leading up to unforeseen consequences for everyone involved. Further, all four of the shows examined in this chapter are nourished by the goal of regaining an Edenic space (closely connected to the figure of Woman). We can also safely say each benefited from being made during the highest peak of the golden age of the epic miniseries, a period when the melodramatic impulse of *Rich Man, Poor Man* and the didactic response of *Roots* and *Holocaust* became wedded to a more lavish and lyrically poetic form of epic artistic expression. The four major epic miniseries considered in this chapter are *Shogun*, *Brideshead Revisited*, *The Thorn Birds*, and *Lonesome Dove*.

Chapter 4, "Visions, Values and the Void," takes up the phenomenon of producer/director Dan Curtis and his obsessive ten-year quest to realize his dream of transforming author Herman Wouk's Tolstoyan sagas *The Winds of War* and *War and Remembrance* into what is, perhaps, the ultimate American epic miniseries. In so doing, Curtis also succeeded in creating what is arguably the definitive portrait of the aging Adventurer as Great Patriarch in the somewhat overdetermined protean figure of hero Pug Henry (memorably portrayed by iconic superstar Robert Mitchum). While *The Winds of War* ranks third in the Nielsen ratings as the most-watched miniseries in the history of television, its mega-miniseries sequel (despite that program's obvious excellences) generated a shockingly poor audience response. In fact, as the overall quality of *War and Remembrance* "rose with every massive installment, its ratings declined just as measurably, and by the time the miniseries was over, so, too, were the boom years for epic TV miniseries."[3] Along with considering why this was the case, this chapter will also take up the matter of some of the interesting ways the form altered over time, until it virtually deconstructed itself toward the end of the 1980s and into the 1990s.

Chapter 5, "Transitional Places," addresses some of the excellent epic miniseries made in foreign lands, as well as the changing nature of those made in this country. Whereas epic miniseries made for American television tended to adhere to codified formulaic conventions, as the 1980s progressed, they also began to exhibit surprising signs of formal and contextual experimentation in terms of their ultimate presentation. At the same time, epic miniseries of other countries tended to exhibit a much bolder, infinitely more experimental creative attitude, resulting in some of the greatest work ever presented on television. Even though this aesthetic and theoretical language would appear to be the very antithesis of that used by the creators of the American epic miniseries, miniseries from foreign countries nonetheless ended up exerting a noticeable influence on the American epic miniseries of the 1990s and 2000s. This chapter will look at three of the best foreign epic miniseries—*Scenes from a Marriage* (PBS, 1974), *Berlin Alexanderplatz* (1980), and *The Singing Detective* (PBS, 1988). It will conclude with a survey of some of the transitional American epic miniseries of the 1980s that helped move the genre into the future.

Chapter 6, "The Lady Is a Champ," addresses the birth of a new kind of epic miniseries experience. Made in the radically altered televisual landscape of the 1990s, which was marked by the ever-increasing fragmentation of the nation's TV audiences, the programs of this decade reflect the dramatic shift the genre made to insure its future survival. With the monopoly of the three major networks considerably diluted, the halcyon days of the epic miniseries of the 1970s and 1980s were all but finished. Faced with the increasingly withering response of the viewing public (evidenced by the dismal showing in the-Nielsen ratings for many miniseries), it became painfully clear that the once mighty televisual genre had fallen out of favor.

That said, this mainly antagonistic climate still saw the creation of some truly amazing miniseries. Curiously, rather than exploring complex interior spaces, these shows journeyed off into creative spaces of a more fantastic and mystic sort of spectacle, both literally and figuratively. (The powerful influence of foreign miniseries contributed to this fact.) A reading of two of these texts, *Tales of the City* (PBS, 1994) and *The Stand* (ABC, 1994), provides us with examples of miniseries that found deeply self-reflective, ironic, post-modernistic approaches to respond to and even escape from the dwindling creative opportunities of the 1990s. Significantly, these, along with several other 1990s texts—*The Kennedys of Massachusetts* (ABC, 1990), *Voice Within: The Lives of Truddi Chase* (CBS, 1990), *Darlings of the Gods* (A&E, 1991), *Queen* (CBS, 1993),

The Oldest Living Confederate Widow Tells All (CBS, 1994), *Liz: The Elizabeth Taylor Story* (NBC, 1995), *True Women* (CBS, 1997), *Joan of Arc* (CBS, 1999) — serve as our introduction to the fifth and final type in the epic miniseries pantheon — the Avenging Angel. This results in a dramatic shift towards a post-racial, post-sexist, gender stereotype–defying utopian world of cosmic possibility and universally. Most important, all these miniseries elevate Woman as never before, while they also look backward in the way they desire to reconnect with the glory of the cinematic and televisual past while pointing the way towards the future of the genre as the new millennium approached.

Chapter 7, "Outer and *Outré* Spaces," examines the late 1990s text *From the Earth to the Moon* (HBO, 1998) and two ultra–post-modern new millennial epic miniseries, *The 10th Kingdom* (ABC, 2000) and *Angels in America* (HBO, 2003). In each, some interesting new developments can be seen. Although Woman, usually in the form of the Avenging Angel, still plays an important role, there is a new ambivalence expressed towards the figure. Along with this, we also see traces of what can best be referred to as the rise of a new, 21st century imperialistic authoritarianism. As a result, a distinctive sense of totalitarian grandiosity seeps into these three new millennial texts and several others.

We conclude the book with an afterword, "Where We Are and Where Are We Going," in which we put forward our belief that the epic miniseries, now often considered dead, is perhaps only playing possum. For despite everything, one thing remains constant: the story of the epic miniseries of America is America's story.

Lastly, we believe this project is of significance since no close, systematic study has yet been carried out on the development of the epic miniseries of American television.[4] If our approach is but one of the many that a work of criticism might possibly take, we sincerely hope it provides readers with a badly needed guide to the essentials and initiates an ongoing critical dialogue.

Chapter 1

Beginnings:
The Melodramatic Impulse

The Form Is Born

The epic miniseries, as we have come to understand the term today, did not begin in this country. Rather it developed out of the enormous success on American public television of such acclaimed British serial dramas as *The Forsyte Saga* (BBC, 1969), *The Six Wives of Henry VIII* (BBC, 1970), and *Elizabeth R* (BBC, 1971). But before going into just why and how these British programs came to influence those of this country, we will first take up the issue of how the former grew directly out of the radio serials made by the BBC during the 1930s and 1940s.

Robert Giddings and Keith Selby explain that the British serial TV miniseries of the 1950s grew out of the radio serial adaptations and dramatizations that were "put together in the early days of radio drama between the two great wars. The genre emerged in the context of the BBC monopoly."[1] The authors then point out that the great prototype of all British radio serial drama was the 1939 adaptation of the lushly romantic novel *The Prisoner of Zenda*. In an article for *Radio Time*, Jack Inglis, the adapter of the book for radio broadcast, laid out what would later become the golden rules of classic serial adaptation:

> The story is simple, with clear cut characters, [and] falls easily into nine episodes.... It always seems to me that it is the first duty of an adapter to reproduce in another medium the original flavour and atmosphere of the book. And so I have chosen the method which is nearest to the novel. Rudolph Rassendyll tells the story himself, introducing each episode.... I have stuck to the dialogue and, what is more important, I have stuck to the story....[2]

However, despite his claim, Inglis did not stick to the story completely. To make it clearer and easier to understand for radio audiences, he found it necessary to compress various characters into one, simplify the plotline, and fold the two great castles of the novel into only one even greater castle. Obviously his changes paid off. The epoch-making *Prisoner of Zenda* not only became an instant sensation from the time of its first broadcast, but also ended up serving as the great prototype for all radio serials that followed it.

So successful did these radio dramas ultimately become, the BBC went on to gain a total monopoly over Britain's public service broadcasting. But that would end, as all good things eventually must, when the post-war Labour government broke the monolithic hold of the media giant, thus ushering in the rise of commercial radio and, later, television, in Britain. Regardless of this governmental victory, the BBC radio serial drama remained incredibly popular with the listening public throughout the 1930s and 1940s.

In the 1950s, the BBC embarked on a most aggressive move into the budding technological realm of television production. Essentially, *The Prisoner of Zenda* prototype was now provided with a new visual dimension. But because of the limitations of early television broadcast, with its technical inability to produce a well-defined image, it was soon deemed necessary that certain adjustments be made to compensate for the lack of visual clarity. This necessity, combined with the economic imperative, led to a strong preference for the use of an interiorized mise-en-scène over a more costly reliance upon elaborate exterior scenery. This stylistic preference established a pronounced emphasis upon theatricality, combined with a heavy dose of soap opera–esque melodramatics. Because the early television camera could not move about with ease, the emphasis was placed on the use of extreme and intensive close-ups in place of lyrical tracking shots. By repeatedly cutting back and forth from one speaking character to another delivering these extended passages of theatrical dialogue, a sense of intense histrionics was conveyed with a minimum amount of technical application.

Like the reliance upon the close-up to convey much with as minimal a means as possible, music was also employed as a way to further intensify narrative, cuing listeners in to those segments of the show meant to convey the strongest dramatic impact. Music also served as a kind of melodic bridge, connecting one serialized weekly episode to that of the following week. Along with adapting the "radio" music model to fit the new dimensions of television, the BBC also adapted radio's sophisticated employment of overall sound technique from one medium to the other. Sound was used much as Russian director Sergei Eisenstein had used cinematic montage in his films, achieving "fades and cross-fades of sound giving similar technical effects as the editing of motion pictures."[3]

Both of these innovations worked so well that the BBC applied them to all the television serials produced, on the assumption that classic novels, colored with liberal amounts of melodramatic excess, made for the very best source material. Among the most favored authors for the process of serialized dramatization were Daniel Defoe, Samuel Richardson, Walter Scott, Charles Dickens, William Makepeace Thackeray, Thomas Hardy, Jane Austen, Wilkie Collins, George Eliot, the Brontës, John Galsworthy, and Arnold Bennett.

In his authoritative study of the history of the British novel, Ian Watt demonstrates the way that serialized novels of the 18th and 19th centuries were principally designed for a predominately female readership:

> Women of the upper and middle classes could partake in few of the activities of their menfolk, whether of business or pleasure. It was not usual for them to engage in politics, business or the administration of their estates, while the main masculine leisure pursuits such as hunting and drinking were also barred. Such women, therefore, had a great deal of leisure, and this leisure was often occupied by omnivorous reading.[4]

But since no creative method is ever totally free of some aesthetic qualifications, in time these British women of the 18th and 19th century came to exert a certain amount of feminine influence on both the choice of subject matter and the way in which the great British novelists designed their episodically constructed novels. The seminal works of Samuel Richardson especially were created, and even altered, out of deference to the opinions made known to the author by his predominately female reading audience. Richardson's legendary pair of literary heroines, Pamela and Clarrisa, were greatly affected by this womanly opinion. The manifestation of the influence of all these 18th and 19th century British women who were avid readers would even come to be felt in the epic American miniseries of the 20th century. One of the ways this influence was realized was in the progressive ideological tendency that ran through several epic miniseries dealing with a marginalized people, such as *Roots* (Blacks), *Holocaust* (Jews), and *Angels in America* (gay AIDS victims). Another less positive way can be seen in the ambiguous attitude often expressed towards the implicit power of female characters in many epic miniseries. Later we shall see how these two tendencies form a dynamic narrative tension that cannot always be so easily resolved.

From the Old World to the New

It should probably go without saying that when the time finally did arrive for the powers-that-be running the three major American television networks (ABC, CBS, NBC) to take up the daunting task of first deconstructing, then re-constructing the model of the multi-part British serial dramas of the 1960s and early 1970s to fit the tastes of American television audiences, they had assumed for themselves a seemingly impossible task. After all, how could they possibly find a way to transform such literary and exceedingly "high-brow" British fare, making it palatable to what they perceived to be the mostly non-literary, "middle-to-low-brow" tastes of the mass of American television viewers? No, theirs was clearly not an enviable task. Fortunately for these television executives, they did at least have before them a more practical, Americanized working model to draw upon for creative influence: the phenomenal box office success of such Hollywood movie blockbusters as *Doctor Zhivago* (1965) and *The Godfather, Part I* and *Part II* (1972, 1974). Like the British television serials, these three epic films were adapted from popular, best-selling novels, resulting in "long complex and historically situated narratives that were both temporally expansive and narratively multilayered."[5]

Thus, after countless corporate meetings, many sleepless managerial nights, and much executive hair-pulling and hand-wringing, an acceptable answer was finally hit upon. Rather than looking to the off-putting literary and historical texts of the British model, the primary inspiration for the epic miniseries made for American television would come from the rather bulky, most popular best-selling novels of the time. It fell to Barry Diller and Martin Starger of ABC to set this course into action. Added pressure was placed on the two men by nervous ABC stockholders. What they wanted with the creation of the new televisual format was nothing less than a way of providing the flagging super-station with some much needed attention and prestige from both critics and the public.

The first part of the Diller/Starger plan began with the purchase in 1971 of the best-selling novel *QB VII* by Leon Uris, which they promptly decided to broadcast over two separate nights. The absorbing tale Uris told on the page was loosely based on his own experience after the writing of his most famous novel, *Exodus*. The story concerns Abe Cady (Ben Gazzara), an American writer being sued for libel in a British court by highly indignant Polish doctor Adam Kelno (Anthony Hopkins) over accusations the writer makes, accusing Kelno of having committed horrific pseudo-scientific experiments on prisoners while a surgeon in a gruesome Nazi concentration camp.

Produced by Douglas S. Cramer and directed by Tom Gries, the television version of *QB VII* was presented over two consecutive nights in 1974 (April 29 and 30) to a respectable critical and public response, going on to receive thirteen Emmy Award nominations and winning five. Part of what made the miniseries so successful was the way it criss-crossed seamlessly, in a most Dickensian style, between the details of the parallel lives of the two protagonists over an expansive thirty-year time period. During this time, Abe Cady almost inadvertently discovers his Jewish roots and goes on to write an important, best-selling book about what the ravages of the Holocaust meant to his people. Meanwhile, Dr. Adam Kelno is seen selflessly (but narcissistically) devoting his life to public service in the near East and the dismal slums of London. For all his noble deeds, Dr. Kelno is acclaimed and eventually knighted by the Queen. Part two of *QB VII* takes up the labyrinthine workings of the British judicial system, chronicling the vicious lawsuit for libel and the subsequent trial the indignant Dr. Kelno brings against Cady in London's Queen Bench courtroom No. 7.

Aside from getting its fair share of attention from both critics and the viewing public the ultimate success of *QB VII* hinged upon the superb use it made of some extremely important and highly influential technical and aesthetic creative decisions, which would be further refined and elaborated upon by all future epic miniseries. First, the thirty-year narrative sweep of the program (which necessitated a leisurely 6½-hours running time) was presented in a considerable amount of narrative detail, allowing viewers to get to know each of the protagonists much more fully and intimately than would have been possible in a standard two-hour feature-length movie. Second, by utilizing striking historical and iconic backdrops such as World War II, the Nazi concentration camps, the Kuwaiti Desert, the squalor of the postwar London slums, and the stately grandeur of the courtrooms of London, the epic action was provided with a more lavish movie-style form of presentation than was typically seen in television fare of the early 1970s. Third, both characterization and storytelling technique were stripped of a certain amount of literary and psychological complexity, which was replaced by a more direct form of stylization, infusing the former with the stuff of pure archetype and the latter with the manner of the epic and immediacy of myth. Fourth, the inventive concept of using multiple rotating guest stars (John Gielgud, Anthony Quayle, Dame Edith Evans, Jack Hawkins, Juliet Mills, Sam Jaffee) throughout the course of the epic narrative worked both to help hold the viewer's interest and to provide the type of high ratings insurance so cherished by anxious television executives. And, finally, as in the British television model, music was employed to an often stunning effectiveness.

Composer Jerry Goldsmith wrote a magnificent musical score for *QB VII* that was one of the longest and most complex of his career. Particularly impressive was the way the composer used traditional Jewish sacred music for the harrowing scenes taking place in the Nazi concentration camps. Using the text of the Kaddish, the traditional Jewish mourner's prayer, Goldsmith had the members of the Sistine Chapel choir perform the words, in perfect Hebrew, alternately sung and spoken in almost abstracted fragments of evocative sound. John Burlingame observes that the final impact of this technique helped to suggest "that the ghosts of the Jewish victims were all around; the soulful wailing of a women's choir were grim echoing reminders of the hideous experiments that had gone on in these and other places."[6] It was only at the conclusion of the miniseries, which was aptly titled "A Kaddish for the Six Million," that Goldsmith allowed the complete choral performance to be heard in its total brilliance, stirring the soul with its pathos and compassion at the finale. Goldsmith was rightly awarded an Emmy for his eloquent musical score.

Rich Man, Poor Man

Buoyed by the impressive success of *QB VII*, Diller and Starger next turned their attention to purchasing the television rights for novelist Irwin Shaw's 1970 best-selling novel *Rich Man, Poor Man*, with the hope of transforming it into the next successful epic miniseries presentation for ABC. With its twenty-five-year narrative span (encompassing such pressing topics as the end of World War II, the Cold War, the McCarthy era, the war in Vietnam), its classic story of sibling rivalry with the Good Brother versus the Bad Brother, and the many twists-and-turns of its admittedly melodramatic plotline, Shaw's novel looked to have all the earmarks of a considerable television hit for ABC. Yet another benefit of the favorable response to *QB VII* was the executive gamble to extend the television adaptation of *Rich Man, Poor Man* from the originally planned six-hour length to a then unprecedented running time of twelve hours of primetime television. Ironically, even this guarded optimism on the part of the network had little effect on either Irwin Shaw or his high-powered literary agent, Irving "Swifty" Lazar. In fact, upon first learning of ABC's interest in acquiring the rights to Shaw's novel to develop into a possible epic miniseries, Lazar told Ross Claiborne, among several others, "A miniseries? Like those British things on public television? It'll never work here." Feeling as negatively as he did about the future prospects of *Rich Man, Poor Man* ever being transformed into a successful miniseries, Lazar foolishly asked ABC for "no further monies when the show aired, or residual for any repeated showings. Nor did it seem to matter to him that the network would retain all future television rights to the novel's fictional characters."[7] After only one up-front payment of $100,000, Shaw was entitled to not so much as one penny more of all the future profits made by ABC on its epic miniseries presentation of *Rich Man, Poor Man*. Lazar's unfortunate lack of foresight also allowed the network to alter Shaw's novel in whatever way it deemed fit. This would later prove to be a source of some displeasure for the author.

Rich Man, Poor Man tells the story of two brothers: Tom and Rudy Jordache (Nick Nolte and Peter Strauss). The rebellious Tom is cruelly rejected by both of his parents early on. Axel (Edward Asner), his violent, German father, and Mary (Dorothy McGuire), his increasingly embittered, religious-fanatic mother, lavish all of their love and devotion upon their favored elder son Rudy. As the action unfolds, each brother acts according to his prescribed family role. When Julie (Susan Blakely), the young woman whom both brothers admire, is seduced by local rich man Teddy Boylan (Robert Reed), Tom responds by burning down the greenhouse on Boylan's lavish estate, bringing about his own abrupt exile from the town. Ever the opportunist, Rudy uses the matter to further his own personal ambitions.

Axel sends Tom off to live with his wealthy brother Harold (Bo Brundin), where he becomes romantically involved with his uncle's sensuous maid Clothilde (Fionnuala Flanagan). When he learns of the affair, the jealous uncle sends the boy away again. While Tom goes on to a promising boxing career, Rudy aligns himself with wealthy department store tycoon Duncan Calderwood (Ray Milland), getting himself romantically entangled with the elder man's neurotic daughter Virginia (Kim Darby). Julie, despite having made a bad marriage to cynical, alcoholic Willie Abbott (Bill Bixby), becomes a successful writer and later a photographer, and gives birth to son Billy. Axel ends up committing suicide, while Mary grows more embittered and fanatical over her lot in life.

Meanwhile, Tom marries the promiscuous Teresa Santoro (Talia Shire), who eventually runs off with their son Wesley, effectively derailing Tom's boxing career and setting in motion a disastrous course of events. The now-wealthy Rudy, who has avoided getting involved with women, finally convinces the widowed Julie to get married. Although Julie becomes traumatized when she miscarries a baby and learns she can have no other children, Rudy remains fiercely determined to become as successful in politics as he had been in business. His ruthless ambition leads Julie to become a depressed, angry alcoholic.

After Tom has an affair with Linda (Lynda Day George), the wife of mob-connected boxer Joey Quales (George Maharis), then brutally beats up Joey, he is forced to leave America. Tom joins the Merchant Marines, befriends fellow Merchant Marine Roy Dwyer (Herb Jefferson), and makes a mortal enemy of the sadistic Falconetti (William Smith). Tom and Roy purchase a luxury yacht (which Tom names the *Clothilde*, in honor of his first great love), becoming partners in a Mediterranean cruise service catering to the idle rich. Kate, the cook Tom hires to work on the *Clothilde*, soon becomes his new love. She also provides some much-needed mothering to young Wesley, of whom Tom has won custody from Teresa.

Back in America, the combination of Julie's drunken cavorting and his own stubborn rigidity lead to the derailment of Rudy's career in politics and Julie's estrangement from her son Billy. The couple escapes to Europe, joining Tom and the now pregnant Kate to celebrate their wedding day. But Julie's alcoholism ruins everything when she runs off, gets drunk, and erotically entangles herself with the vengeful Falconetti. Although Tom does rescue Julie from Falconetti's evil clutches, Falconetti gets his final revenge when he sends his henchmen to stab Tom to death. While the bereaved Kate scatters Tom's ashes into his beloved Mediterranean, Rudy and Julie move towards reconciliation.

As this summary indicates, the plot of *Rich Man, Poor Man* is crammed full of so many moments of pure melodrama that much of it comes across like a romantic-opera-novel-for-television, jam-packed with passage after passage of absurdly lyrical, operatic intensity. At times it even looks as if the televisionmakers are aiming for the narrative naïveté we associate with classic operas by Verdi, Puccini, Wagner, and Bizet. With this, they also seem to be quite willing to cast aside such matters as psychological believability and logical reason in favor of full-scale utopian romanticism, lyrical visualized poetry, and fantastic myth. Yet when *Rich Man, Poor Man* premiered in 1976, audiences had no problem accepting the show's lapses in probability, operatic characters, and the breakneck twists-and-turns of its melodramatic plot. Like heroic figures out of classic opera and myth, the lives of Rudy, Tom, and Julie become a compellingly addictive viewing experience, even when what is happening to them does not always remain in the realm of the believable. Perhaps because all three characters were so quickly established as larger-than-life mythic types, audiences had no trouble with their drawing freely upon metaphorical images of charged-up power and spectacular passions. In fact, it is this operatic and mythic conceptualization of character that provides the epic miniseries with its unique center, giving it a distinctive and at times even oddly subversive eroticized, emotional aura of its own. So even if *Rich Man, Poor Man* is one of the most wildly melodramatic, absurdly over-the-top, baroquely operatic of all the great epic miniseries, it clearly possessed the ability to strike some deep, secret psychic chord in audiences, which comes close to the deliciously sublime and strangely exultant. Once again, mythic archetypes resonate in our collective consciousness.

It is worth saying something about three important assumptions that underline the perspective of the agenda of melodrama. These three assumptions will also play a major role in many of the epic miniseries later documented in this book:

(1) As a Hollywood genre convention, melodrama breaks away from the traditionally more realist codes that dominate classic Hollywood films and television, and can therefore disrupt the ideology that informs them.
(2) The audience can then suddenly be "distanced" from its ideological position by the operations of the film or television production.
(3) Most essentially, the ideology can be defined through the analysis of film and television.[8]

The view that Hollywood film and television drama has a critical, self-conscious potential is signified by the melodramatic view of life put forth by *Rich Man, Poor Man*. Such a view is not always happy and even has a decidedly reactionary aspect that connects it to the conventions of an archly conservative 19th century ethos. At it best, this ethos can surprise us by taking on a more generous and forgiving sensibility, like that of Dickens in his mode as a great social critic of the darker aspects of the Victorian era.

The question boils down to this: how are we supposed to read a text like *Rich Man, Poor Man* anyway? It should be remembered that despite all of its operatic excesses and the unbelievable machinations of its supercharged plot, the show remains one of the most influential and successful of all the epic miniseries. By "influential" in this context, we mean the expert way epic narrative has been crafted to work out its combustion of images and emotions, while getting the most mileage it can out its classic theme of Good Brother versus Bad Brother and its other mythical characters. Schnayerson relates that the show's exceptionally long gestation period (close to five years) allowed writer Dean Riesner a solid block of time to craft a final script that "had been more carefully written, and rewritten, than those of standard television drama."[9] Riesner's careful crafting of the script aside, it still takes a considerable amount of time to warm up to the problematically drawn, often anti-operatic but still mythic character of Rudy, and to a far lesser extent that of Julie. Much of the time, the ultra-conservative Rudy comes off as so emotionally repressed and pinched, he seems on the verge of shutting down completely. Julie, for all her admittedly appealing larger-than-life, mythic attributes, goes through so many changes in personality, she cannot help but lack a certain psychological credibility. (The exact reasons for the problem with Julie's character are detailed further below.) Only Tom, then, with his always going-against-the-grain, bad-boy attitude, Marlon Brando–esque intensity, and operatic lack of control or restraint of his actions and deeds, always commands our full attention while adding a welcomed edginess to the proceedings.

Perhaps the best way to characterize the epic narrative structure of *Rich Man, Poor Man* is by focusing on the ironic, iconic surface beneath which the life of a character can and does drop off, plunging him or her into endless hidden tunnels of melodramatic pain and operatically pitched despair. These tunnels also function as mysterious Gothic subterranean passages and emotion-laden minefields in wait of some poor, unfortunate victim. The main trick of why this works as well as it does in *Rich Man, Poor Man* has to do with the way mise-en-scène, spectacle, and a certain Douglas Sirkian distanciation[10] is used to keep audiences perched on the edge of their seats and guessing what is going to happen next for the full twelve-hours of its running time.

Closely connected to this device is the way the program draws upon, and further embellishes, the four of the narrative tropes first established by *QB VII* in 1974. The first of these tropes comes in the form of the narrative patterning, which takes full advantage of the rather broadly drawn panoramic sweep of post–World War II American history to create a dazzling televisual backdrop with which to illuminate and contextualize the actions of the central characters. Although much of this comes directly from Irwin Shaw's novel, the makers of the miniseries do deserve credit for the way they have stylized and eroticized Shaw's words to create an even stronger visual sense of period feeling and detail, summoning up an entire country and generation. In other words, these artists have developed a highly codified televisual style that has the power to form the constantly changing, forever shape-shifting mise-en-scène into a thrilling backdrop, insuring that the extravagantly theatricalized, spectacle-laden aspect of the action is kept moving along at a good clip.

An example of this happens in the extended opening, which takes place at the end of World War II on VE Day in 1945. To mark the Allied victory over the Nazis, the townspeople of Port Royal, New York, are out uproariously celebrating the historic milestone in the streets. Suddenly a dazzling display of multi-colored fireworks illuminates the nighttime sky. As drunken soldiers and sailors kiss every attractive young woman in sight, a brass band fills the night air with melodic patriotic tunes. The visual spectacle of the scene and the sexually pumped-up atmospherics have an explosive vitality, an intoxication of movement, music and rhythm. In sharp contrast, the rapid cutting and wide camera angles of the teeming outdoor scenes are replaced by oppressive, statically composed scenes of Axel Jordache toiling away in the shadowy depths of the dark, dank basement of his bakery. As he bakes his multiple loaves of bread in huge fiery ovens, he consumes large quantities of alcohol, loudly singing German songs. Mary appears nervously at the top of the basement stairs to reproach her drunken husband for his behavior. In his own defense, he rudely informs her he is neither American nor German. Instead, he has become merely a miserable man, trapped in Hell forever, baking Parker House rolls. Thus Axel's negative, abrasive nature is firmly established, signified by his heavy consumption of alcohol, profuse sweating, and the raging of the ovens. Is it possible that under a different set of circumstances we might have even found Axel humming Wagnerian tunes over the ovens of Dachau?

Not coincidentally, similar images are also used as signifiers for his son Tom. While the townspeople throw discarded furniture and bundles of wood onto a raging celebratory bonfire, Tom and Claude — his partner-in-crime and best buddy — sarcastically mock the surrounding patriotic fervor. Next comes a scene of Rudy in his bedroom narcissistically examining his reflection in a mirror (this begins a recurring visual association of Rudy to the surface allure of hard-edged, material objects). Mary joyously enters her favored son's bedroom, wraps her arms around him and kisses him. Finally, the third major character, Julie, is introduced. Dressed in a crisp nurse's uniform, she sits by the bedside of a severely wounded soldier, reading from *Gone with the Wind* in a not totally believable, actressy style of voice. With her appearance the use of woman as nurturing, subservient mother-like stereotype is opened up in the order of the epic narrative. Instantly, Julie is linked to the figure of the Good Wife. Later, the mise-en-scène and precise nature of her meaning changes considerably as she is made to signify a different type of narrative agent entirely.

With this technical tour-de-force of televisionmaking, the dynamics of the spatio-temporal framework are memorably established, preparing us for the way the complex sweep of historicity will be transformed into a highly stylized mise-en-scène. Now the story proper can begin. The interplay of history, epic narrative and spectacle provides us with crucial narrative information about character and plot. Not only does this act as a needed form of insurance to keep the sometimes creaky mechanics of the melodramatic storyline moving along, it also helps keep audiences from reaching the conclusion that despite the historical detail being depicted, history is basically being used as a means of transforming "complex historical debates into little more than sexy soap opera fare."[11] Yet even if there were a part of the audience put off by such a reductionist attitude towards historical veracity, the largest part of that audience could not resist the pull of such a specularization of history on the lives and loves of Tom, Rudy, and Julie.

After Tom, the disillusioned patriarch Axel is the second most fascinating character. While serving in World War I as a German soldier, he is badly wounded and left to suffer from a painful, lifelong limp. But far more disastrous than his physical disadvantage, for both himself and his family, are the deeply inflicted psychological wounds that life has inflicted upon him. These inflictions make him a cynical nihilist who mocks the values placed on abstract entities such as the belief in either God or country. Even after he leaves his native Germany, marries the lovely Mary, raises two sons, and opens a successful bakery, none of it helps to temper his inherent dark cynicism. Faced with her husband's profound negativity, heavy drinking, constant womanizing, and boorish behavior toward her, the embittered Mary is sent fleeing into a delusional state of religious fanaticism. The ways their sons respond to the dysfunctional parents is another matter entirely. But as we shall see, the individual responses of Tom and Rudy ascribe to the epic narrative the specifications of the binary scheme that gives *Rich Man, Poor Man* the style and authority to make it the first of the truly great epic miniseries.

RUDY AND TOM—The second of the tropes that *Rich Man, Poor Man* appropriates from *QB VII* concerns the way Reisner has taken the characters of Shaw's novel and re-imagined them to fit the requirements of a televisual context. This is achieved first by stripping them of some of the more complex psychological nuances they possessed on the written page. Next, he fires them up with just enough melodramatic passion and operatic despair to transform them into sheer mythic archetypes. This accomplished, all the ecstasies and dooms of the characters take on the stylized amplification of form over substance in the obvious preference for an exaggerated style of acting and overly dramatic detail. That each of these points has its own value is evident in the way Rudy has been conceived for television. True, he is still the proverbial "Rich Man" of Shaw's novel, only now he is much more than that. He is obviously the "Good Son" as well. It is Rudy who is ostentatiously favored and adored by his parents. And how could they not favor and admire such a son as Rudy? Is he not a perfect example of the "All-American Boy" growing up into the "Super-Rich All-American Tycoon"? This point is signified in the mise-en-scène by the continual association of Rudy with images of wealth and power. The hard-edged perfection of glass, steel, marble, the impeccably manicured lawns and well-appointed estates form the tactile materialization of his most desired vision of a closed-off, perfect world of rigid boundaries, exclusive privilege, and class-conscious affectation. On the surface, Rudy's dubious achievement does seem to invoke the spirit of both the perfect Adventurer and Appollonian Man.

In dialectical opposition to Rudy and everything he signifies, there is the transgressive figure of Tom, the "Poor Man" of the title and the "Bad Son," damned at birth by both parents. Tom's inferior positioning gives his story an incessant furor and intensity. After Tom burns down the wealthy Teddy Boylan's greenhouse, Axel uses the incident to run his son permanently out of town, thus making Tom the Prodigal Son no one ever wants to come home again. And since Tom is usually depicted as such a promiscuous character, forever smoking, drinking, performing badly in school, making trouble, and challenging authority in every way he can, he signifies the uncontrollable force of Dionysian Man. Camille Paglia defines the principles of the binary opposition between the Apollonian and Dionysian in this way:

> The Apollonian and Dionysian, two great Western principles, govern sexual personae in life and art.... Dionysus is identification, Apollo objectification. Dionysus is the empathic, the sympathetic emotion transporting us into other people, other places, other times. Apollo is the hard, cold separatism of Western personality and categorical thought. Dionysus is energy, ecstasy, hysteria, promiscuity, emotionalism — heedless indiscriminateness of idea or practice.... In the West, Apollo and Dionysus strive for victory. Apollo makes the boundary lines that are civilization but that lead to convention, constraint, oppression. Dionysus is energy unbound, mad, callous, destructive, wasteful. Apollo is law, history, tradition, the dignity and safety of custom and form. Dionysus is the *new*, exhilarating but rude, sweeping all away to begin again.... Our story is vast, lurid, and unending.[12]

Of course the fundamental paradox is that for all of Rudy's Apollonian traits, he can still never escape the fact that part of his unwanted and disowned birthright is his inheritance of the worst aspects of both his parents. Like his father, Rudy fails to understand or accept either his own personal identity and autonomy or that of others. This character flaw translates into his failing at everything he attempts in life, except of course when it comes to acquiring more wealth and status. But no matter what he achieves materially, Rudy is left to experience profound disappointment.

From his mother, Rudy lacks the ability to come to terms with the true nature of his own sexuality. After refusing to sleep with the young and nubile Julie, whom he loves, Rudy deals with his sexual frustration by channeling his energies into acquiring more and more wealth and status. But since another part of his birthright includes what his mother refers to as "the family curse," everything

The Proverbial Poor Man: Tom Jordache (Nick Nolte) scraping by in his stint as a boxer. *Rich Man, Poor Man* (ABC, 1976). (Photofest).

Rudy accomplishes in his life is defined by the disasters of his past. In a strange way, such a definition is fueled by both genetics (the sins of the father and mother visited upon the son) and environment (not unlike the tragic fates of the doomed characters trapped in the harsh brutalities of the naturalistic novels of Émile Zola, Frank Norris, and Theodore Dreiser). For much of the time, Rudy is left a vivid figure standing on the threshold of some serious disconnect. Then, making matters even worse, he usually does all he can to deny the reality of his predicament. Although he might see himself as an Adventurer, in actuality he is not a heroical creature. He is much closer to the type of the Slave. Because of the lethal combination of his enslavement to the power of the almighty dollar and his tightly bottled-up emotions and sexuality, his good common sense is impaired. This diminishes him, binding him up in chains even stronger than the ones that confine Kunta Kinte in *Roots* (discussed in Chapter 2).

A key to Rudy's behavior is offered in the writings of one of the most influential social analysts of the mid–1950s, sociologist C. Wright Mills, the author of *White Collar* and *The Power Elite*. Mills believed that a broad "power elite" commanded all of the major hierarchies and organizations of modern American society. This elite "ruled the corporations ... ran the machinery of state ... directed the military establishment."[13] American pressure toward complete conformity as a profoundly damaging malaise that became "deep-rooted" and which led to a generation of men and women who were "alienated from their work, and on the personality market, from the self."[14]

The Mills-defined Rudy is the polar opposite of his brother Tom. Whereas the world Rudy inhabits is a site of cold, hard-edged, Apollonian materialism, the nature of the mise-en-scène surrounding Tom is a virtual panorama of elemental force and cosmic reality: Earth, sky, sun, water, blood, sweat, tears— these are the primal elements that signify his epic narrative space. Much of the time, he stands in direct contrast to the cold light of his brother's Appollonian severity. In an early scene, Tom returns home late one night after a bloody fistfight with a soldier in a movie theater. Upon entering the dark, drab, claustrophobia-inducing bedroom he shares with his brother Rudy, the sweaty, blood-stained Tom strips down to his underwear and climbs into the bed he also shares with Rudy, without first washing. Highly indignant over what he considers his brother's lack of good personal hygiene, Rudy tells Tom he smells foul, like a wild animal. From that point on Tom does everything he can not only to smell like a wild animal, but to act like one too.

Nevertheless, such qualities did not prevent Tom from becoming the character the audience embraced most warmly, nowhere more so than in America. But then again, how could an American audience not have warmly embraced him? He is the most quintessentially American of characters. For implicit within Tom is the American ideal of the mythic pastoral, of the promise of the limitless expanse of space — shooting out, all around, vertically and even more so horizontally — into the endless, far-off distance, an Eden without ending. Moreover, this ideal dates all the way back to the founding of America itself. It is implicit in the ideas and ideals of such great American writers and thinkers as Thomas Jefferson, Ralph Waldo Emerson, Henry David Thoreau, Walt Whitman, Herman Melville, Nathaniel Hawthorne, Stephen Crane, Emily Dickinson, Mark Twain, and many countless others. Space is the American experience. And space also plays into the compulsive drive toward the picaresque, which harkens back to the wide openness of the utopian Eden: the connection between the pastoral vision of Eden and the sense of wide open spaces — the deep blue sea, the fields of golden wheat and grain, the endless, treeless spaces of the Old West — all spreading out forever into an eternity.

Inevitably, Tom's behavior and wanderlust cannot help but get him into big trouble. Yet even on those occasions when things seem on the verge of spinning out-of-control for him, Tom's Dionysian zest for life saves the day. He never abandons the American sense of hope for the future as both his parents have. According to James R. Giles, this happens mainly because "Tom is the very personification of a potentially healthy Dionysian principle in the Jordache family, and he exhibits the capacity to attain a saving totality of self." However, Giles later points out that because Tom is "never shown anything but brutality and rejection by his parents, like his father he starts his sexual education with prostitutes, and he can hardly help but resent the favored Rudy.... Further, he understands the social stigma attached to the family and so constantly lashes out against the world."[15] It is this aspect of Tom's "damaged" personality that makes him a figure of a singular dramatic and tragic power.

Through the character of Tom, we can see how the ideal of American spatiality leads to a compulsion for constant motion, energy, vitality, speed, and space, resulting in the hope of regaining the lost sense of the Edenic. Tom gets a taste of this through the mystical intercession of two remarkable females: Clothilde and Kate. While living in the home of his wealthy uncle Harold, Tom begins his idyllic erotic interlude with the lushly sensuous Clothilde. With her full, voluptuous breasts, fleshy belly, and curvaceous hips, her identity as Uncle Harold's housekeeper drops off. She is transformed into the Mystery of Woman. Closely associated with the attribute of physical nurturance and sustenance, Clothilde signifies Woman as great Earth Mother, canceling out the earlier painful image of Axel as Tyrant Father. But later, when Clothilde strips off her robe, climbing into the bathtub to join Tom, she signifies Woman as pure Erotic Spectacle, opening up the promise of an Edenic paradisiacal garden of fleshly delights. Paradise is regained. No sooner has the mise-en-scène shifted into the luxurious opulence of sexual desire than does Tom's God-like, all-controlling Uncle Harold intervene, spoiling his nephew's chance at being humanized by the healing power of Clothilde's love. With this, taboo becomes totem. The procreative power of Clothilde's womb is transformed into the reactionary force of Uncle Harold's contribution to Tom's doom.

Tom's post–Clothilde existence consists of one picaresque misadventure after another, enslaving him to a chain of confining incidents leading to chaos for himself and others. And as Tom's story becomes this series of misadventures, lacking any clear sense of purpose, the epic narrative feels constructed more as a fragmented mosaic-like structure than a chain of interconnected dramatic events. Strangely, such a structure does have its advantages in that total incoherence gets canceled out as a factor in contributing to confusion, "since disconnection except where edges touch becomes the rule, not the exception."[16] The mosaical arrangement of events also becomes a correlative for Tom's condition, as all the energy he extends produces nothing but more chaos for himself and others.

All of that changes for the better when the wondrous Kate enters his life, who "becomes the virtual reincarnation of Clothilde."[17] Yet, while Clothilde is a signifier for the regaining of the pastoral Edenic idyll, Kate is more a Melvillian signifier of the allure of the vast open seas of *Moby Dick* and *Billy Budd*. Fittingly, the love between Kate and Tom flourishes on the vastness of the open seas. Thus it is through his connection to these two amazing women that Tom is afforded the real possibility of conversion, and therefore a reassuring means of escape from the teleologically closed-off world of *Rich Man, Poor Man*. With this surprising turns of events, hopelessness becomes hope, hate love, chaos celebration, the *Poor Man* rich and the *Rich Man* poor. A final sense of narrative order is restored, and so *Rich Man, Poor Man* is made to seem new (at least as far as Tom is concerned).

JULIE— When Julie appears, clad in only the flimsiest of lingerie and seductively slouching her much-desired body onto the bed, the first great Whore of the epic miniseries is born. That she is also seriously considering the bold offer made by the filthy rich Teddy Boylan of $800 for sleeping with him only reinforces this fact. Although the scene signifies the start of Julie's pragmatic understanding that her beauty and sexuality will gain her entrance into the now closed-off-to-her world of rich and powerful men, there is still an inherent problem with such imagery. It does not jibe with the earlier image of Julie as a warm-hearted schoolgirl administering to the needs of the sick and wounded GIs at the Veteran's Hospital. In that scene, Julie was the symbolic embodiment of the All-American Girl-Next-Door acting out the role of a teenaged Florence Nightingale; in the scene in her bedroom, she is like an American, small-town Moll Flanders or Emma Bovary. As hard as it is to reconcile these two quite different "faces" of Julie (whom we will refer to from here on as Julie #1 and Julie #2), that is only the beginning of the difficulty.

Later, with the $800 she made from sleeping with Teddy Boylan firmly in hand, she heads off to the New York City of the 1950s with the hope of becoming a serious actress in the theater. When this does not pan out, for no apparent logical reason she agrees to marry the frail, emasculated figure of Willie

Abbott. Before our unbelieving eyes, Julie #2 metamorphoses into Julie #3, the long-suffering wife and loving mother, who supports her family of three by working as a writer. After we have had a chance to come to grips with Julie #3, the rug gets pulled out from us yet again, and Julie #4 is born. In this incarnation, she assumes a freer, more liberated stance. Single, sensational, and so very sure of herself, Julie #4 is the Modern Woman as independent divorcée and single mom, supporting herself and her young son with the money she earns as a successful, world-class photographer.

Most inexplicably, Julie #4 suddenly shifts into a more erotically passive mode, becoming Julie #5, the pampered wife of the super–*Rich Man* Rudy Jordache. As Mrs. Rudy Jordache, Julie seems to exist for four purposes only: to nag Rudy; spend his money; drink excessively; and have a series of disastrous, most indiscreet extramarital affairs. Not surprisingly, her over-the-top, self-indulgent, self-destructive behavior leads to one catastrophe after another, similar to the ones Tom creates.

As can only be expected, it becomes nearly impossible to accept such a fragmented character as real. After all, how can five such distinct and different personalities exist within the psyche of one poor woman? A clue to this baffling mystery is found by returning to Shaw's original novel. There we discover that the Julie of the epic television miniseries is actually a composite character, created by folding three of the book's female characters into one. Thus for television, the totality of Julie's personality is actually constructed out of aspects of three totally separate characters: Julie Hornberg, Rudy's first great love; Gretchen Jordache (the elder sister of Rudy and Tom, who even after having had all traces of her existence erased from the text, still manages to survive in the psychological exigencies of Julie #1, #2, and #3); and Jean Prescott (Rudy's alcoholic trophy wife). Shnayerson posits that these three female characters have been folded in a single female character, chiefly as a way to make "the story line easier to follow and perhaps even more compelling for television audiences to follow."[18] Although we do agree with the essential veracity of Shnayerson's claim, we would also propose that in the process of making three women one, scriptwriter Riesner has reached deeply into the dark, hidden recesses of the male creative psyche to envision a single female character of unbelievably excessive sensuality. Moreover, he then projects her into an imaginary televisual site, where it becomes possible to indulge in a certain amount of unrestrained gender essentialism.

Under these conditions, Julie, for better or worse, ends up embodying the concept of Woman as Fetishized Spectacle. As a result, the whole idea of her character gets expressed through the obsessively fetishized motifs of female fashion and glamorous allure, both of which are charted through the various changes in her appearance and style. Every aspect of her makeup, hair, and clothing ultimately connects her to the same sweep of epic history that is the highly stylized, spectacular mise-en-scène, which is also the narrative flow of the epic miniseries. Yet, while the epic narrative of *Rich Man, Poor Man* obsessively documents the continually changing figure of Julie, her presence at the narrative's center does not in any way suggest her centrality to the historical process depicted. True, Julie may personify the young American woman of the 1940s, 1950s, and 1960s to a certain extent, but her behavior is more like that of a young woman of the 1970s, only in historical disguise. Her transitory control of the narrative as she slides in-and-out of the action stands in sharp contrast to her distance from the overall sense of history. The televisionmakers attempt to conceal this distance from both narrative and history by giving her a false sense of authenticity based upon the many different costume changes she assumes over twelve-hours of screen time.

Thus, Julie #1 possesses a free-flowing natural beauty. Everything about her comes off as simple and sweet. Besides the crisp utilitarianism of her nurse's uniform, she wears practical clothing consisting of pleated skirts, pastel-colored sweaters, white ankle socks and saddle shoes. Her golden blonde hair and schoolgirl-like clothing signify the country-fresh beauty and youthful, naïve appeal she holds for men. Like such popular Hollywood ingénues as Doris Day, Debbie Reynolds, and June Allyson, this first incarnation of Julie is exactly the sort of a girl any red-blooded American boy would love to take home to his mother and even make his wife. Later, however, after accepting Teddy Boylan's money for sex, Julie's youthful appeal cannot help but be tarnished. When this happens, what was simple becomes complex. Although Julie's transition from the girl-next-door to small-town slut is short-lived, she is next quickly transformed into Julie #3, perfect wife and mother. Once again, the staging of this transformation of Julie into the epitome of 1950s womanhood is expressed through the motifs of fashion and glamour.

More deeply confined by the circumstances of her life than were either Julie #1 or Julie #2, Julie #3's hair, clothes, and makeup all reflect this aspect of her situation. Now her face is heavily made-up, with an over-abundance of rouge and powder. Her clothes, too, reflect the confinement of her new status, as she tends to favor conservative suits, tapered sweaters, tight-fitted skirts and hoop skirts over full, stiff petticoats. Both her lips and her fingernails are painted bright red as she is seen endlessly typing away at the magazine articles that earn her the money to support her out-of-work husband and young son.

When all the stifling confinement of her 1950s working wife and mother guise becomes unbearable for so much as another second, Julie #4 comes bursting onto the scene. Since there is an overwhelming change in the world in the "Swinging" 1960s, so too does Julie's appearance reflect such change. Now anything seems possible for her. She is a charged-up screen presence. Whether clad in halter tops and blue jeans, skintight miniskirts and thigh-high boots, or swirling Indian-style skirts with loose peasant blouses and strands of love beads around her neck, Julie #4 never goes anywhere without her constantly clicking camera around her neck. With her move from writing to photography, the bold, graphic image takes precedence over the densely textured written page. Having finally broken free from Willie, she is in no hurry to marry again, much to the persistent Rudy's chagrin. Her golden tresses flow freely around her beautiful, makeup-free face. She has no more need of makeup. Her natural complexion gives off a radiant, revolutionary glow. She has discarded her confining 1950s bra and girdle; she demands a woman's right to control her own body and destiny.

Sadly, all the high spiritedness of Julie #4 gives way to Julie #5, who contradicts much of her former meaning. When this happens, the Feminine Mystique becomes one big Feminine Mistake. As the narcissistic trophy wife of the super-rich Rudy, Julie's pampered appearance and demeanor give off a cool, forbidden quality. Now, in her final and most problematic incarnation, she is a Super-rich-Bitch-Goddess, with a painted on, mask-like face and a puffed-up bouffant of bleached blonde hair. Her clothes are more confining than ever before, consisting of stiff-looking garments reflecting her newfound obsession with meticulously designed haute couture. Her infatuation with luxury and her complete lack of concern for others give her an air of both ultra-refinement and complete self-absorption. If one part of her seems to enjoy the admiration her well-tended perfection invites from others, another part of her looks upon such attention with downright disdain.

Super-Rich Rich Man & Trophy Wife: Rudy Jordache (Peter Strauss) unhappily married to Julie Prescott Jordache (Susan Blakely). ***Rich Man, Poor Man*** (ABC, 1976).

But great excess exacts great cost. Almost inevitably, it is revealed that behind the flawless perfectionism there beats a wild, rebellious heart. For all her icy reserve, this Julie harbors much resentment and recklessness deep within her soul. In time, this inner storminess rises up in the form of a tidal wave of orgiastic, alcohol-fueled fantasies of subversive female sexuality, which can no longer be controlled or contained by anyone, least of all her husband Rudy. With such a development, recklessness grows out of pain, desire out of need, spectacle out of lack. And it is this absence that becomes the defining characteristic of Woman as Fetishized Spectacle, the ultimate presence of the epic miniseries. True, it may have been Rudy's wealth and power that constructed her meaning, but in the end, that meaning is meaningless for Julie. In the face of her existential crisis, she sets out to destroy Rudy's defining, meaningless meaning through her own spectacular excess and, perhaps, replace it with a more meaningful meaning of her own creation. In this regard, she is personality as sex and power, and the epic miniseries, at least in this instance, can be interpreted as the unexpected triumph of the subversive feminine over the restriction of a closed, repressive patriarchal system gone bust. As Julie assumes for herself the empowering position of center stage, she dominates the eye. The narrative devices of the epic miniseries are forced to take on a whole other function. With Julie's florid and theatrical acting out against all that her husband represents—his ruthlessness, his greed, his indifference to her—she is a cultic epiphany totally unto herself. She forces a shift from a phallocentric to a feminine-based narrative, providing the text with some of its most spectacular Woman as Fetishized Spectacle moments. These include the drunken Julie's sadomasochistic destruction of her no-longer-used camera and award-winning photographs; her drunkenly and brazenly appearing nude at the door so that angry students protesting Rudy's reactionary political views can better snap pictures of her newly found erotic grandeur to destroy his political future; and her unwisely taking up with the sadistic Falconetti in France for a wild night of drugs, drinking, and sexual debauchery.

But even though such scenes depicting Julie's destructive rise and eventual fall do provide the text with some of its most spectacularly melodramatic moments, ironically they also end up working as a safeguard, protecting against the complete dissolution of the narrative through the spectacularization of the figure of Woman. That is, until Julie can be sufficiently contained into the epic narrative again.

With storytelling such an essential part of the epic miniseries, the televisionmakers eventually find themselves needing to make a crucial decision. Having put Julie through such a haphazard profusion of negative incidents, the choice comes down to two alternatives: (1) to go on exploiting her character along much the same lines or; (2) to provide Julie with the same possibility of conversion allowed to Tom. Although we cannot truthfully say that all of the morally and narratively problematic aspects of Julie's character get fully resolved in any sort of believable, teleological way, at the very least the epic narrative concludes matters on a relatively sound, affirmative note in the final scene. After the very pregnant Kate tearfully scatters Tom's ashes into the sea, the camera pulls back, revealing a long shot which in turn creates a tableau-like image of Julie standing apart from Rudy on the stern of the *Clothilde*. With their backs turned away from the camera's too-penetrative gaze, they stare out into the velvety expanse of the blue-on-blue sky—dotted with brilliant white clouds—and the hypnotic rhythm of the infinite, deep blue sea. The serene natural beauty of the frame becomes a lyrical, poetic gesture to similar passages found in the revelatory cinema of the great Russian film poet Alexander Dovzhenko. When Rudy reaches over for Julie's hand, she graciously accepts. With this, female desire returns to a private, natural space. And the final image we are left with is one of the couple, united in complete harmony with the elemental forces and cosmic reality of nature: wind, sun, sky, and sea, all signifiers for Tom's exuberant Dionysian spirit. Such an ending pays homage to the great chain of being or the mythic cycle of life and love born out of pain, misery, death, and finally rebirth.

Music by Starlight

We conclude this chapter with a few comments about the use *Rich Man, Poor Man* makes of two of the other formalistic tropes first introduced by *QB VII*: (1) the concept of employing multiple revolving guest stars to hold the audience's attention; and (2) the application of music to help unify and smooth out the choppy spots of the long, episodic narrative, creating a more heightened sense of dramatic impact.

Since three unknown actors had been cast as the leads (Nolte, Strauss, and Blakely), ABC demanded several actors more familiar to television audiences be cast in supporting roles. This executive decision created a stellar televisual dialectic in which seasoned actors such as Edward Asner, Dorothy McGuire, Ray Milland, and Bill Bixby were provided the opportunity to deliver memorable star-turns in substantial dramatic roles. Other, equally well-known stars such as Oscar-winning actresses Gloria Grahame (as Sue Prescott, Julie's mother) and Dorothy Malone (Irene Goodwin), along with Fionnuala Flanagan, George Maharis, Steve Allen (Bayard Nicholas), Van Johnson (Marsh Goodwin), Talia Shire, and Lynda Day George all make lively impressions in either stand-out supporting roles (Grahame, Malone, Johnson), or brief appearances (Maharis, Allen, Shire, Day George).

The 1976 Emmy Award for Excellence in Musical Scoring was awarded to Alex North for his rich and varied score for *Rich Man, Poor Man*. As he explains in his liner notes to the soundtrack album, "The treatment of the score called for a virtual musical anthology spanning over twenty-five years in the lives of the Jordache family." To achieve this effect, North incorporated a wide-ranging collection of such different musical styles as big band sounds of the 1940s, jazz-oriented motifs of the 1950s, and the explosive sounds of rock and roll of the 1960s. North's distinctive sound and style beautifully conveyed the many complex moods that America and all three of the key protagonists go through. On the album, he also explains that he gave each character his or her own individual musical theme: for Rudy, North created "a rather sophisticated waltz-like sound"; for Tom, the music shifted into more of a loose "bluesy, virile and jazz-oriented 'carnal' sound"; for Julie, the composer achieved a lyrical tonal portrait "of a lovely adolescent girl, her desires and sensual curiosity."[19]

The music North composed for the main title possessed " a slightly Americana theme," which both nostalgically evoked a past era and helped keep television audiences deeply involved with the various lives and loves of the characters. In addition to the main title, North's opening music was later used as a memorable recurring motif for Tom's newfound love and happiness with Kate in France. Especially moving is the way the haunting melody accompanies the poignant finale, when Kate scatters Tom's ashes into the sea. Here the full utopian potential of North's music perfectly unites sound and image, characters and narrative motifs, location and event, to envision an elusive, privileged image of a visionary televisual space without any discernable limitations or boundaries.

When the first part of *Rich Man, Poor Man* aired on February 1, 1976, it met with impressive Nielsen ratings. With well over 50 million viewers thoroughly captivated by the mythic storytelling technique of *Rich Man, Poor Man*, it was clear to all: The epic miniseries and American television were a perfect fit. As Donna McCrohan writes, "A genre (the episodic television soap opera) that the 1950s had dismissed as trite and shallow became — thanks largely to bigger budgets and more advanced technology — state-of-the-art in 1970s hands."[20] And so, by the time the series concluded on March 5, 1977, Strauss, Nolte, and Blakely had all gone on to become household names in America, "supporting actor Edward Asner was poised to win an Emmy (which he did); and the major strengths of 'long-form TV' were demonstrated for all to see." For these and other reasons, we fully endorse David Bianculli's claim that *Rich Man, Poor Man* has most deservedly won for itself a very special place in the history of American television, and it has, indeed, gone on to "cast a tall shadow of its own."[21] Amazingly, even that achievement would be overshadowed in January of 1977 by the even more phenomenal critical and popular success of the epic miniseries that still stands in a special class of its own — *Roots*. If *Rich Man, Poor Man* can be said to be the reason the epic miniseries ended up on the televisual map, then it would be left to *Roots* to take it from that map, and launch it straight into the broadcasting stratosphere.

Chapter 2

The Triumph of the Heroic Slave

Following the huge impact of *Rich Man, Poor Man*, all three of the major American television networks had to make some important decisions relatively quickly. Either they could ignore the promising future potential of the epic miniseries as a new televisual art form, or else they could attempt to replicate the success of the 1976 blockbuster hit. NBC seemed to have gleaned all it could from *Rich Man, Poor Man*; in an obvious attempt to beat rival ABC at its game, in the fall of 1976 the Peacock Network broadcast its own stylish 9-hour presentation of the lavish, excessively melodramatic, generational saga *Captains and the Kings*. Based on the best-selling 1971 novel by Taylor Caldwell, the epic miniseries told the very *Rich Man, Poor Man*–like tale of a rich and powerful Irish-American family bearing more than a passing resemblance to the uber-famous Kennedys (this text will be further detailed in Chapter 3).

This second chapter will consider two important epic miniseries of the 1970s, *Roots* (ABC, 1977) and *Holocaust* (NBC, 1978), which translated the lessons of *Rich Man, Poor Man* in ways that proved to be innovative instead of simply imitative. Actually, so influential are all three texts, many now place them together in a dazzling triumvirate of televisual masterpieces. Although it is true that both *Roots* and *Holocaust* draw upon many of the same formal principles of display established by the earlier success, we shall see that they take those principles to a whole other creative realm. Part of this comes from the way each reconfigured the marginalized "Otherness" of the Black and Jewish experiences, much the same way *Rich Man, Poor Man* reconfigured the "Otherness" of Woman in the figure of Julie. What ABC and NBC did was to set in motion a system of transformation through which the previously narrowly defined sectarianism of the "Other" was further refined and redefined into a more universal and therefore more popular archetype. Of course, none of this should come as a big surprise to us, since plays, films, and television programs that aim for the mythic goal of such universalization tend to "garner acclaim, awards, and financial rewards for the artists and producers who generated them."[1]

This chapter will consider the ways that *Roots* and *Holocaust* employ the combination of a didactic agenda with the same melodramatic impulse that informed *Rich Man, Poor Man* to negotiate a new, exciting way of reading the potential of the epic miniseries. Along with avoiding the obvious pitfalls such a project would seem to entail, both texts succeed in acknowledging the central importance of the Black and Jewish experiences, while simultaneously connecting those experiences to the broader context of the American experience, and beyond that, the super-colossal system of the universalized network. As a result, what had previously been viewed as only the minority status of the marginalized, historical "Other" is suddenly brought into closer alignment with the intimacy of the popularizing process of the known for a mass audience.

Roots and *Holocaust* also demonstrate how the project of the epic miniseries can operate as something more complex than just lavish televisual entertainment or an attempt to concretize the idiosyncratic personal vision of its televisionmakers. In both cases, we see the form aspiring to the dimensions of a visionary epic designed to provide audiences with a series of challenging words and images, with the mission of actually altering perceptions. In the process, the epic miniseries becomes, along with everything else it can be, a tool to educate and enlighten.

Roots

Roots is a densely textured, expansive work of televisual pop art, with the capacity to mean many different things to many different people. For example, *Roots* is a multi-generational saga about the lives of several members of one remarkable African American family. The main impulse of the text is not unlike that which inspired Margaret Mitchell to write *Gone with the Wind*, and D.W. Griffith to make *Birth of a Nation*. The most significant difference between *Roots* and those texts, however, is that *Roots* tells the flip-side of their stories, "revealing all the horrors and tragedy of slavery, taking viewers from the mist and magnolia to the slave quarters, the family separations, the beatings, the wholesale trading of Black lives."[2] *Roots* is also a fantastic oral historical-biographical construct dedicated to the remembrance of a proud but almost completely forgotten people. And in the act of remembering what the dominant White culture wants forgotten, *Roots* provides a clear, defiant voice for all those forgotten. In effect, *Roots* is a televisual resurrection of the past, providing knowledge, wisdom, and hope for those of the future.

Through the writing of *Roots*, author Alex Haley became a mythopoet, pulling off a stunning literary feat: he transposed a great oral narrative into written text, then re-constructed the historical mythos in which to place it. Based on his arduous twelve-year journey to find his own lost family roots, Haley's epic tale begins in Gambia, West Africa, with the birth of Kunta Kinte (played by LeVar Burton as a young man, and later by John Amos, of the heroic physical stature) to Binta (Cicely Tyson) and Omoro (Thalmus Rasulala). Initially, Kunta's life is impossibly idyllic as he grows up happy and free. At the age of sixteen, this changes forever. He is captured by ruthless White slave-catchers and shipped off in chains, to be sold on the auction block in America. Subjected to countless acts of cruelty, Kunta grows angry and rebellious. On many occasions he attempts to escape. To prevent him from running off again, his owners chop his foot off as punishment. Eventually, through his friendship with the shrewd, older slave Fiddler (Lou Gossett Jr.), marriage to the goodhearted Bell (Madge Sinclair), and the birth of their daughter Kizzy (Leslie Uggams), Kunta attains a form of spiritual solace.

Next the miniseries becomes the story of Kunta's daughter Kizzy. In womanhood, Kizzy, first betrayed by her spiteful white mistress Missy Anne (Sandy Duncan), is later sold off to the spiteful Master Tom Moore (Chuck Connors), who repeatedly rapes and abuses her, even after she gives birth to her son by him, Chicken George (Ben Vereen). Although George becomes the best trainer of fighting gamecocks in the South, he too is sold off by Master Moore to an Englishman to pay off Moore's extensive gambling debts.

Thirty years later George returns home, now old but free, only to find America in the throes of the Civil War. His son Tom (George Stanford Brown), a successful blacksmith, is recruited into the army to work on Confederate cavalry horses. Later Tom, who has married Irene (Lynne Moody) and raised a family of his own, is profoundly disappointed to find emancipation brings little freedom from either the White man's terror or his control. However, *Roots* concludes on a triumphant image of Chicken George, accompanied by his loving wife Matilda (Olivia Cole) and their family, setting out for a new and hopefully better life in the promised land of Tennessee.

As this summary makes evident, *Roots* is not without its fair share of *Rich Man, Poor Man*–like melodramatics. Nor is *Roots* without its other aesthetic flaws.[3] But the attainment of some sort of aesthetic perfection seems beside the real point here. Far more important is that with his creation of *Roots*, Alex Haley set in motion the dynamic projection of a system of re-construction, overflowing with grace note upon grace note, until a certain mythic epiphany is attained, sustained, and maintained. This is doubtless what television audiences in unprecedented numbers found themselves responding to so eagerly when the show premiered in January of 1977.

Unbelievably, even after reaping the lucrative benefits of the huge, blockbuster ratings of *Rich Man, Poor Man* the year before, several executives at ABC voiced grave misgivings at the idea of producing a 12-hour primetime epic miniseries devoted to an African American family of slaves. With little if any "starry-eyed expectations for it,"[4] these same top executives approached the whole matter with extreme trepidation, right up to the point of its eventual television broadcast.

The reason for all this corporate anxiety, and the effects it ultimately had on the show, will be returned to later in the chapter. For the time being, we shall consider the four main reasons *Roots* become such a legendary epic miniseries. First, *Roots* introduced us to the first and still greatest example of the mythic type of the Heroic Slave embodied in the figure of Kunta Kinte. Second, the epic narrative is structured so as to reconfigure the traditionally marginalized figure of the Slave into a more universalized (and thus Americanized) archetype. This allowed the vast majority of the White television audience of the time, both in America and around the world, to care about and more importantly to fully identify with the fate of Kunta Kinte. In a very real sense, the Black experience of slavery became the symbol for the suffering of all mankind. Third, as with *Rich Man, Poor Man*, *Roots* uses the stylistic tropes of mise-en-scéne, music, and a revolving cast (in this case, a predominantly White cast) of famous guest stars to particularly brilliant effect. Fourth, the apprehension over the reception of *Roots*, expressed by several of ABC's top executives, ended up helping rather than hurting the show.

A Dream of Africa

The epic narrative patterning of *Roots* operates along the lines of the classic quest myth. Kunta Kinte (and later several of his descendants) sets in motion the elaborate process of remembering and aspiring to his revolutionary vision of re-attaining the Dream of Africa, which becomes a promise, a memory, and a signifier for all that has been taken from him (his identity, heritage, and religion) when he is captured and brought to America in chains. Despite all he is subjected to, he never once relinquishes the idea of transforming his magnificent Edenic dream of African freedom into an American reality. In this way, the power of myth is used, much as it was in *Rich Man, Poor Man*, to assist audiences (through Kunta and his family) in gaining a clearer understanding of the universal human condition. This, in turn, helps shape the cruel and baffling chaos life becomes for the Black man and woman in White America into more "ordered, predictable, comprehensible patterns of events—patterns which allow the mind to perceive a kind of meaning, or answer, to the riddle of human existence."[5]

In keeping with the concept of epic narrative being shaped into "ordered, predictable, comprehensive, patterns," *Roots* begins in a supremely orderly space, worthy of 18th century French philosopher Jean-Jacques Rousseau. In his famous treatise *The Social Contract* (1776), Rousseau writes: "Man is born free, and everywhere is in chains." With the idyllic depiction of Kunta's boyhood in pastoral Africa, he is free and unchained. Africa is depicted as a utopian dream space in which a benign Romantic nature creates a vision of paradise. Like Rousseau's rejection of the Western concept of original sin, "Christianity's pessimistic view of man born unclean with a propensity for evil,"[6] the Africa of *Roots* recalls more the empirical thinking of English philosopher John Locke, who advocated mankind's innate goodness.

This principle of display makes the opening African scenes of *Roots* the closest approximation American television will probably ever get to producing a visual correlative of the humanistic philosophy of Rousseau and Locke.

With the fusing of this progressive strain of 18th and 19th century Western thought onto the depiction of Kunta's 18th century Africa, the televisionmakers subtly shift the specificity of the young man's condition away from an exclusively Black experience to one of a greater universal appeal. This new metaphoric configuration allows traces of other Westernized utopian spaces—such as the Garden of Eden, Shangri-La, and El Dorado—to be evoked. Thus, as were Adam and Eve, so too are Kunta and the members of his tribe naked, unashamed, and free of the concept of original sin. Similar to the microcosmical world Tom creates for himself at the end of *Rich Man, Poor Man*, Kunta's Africa is a macrocosmic version of paradise.

In a much less optimistic vein, like the characters of *Lost Horizon*, the Africans of *Roots* are also destined to suffer grave repercussions when they are taken from the vastness of their African Shangri-La. This happens with the arrival of the White man in the form of destructive slave-catchers, through whom profanation, corruption, and violation come crashing into the utopian space of *Roots*. With the White man's unwelcomed appearance, the innate goodness of the Rousseavian/Lockian paradigm shifts into the more pessimistic view of human nature espoused by 17th century philosopher Thomas Hobbes. In his magnum opus *Leviathan*, Hobbes wrote: "The life of man is solitary, poor, nasty, brutish, and short." And since the White man is so inclined to establish rigid Apollonian hierarchies, he is also inclined to elevate himself to the highest level while relegating the Black man to the very lowest. Suddenly, in a paradigm of Darwinism, survival of the fittest and the fiercest becomes the new law of the African land. The fact that the White man possesses the advanced technological weaponry of swords, guns, and cannon fire seals the fate of Kunta Kinte. His own father, Omoro, understands this completely. When he learns his eldest son has been captured by the White slave-catchers, he informs his wife, Binta, that their son is now lost to them forever. Precisely because *Roots* has so successfully emphasized the universal aspects of Kunta's story, we have no trouble identifying with the Black young man against the White slave-catchers.

In this regard, *Roots* contains a particularly daring sequence, depicting the extent of the White man's total inhumanity to the Black man and woman. The scene takes place on the *Lord Ligonier*, the slave ship carrying Kunta and the other captured Africans from the Dionysian paradise of Africa to the cold, oppressive Apollonian world of the White man's America. In one extended, continuous movement, the camera tracks along the ship's glistening, polished decks. It comes to a full halt at a heavy grating from which the sounds of human pain and suffering emanate. Then the camera passes right through the heavy grating into a seemingly impenetrable blackness. After descending further downward into the shadowy depths, the camera reveals a shocking image of the ship's narrow, claustrophobic interior. There, in the stench-filled bowels of the *Lord Ligonier*, a scene straight out of *Dante's Inferno* is being played out. In this godforsaken, oppressive space, the enslaved Africans—chained and shackled together, their pain-wracked bodies whipped, beaten, tortured, covered in blood, vomit, excrement, and filth — are held captive, bound for the New World.

And just as Dante is warned as he advances into the Inferno, "Abandon all hope, ye who enter here," Kunta must do the same as he approaches American soil. Upon his arrival, he is subjected to further degradation and humiliation. First he is sold off to wealthy plantation owner John Reynolds (Lorne Greene). Then his identity is totally obliterated and his name changed from Kunta Kinte to Toby. Worst of all, he is forced to witness the unbridled racial and sexual licentiousness with which the White man typically views the Black man and woman. The fact that much of this sexual debasement occurs

Paradise Lost: The Heroic Slave, Kunta Kinte (LeVar Burton), brought to America in chains. *Roots* (ABC, 1977).

in these statically composed scenes of lush pictorial beauty, possessing an almost John Ford–like evocation of the spatial-pastoral experience of the American landscape, only adds to their overall intensity. It often seems impossible to believe such unnatural ugliness could actually be happening within the context of such natural, promising beauty. Much of this goes back to the way the White man views the African slave. The Black man is looked upon as his social and spiritual inferior in every possible way. However, the Black woman in *Roots* is a signifier for something quite different. The White man views her as the mythic type of the Whore. In other words, we see characterization mythically delineated in *Roots*, just it had been in *Rich Man, Poor Man*, in terms of binary dialectic. Such Heideggerian dialecticism results in a dynamic, dualistic tension between Black/White, good/evil, natural/unnatural, innocent/corrupt, hero/villain.

One of the major ways this binary dialectic manifests in the narrative is in the form of historical sexual memory. Towards this end, the abused Black woman is universalized into a kind of collective historical, sexually victimized symbol of Woman. Thus, as the White man elevates his White woman high onto a pedestal, safely protected from his own baser erotic needs, the Black woman is made the prime target of those very needs. Concurrently, through this harsh treatment of the Black woman, the Black man is further reduced to the figure of a powerless "emasculated" male, no longer capable of protecting his woman, his home, or even his own manhood. In one harrowing scene, this aspect of the Black man's plight is crystallized in an image of primal Freudian horror. As punishment for trying to run away once too often, Kunta must choose between having either his penis or foot chopped off. For all its gruesome excess, the scene attains a Shakespearean ripeness, pulling together several narrative strands at once, which leads to Kunta's introduction of the resourceful figure of Bell, the cook in the household of Dr. William Reynolds (Robert Reed).

After being symbolically castrated by the sadistic slave-catchers, Kunta is left totally drained of the Lifeforce. Fortunately, Bell is determined to give him back his life at all costs. She expertly heals him with her nursing and culinary skills, and later provides him with the greatest happiness he has known since being taken from Africa. Bell accomplishes this by marrying Kunta and giving birth to their beautiful daughter Kizzy. Bell goes on to symbolize one of the most memorable depictions of the mythic type of the nurturing Wife in the epic miniseries. However, Bell also has a secret tragic side: her two other daughters were brutally sold away from her.

Still, Bell does signify grace, comfort, and female power. This symbolically connects her to the two great matriarchal figures of Kunta's mother, Binta, and his grandmother, Nyo Boto. It also makes Bell the forerunner of the next two great matriarchal figures of *Roots*: her own daughter Kizzy, and her grandson Chicken George's wife, Matilda. Taken together, this remarkable quintet of African American women provide *Roots* with a steady, calming center, a nexus of female clarity around which the tempestuous narrative forces of the epic miniseries and history converge, organize, and re-focus. Stripped of the artifice that sometimes marred Julie's character in *Rich Man, Poor Man*—shorn, unadorned, refined, and never less than spiritually beautiful or symbolically true at any point—Binta, Nyo Boto, Bell, Kizzy, and Matilda are each distinguished by a mythic power, serenity, and sense of character that is completely her own.

The undeniably strong investment of the centrality of these women is paid tribute to by Jahna Cole and the unsurpassable Quincy Jones, the composer originally hired to write the evocative music for *Roots*, which was then completed by composer Gerald Fried. Also, as Cole observes: "Without really trying, *Roots* killed the age-old myths about the Black family by showing how and why Black families were torn apart, often leaving the Black woman alone as head of the house-hold. The program also shows just how important children were and are in the legacy of the Black family."[7] Jones was obviously thinking along similar lines as he composed the opening music for *Roots*: "Conceptually, what I was trying to do was let Letta Mbulu, with her great voice, be the symbol of the great Motherland, Africa. When Letta Mbulu sings, you know that she is an extraordinary African woman."[8]

There is then something of this same mythic complexity and extraordinary power Jones speaks of in the five Black women of *Roots*. Binta and Nyo Boto provide the young Kunta with the singularity and dignity needed to keep his great utopian Dream of Africa alive during his American ordeal. Later, after Kunta marries Bell, she provides him with a safe, loving home, and blesses him with their daughter Kizzy. This is not meant to imply that the relationship between Bell and Kunta is without its problems. Since she considers herself a fully assimilated American Black woman, Bell cares nothing of Kunta's Dream of Africa. All she wants is for him to put such thoughts out of his mind for good. Although the couple does successfully work out its differences, Kunta can never relinquish his great dream altogether. He does, however, learn to take tremendous personal pleasure in his sense of family, love for Bell, and deep pride in Kizzy, the radiant, new light of his life.

Upon becoming a young woman, Kizzy is sold off to Tom Moore, who repeatedly rapes her and impregnates her with her son George. As a mother, Kizzy assumes her rightful place at the center of the epic narrative, becoming the site of the mythic memory of the past and also the hope and promise of the future. *Roots* becomes Kizzy's story. She is now the daughter of African American myth and history. Through her, just as they had been in her father memory, history, and myth are suffused together into an eternal generational mythos passed down from one to the next. Furthermore, this forms a kind of organized remembrance: history, myth, epic narrative, and visual spectacle are all signified in the figure of Kizzy, and later her son, Chicken George.

We see a powerful example of how this is achieved with the simplest of means when Kizzy visits Kunta's gravesite. In the scene, three basic elements—woman, epic narrative, and mise-en-scène—form a classical triptych. Dressed in warm, womanly earth colors, Kizzy approaches her father's grave. Dropping to her knees, she tells him how much she loves and misses him. With a graceful tracking shot, the camera moves in for a close-up of her face. She grows more emotional as she tells her father of her son George, to whom she has passed on Kunta's Dream of Africa. Her face framed in tight close-up, Kizzy promises to have other children whom she also vows to tell of Kunta's Africa and freedom. Overwhelmed with mythic emotion, Kizzy promises to devote the rest of her life to making certain her father's great dream shall never die. Then she picks up a rock, and defiantly inscribes something on the tombstone. After she leaves, a close-up of the inscribed tombstone shows that the name Toby has been scratched out. In its place, she has boldly written "Kunta Kinte." Kizzy's act both simplifies and complicates her meaning. She is simplified in the way she identifies herself so straightforwardly as daughter, mother, and future wife. Yet Kizzy is complicated at the same time. Although she has been enslaved, abused, and sexually objectified by the White man, inwardly she has turned against the injustice of that symbolic order. It will never destroy her. She will not let it.

Once Kizzy's son Chicken George assumes his place at the center of the epic narrative, *Roots* shifts focus dramatically. Being such a fast-living, hell-raising ladies' man about town (which is visually signified by his stylish derby and rakish emerald green scarf), and widely acknowledged as the finest trainer of gamecocks in the South, the flamboyant George is offered a greater level of personal freedom and autonomy than his grandfather or mother ever had. Growing increasingly frustrated with being merely a slave for the rest of his life, George develops a restless, dialectical spirit. Rather than simply "staying put" on Master Moore's oppressive Southern plantation, he longs to experience even more personal freedom: the freedom of the endless open road, stretching out before him in all its glorious vastness, becomes an alluring Siren's song, a celebration of escape, a hymn to uprootedness, an endlessly panoramic vista of hope and promise. In effect, he possesses a Walt Whitmanic or Jack Kerouacesque vision of America and all it holds for a man such as himself.

This pastoral dimension refines and romanticizes George to the hilt. It also connects him to the Emersonian/Thoreauvian ideal of the American experience. All of America, and beyond that, all of the world, becomes a vision of wide open spaces, without any fences, boundaries, or chains. There is nothing to hold George back or keep him down anymore. In space, there is only inspiration, aspiration, mobility, and nobility. The possibility of self-purification, self-renewal, and self-fulfillment awaits George, if only he opens himself up to that electric expectation of expansion, that seductive spectacle of spatiality. Like Mark Twain's Huck Finn, George must do what he must do. After all, in doing so he can in his own way pay tribute to his grandfather Kunta Kinte's great dream, which was stolen, defiled, and wasted, and which now compels George to regain that majestic, ancestral sense of paradise lost: Africa.

When Master Moore, whom George ironically views as something of a father figure, offers him an opportunity to gain his freedom, George jumps at the chance, much to his mother's dismay. Justifiably fearful of her son being hurt and disappointed by the ever-deceitful White master, Kizzy persuades him to focus his sights on his grandfather's mythic Dream of Africa instead. Her words trigger a lifelong, internalized conflict within George. Although he still cannot help longing to see the whole wide world, he nevertheless understands the importance of family and "roots." Since he is such a resourceful man, George eventually experiences both. Not only does he get to see America, but he also spends considerable time traveling through Europe. If the reasons for his going are harshly negative ones (George is sent to Europe to pay off a twenty-thousand dollar bet made by Master Moore), it does insure his freedom. Although fifteen years pass before George returns home, his reunion with his family is a joyous occasion for them all. But when his wife Matilda learns her husband is in danger of being made a slave again if he stays with her, she movingly persuades him to leave her and their family once more. After all, George has become the bona fide living reality of the great promise of Kunta Kinte's Dream of Africa for all of them.

As the epic narrative of *Roots* draws to a close, we are presented with a succession of epic images of both horror and celebration, featuring the waging of the Civil War, the emancipation of the slaves, the fascistic rise of the Klu Klux Klan, and the assassination of Abraham Lincoln. Through it all, the descendants of Kunta Kinte persevere.

The narrative patterning of *Roots*, which then began with images of the symbolic order and tranquility of Africa only to descend into long stretches of confusion and disorder, shifts back into a suggestion of a serene sense of order and harmony once again. With the radiant light of dawn breaking over the distant hills, the family's caravan of wagons sets off for the shining, promised land of Tennessee. Reveling in the well-earned role of paterfamilias, Chicken George begins his recital of the now-legendary family litany, beginning with the birth of Kunta Kinte, who was born in Africa, and called a river Kamby Bolongo, only to be captured by slave-catchers and sold off as a slave in America, where he married the woman named Bell, who gave birth to a daughter named Kizzy.... As George's voice intones the words, it becomes a luminous mantra of hope, a cherished ritual, a sacred text of mythic grandeur, for both him and his family.

Perhaps the most peculiar aspect of this ending, however, is that although it certainly does work at concluding matters in a relatively coherent and acceptable way, we cannot help feeling there is still more that needs to be said about this particular set of mythic characters. In this respect, the epic narrative itself seems to call out for a different, more conclusive way to end. And perhaps this is as it should be. For despite the appearance of a sense of order being regained — again, of a return back to the Edenic — we know from having viewed the preceding twelve hours of *Roots* that concepts such as "freedom," "conversion," and "happy ending" are relative at best for the Black man and woman in White America. By acknowledging this fact, the epic narrative begs for a more forceful sense of thematic and teleological closure.[9]

Eight Days a Week

Earlier we mentioned that all the apprehension and nervousness on the part of the network executives at ABC aided rather than hindered *Roots* in becoming the phenomenal television blockbuster it ultimately did. If success is the child of many fathers, ABC provided *Roots* with three wonderfully supportive fathers. The first two were Barry Diller and Martin Starger, and the third was Fred Silverman, chief programmer and Vice President in charge of all primetime entertainment. It was at his persistence ABC greenlighted *Roots* in the first place, committing itself to the expenditure of $6 million for the full twelve-hour epic miniseries production. Although Silverman's first order of business was to devote himself to the network's weekly primetime scheduling, he kept a close, watchful eye on the progress of *Roots'* filming. When the series was completed, Silverman and his wife spent an entire weekend watching the full twelve hours—five hours one day, seven the next. As the end credits rolled,

> The Silvermans felt overwhelmed by the show's emotional wallop. Instead of scheduling *Roots* over a period of weeks (as ABC had scheduled *Rich Man, Poor Man*), Silverman decided to run it on eight consecutive nights. "To spread it out would have dissipated the impact," he said.[10]

Still not fully comprehending the trailblazing work of popular art they possessed, the shortsighted executives of ABC more or less jumped at Silverman's unorthodox idea. Rather cynically, they reasoned that in disposing of the program in one fell swoop, they would be protecting their valuable corporate necks. This way, if *Roots* tanked in the ratings, it would only destroy the network's ratings for a single week in the godforsaken month of January. In hindsight, what those foolish executives could not comprehend was that by broadcasting the show in such a new and radical "Eight Days a Week" presentation, they were only making it seem even more of a whole new kind of televisual experience for viewers.

In his informative autobiography, *Producer*, David L. Wolper remembers what occurred following the broadcast of the first episode of *Roots* on the evening of Sunday, January 23, 1977. Early the next morning (Monday, January 24), he received an ecstatic telephone call from Silverman. *Roots* had received a sixty-one-point share, which translated into an audience of upward of 100 million viewers.[11] From that point onward, the ratings for *Roots* only got bigger with each consecutive night:

> By the time *Roots* concluded, it had become part of America's cultural history. More than 130 million Americans had seen the show—making it the most watched program in television history. Of the thirteen most watched individual programs in TV history, *Roots* captured eight spots. It became a cultural phenomenon: for one week in January it captured, completely, the attention of the entire nation.[12]

The Peacock Also Rises

Following the unprecedented success of *Roots*, neither ABC nor its two rival networks, CBS and NBC, wasted any time jumping on board the swiftly moving epic miniseries bandwagon. NBC displayed especially tremendous showmanship in developing the aforementioned *Captains and the Kings*, which found an appreciative televisual audience. Less appreciated by viewers, sadly, was the network's beautifully made, journalistically detailed *King* (1978). Consistently powerful, *King* was skillfully written and directed by Abby Mann and contained several standout performances, such as those delivered by veteran character actor Ossie Davis (as Dr. King's dominating father) and the splendid

Mythic Walk to the Promised Land: Martin Luther King, Jr. (Paul Winfield) and loyal wife Coretta (Cicley Tyson) lead a Civil Rights march. *King* (NBC, 1978).

Cicely Tyson (as Coretta Scott King), one of the first of the great mythic figures of the Wife in the epic miniseries. Relying extensively upon elements of Old Testament narrative technique, the undeniable high point of *King* came with the commanding performance of Paul Winfield as Martin Luther King. Winfield's breathtaking recreation of the soaring rhetoric used by Dr. King in several of his most famous speeches is not only a fine example of Mann's meticulous attention to detail, it is also part of an irreplaceable record, attesting to the peaks of artistry the epic miniseries could achieve when in the hands of the right visionary televisual artists.

After witnessing the dismal audience response to the masterful *King*, "NBC was seriously considering surrounding the whole of the RCA building with safety nets"[13] to keep all its withering executives from plunging to their deaths below. If the public failed to respond to such a protean historical and American figure as Dr. King, how could they possibly be expected to embrace the nightmarish story of a fictional family of upper-middle-class Jews' experience in Nazi Germany between the years of 1935 and 1945? Little did NBC realize the triumph it would soon have on its hands with the broadcasting of its next epic miniseries, a mere two months after *King*, on April 16, 1978.

Holocaust

Taken together with *Rich Man, Poor Man* and *Roots*, *Holocaust* remains one of the greatest of all epic miniseries. And this despite its flaws, which many of its critics claim include its tendency to vulgarize and trivialize its tragic historical subject, its too simplistic merging or blurring of fact and fiction to melodramatic effect, and the fact that non–Jewish actors were cast in many key roles. And yet *Holocaust* is so exceptionally well-crafted, so strong is its epic narrative drive, so moving and accomplished are several of its featured performances, so all-encompassing in its masterful evocation of time and place, that it proves itself fully deserving of the canonical recognition it has acquired.

The main focus of the epic narrative is on the catastrophic effects of the Holocaust on five members of the Weiss family. Fully assimilated Jews living in Nazi Germany, the Weisses consist of Dr. Josef Weiss (Fritz Weaver), a highly successful physician of Polish descent; his aristocratic German-born wife, Berta (Rosemary Harris); and their three grown children: Karl (James Woods), a talented artist; the rebellious, athletic, devil-may-care Rudi (Joseph Bottoms); and their overly-sensitive, musically gifted daughter Anna (Blanche Baker). Although Karl marries the Catholic Inga (Meryl Streep), her working-class family have little sympathy for the fate of the Jews in Hitler's new Nazi Germany. Soon after the wedding, the government outlaws mixed marriages. Thus begins a series of horrific events, plunging the Weisses ever deeper into the unimaginable Nazi nightmare.

While the Nazis intensify their wanton persecution of the Jews, Berta persists in defending the civility of her beloved country. When she finally realizes the true intent of the Nazi party, it is too late for her to save either herself or her family. Her dignified, elderly parents become early victims of the infamous *Kristallnacht*; her son Karl is arrested, tortured and sent to Buchenwald; her daughter Anna, after being brutally raped by Nazi thugs, withdraws into a catatonic state and gets committed to an insane asylum, where she is gassed to death; and her husband is deported to Poland, placed in a ghetto, made a member of the Warsaw Jewish Council, and eventually reunited with Berta.

Remaining true to his rebellious spirit, Rudi runs off, cleverly eluding the Nazis, and joins a group of fighting partisans in Russia. Along the way he meets and marries Helena (Tovah Feldsuh), a Czech Zionist, who teaches Rudi of Israel. He also reunites with his Uncle Moses (Sam Wanamaker).

Juxtaposed against the fall of the Weiss family is the ruthless rise of Erik Dorf (Michael Moriarty), an unemployed German lawyer. Pushed along by his ambitious, calculating wife Marta (Deborah Norton), Dorf joins the Nazi party mainly to further his floundering legal career. His obsequious nature results in his becoming chief counsel to Reinhard Heydrich (David Warner) and puts him in close contact with the upper echelon of Nazi high command, such as Heinrich Himmler (Ian Holm) and Adolf Eichmann (Tom Bell). Soon Dorf is inventing the insidiously euphemistic language the Nazis use for the Holocaust: "special handling" (mass deportations to concentration camps); "quarantine" (death camps); "autonomous Jewish territory" (ghetto); and "Final Solution" (the genocidal slaughter of all Jews).

As a result of his superior artistic ability, Karl is sent to the model camp of Thersienstadt, where his anti-fascist artwork leads to his being beaten, tortured, and transferred to the eventual place of his death—Auschwitz. The pregnant Inga and his parents are also later sent to Auschwitz. Shortly after, Helena is killed in a Nazi ambush, and Rudi is captured and imprisoned in Sobibor. Participating in what would become one of the greatest escapes of all in Holocaust history, Rudi then goes off in search of his family.

Meanwhile, Dorf kills himself rather than be taken prisoner by the Allies for his many crimes against humanity. After he learns of the tragic fates of his family, Rudi is reunited with Inga and her young son Josef. While Inga makes plans to return to Germany temporarily, Rudi escorts a group of refugee orphans to Israel.

At the miniseries' inception, the powers-that-be of NBC intended *Holocaust* to be that network's response to the unexpected ratings coup ABC had with *Roots*. Like *Roots*, *Holocaust* looks at another of the most tragic events in human history. When Jacob Neusner formulates "*Roots* = *Holocaust*,"[14] he correctly acknowledges the symbiotic connection between the two. For this reason, we are aware of many striking similarities. For example, just as *Roots* began with Kunta Kinte existing in a harmonious space of paradisiacal serenity in

Roots, the opening of *Holocaust* begins in a similar space. In an extended *Godfather*-like sequence, Karl and Inga Weiss, with their families and guests, celebrate the couple's lavish wedding party (in a foreboding touch, a Nazi or two is among the guests). Importantly, we immediately understand that the Weiss family is fully assimilated, educated, and civilized. Music, art, and literature are highly valued in their luxurious home. In fact music, in the form of Anna's piano-playing, becomes a signifier for the Weisses and the forces of high culture. But as we shall soon see, music can also become a symbol of disharmony. With the Nazis' brutal assault on European culture, the harmonious music of the cosmological spheres is thrown totally out-of-whack.

Originally, teleplaywriter Gerald Green had envisioned the Weisses as a working-class family of Polish Jews, which he believed more indicative of the majority of Jews killed by the Nazis. However, producer Herbert Brodkin (who also produced the excellent telefilm *Judgment at Nuremberg* [1959]) saw things very differently. Rather than working-class Poles, the Weisses were transformed into wealthy, aristocratic, fully assimilated, totally indulged German Jews. In this way, Brodkin believed the family would be much more in keeping with the way American television audiences typically viewed Jews. Also, Karl was provided with a righteous, blonde-haired Christian wife, Inga (superbly played by Meryl Streep in a star-making, Emmy Award–winning performance). With Brodkin's alterations of Green's original concept, we see *Holocaust* being carefully tailored to fit in with other previous television models dealing with the Holocaust. Which, according to Jeffery Shandler, helped American television

> establish a distinct Holocaust iconography and recurrent thematic approaches to the subject. In particular, American television tended to use the Holocaust as a point of entry into more universal issues — the limits of justice, the consequences of intolerance, or the nature of evil — demonstrating the Holocaust as a moral paradigm in general American culture.[15]

In *The Age of Television*, Martin Esslin stresses that "the identity of a culture, the self-image of a nation is formed by the concepts, myths, beliefs, and patterns of conduct that are instantly recognized by the members of that social entity as being peculiarly theirs."[16] Thus, the central goal of Brodkin and Green was to make *Holocaust* function as both the "moral paradigm" Shandler refers to and a universal identifier "instantly recognized" by the broadest possible spectrum of the American television audience of 1978. This concept is further echoed in the advice given by Rabbi Marc Tannenbaum of the American Jewish Committee. Not wanting *Holocaust* to be perceived as solely "a Jewish obsession," Rabbi Tannenbaum impressed upon Brodkin and Green that the epic miniseries had "to be used as a tool that would ultimately raise the consciousness, deepening the moral commitments of the American people not to stand idly by while hatred, prejudice, verbal violence, and actual murder are being unleashed against Jews, and against any other human beings."[17]

Along with the processes of universalization and Americanization (which in the case of *Holocaust* are one and the same), the Weisses undergo yet another process. Although it is true that each family member is noble and gifted, it is highly unlikely that the televisionmakers ever intended to bestow upon them any sort of godly or superhuman powers. Still, we cannot help but feel there are strong similarities between what happens to them and the mythic stories of ancient dying gods and goddesses. In this respect, their story becomes a tragic *Götterdämmerung*, a Twilight of the Gods, a somber mediation on the nature of good and evil in the universe. This reaches a great climax with the individual life-and-death choices each character must make when confronted with the face of total evil on the monumental battlefield of European civilization. Such a battle is not simply between two human forces. There is a much greater cosmogonic, epic battle at stake between the forces of light and darkness, good and evil, life and death, the sacred and profane. Here the true ambitious nature of *Holocaust* comes into sharper focus: as the Jews of Europe are destroyed, so too is the civilized world.

We considered how, in the opening scenes, the epic narrative structure of *Holocaust* owes an artistic debt to *Roots*. We soon realize that, like the young Kunta in his idyllic Africa, the Weisses are not quite prepared for the cataclysmic future that lies ahead of them. Jennifer Ring points out, "the more unprecedented and inhuman the deeds carried out by the Nazis, the more difficult it was for 'ordinary' people to absorb, accept, and defend themselves."[18] This cruel irony receives its fullest expression in *Holocaust* through the character of Berta Weiss. Berta is totally caught up in her well-heeled role as upper-middle-class German *hausfrau*, she foolishly refuses to acknowledge the deadly forces gathering around her and her family. Somewhat reminiscent of Julie in her incarnation as Rudi's trophy wife in *Rich Man, Poor Man*, Berta thrives on her identity as a cosmopolitan German sophisticate and cannot comprehend that in Hitler's new Germany there is no longer a place for someone like her. Fortunately, when circumstances go far beyond her control and she is forced to face the brutal reality before her, she discovers she is a much tougher woman, with infinitely stronger survival skills, than even she ever realized. As a result of this realization, and despite the fact she is ultimately doomed, she is elevated to the status of the mythic type of Wife, making her the first in the triumvirate of good Wives in *Holocaust* (Inga and Helena being the other two).

The geography of Europe plays a key metaphoric and mythic role in *Holocaust*. As the action unfolds, "each family member's fate brings him or her to different sites that have come to be widely acknowledged as landmarks of the Holocaust master narrative."[19] For example, Josef and Berta are deported from Berlin (where they witness the horrors of *Kristallnacht*) to the Warsaw Ghetto, and finally to the place of their deaths, Auschwitz. Karl is initially imprisoned at Buchenwald, then Thersienstadt, then like his parents is sent to Auschwitz to be killed. After she is raped and her psychological state deteriorates, Anna is sent to the insane asylum at Hadamar, where she is gassed to death. Rudi is imprisoned in Sobibor, where he participates in the camp's heroic uprising against the Nazis, becoming the only member of his family to fight back and survive.

However, since all the places and spaces of Europe have become so thoroughly desecrated by the violating Nazi presence, neither those places nor spaces can sustain a survivor of the Holocaust such as Rudi any longer. And so, with the Old World turned against him and the New World seemingly off limits, Rudi views the Jewish homeland of the utopian Israel as the only place left to provide him the sustenance he needs. Just as the transcendent Dream of Africa filled Kunta Kinte and his descendants with a sense of hope in *Roots*, Israel serves a similar function in *Holocaust*. At the conclusion of this chapter, we shall consider the meaning of this strong connection between Rudi and the state of Israel.

The Perversity of Evil

In her controversial book about the trial of Adolf Eichmann, *Eichmann in Jerusalem: A Report on the Banality of Evil*,[20] philosopher Hannah Arendt describes the infamous Nazi anti–Semite, responsible for sending thousands upon thousands of Jews to their deaths, as not being an inhuman, evil monster. To the contrary, Arendt characterizes Eichmann as a rather drab, innocuous, completely business-like civil servant, so intent on currying favor with his Nazi superiors that he willingly destroys his innocent victims just to gain the attention he so desperately craves. On a basic level, there is an aspect of this same sort of petty, civil servant obsequiousness to Michael Moriarty in his chilling, Emmy Award–winning portrayal of Nazi Erik Dorf, which makes him a more popularized signifier of Arendt's complex psychological thesis.

Yet on a deeper level, there is a more disturbing quality of evil that is infinitely greater than the banal sort of evil Arendt so eloquently writes of — an evil even greater than any form of epic miniseries evil that came before, or indeed will come again until the broadcast of *War and Remembrance*. This is evil on such an unimaginable scale, it eventually affects the entire Earth, all its people, places, and history. It is a totally mythic, epic evil. In *Holocaust*, this mythic evil begins in the unholy alliance of Dorf and his constantly cunning, Lady Macbeth–like wife Marta. Hairless, pampered, prissy, and with no real sense of self or moral substance, Dorf is depicted as the major Nazi villain single-handedly responsible for masterminding the mechanics of the Final Solution. In a way, this makes Dorf the mythic symbol for "all the Nazis who ever attempted genocide against the Jews."[21] His wife Marta's main aspect is equally selfish and sinister, if not even more so. So manipulative and menacing does she become in her ruthless ambition for her husband, their intimate scenes together explode into shockingly disturbing episodes of mass killing, which end up taking on an apocalyptic sexual charge. At times these scenes become so overheated with elements of melodrama and fascistic power plays, the Dorfs become an unholy intermingling of Eros and Thanatos polluting the entire continent of Europe.

Like *Rich Man, Poor Man* and *Roots*, *Holocaust* is structured in terms of binary dialectic, and thus takes place in a Manichean moral universe. The good-innocent-life affirming Jews are pitted against the evil-corrupt-death monger-

In the Face of Absolute Evil: Loyal wife Inga Weiss (Meryl Streep) confronts Nazi aggression head on. *Holocaust* (NBC, 1978).

ing Nazis. Although this codified structuring device helps make complex philosophical, moral, and ethical issues easier to grasp, it also triggers an ironic effect. Beginning with the nightmarishly sadistic behavior of Dorf and Marta, this ironic effect is present in all of the other Nazi characters. Eichmann, Heydrich, Himmler are all portrayed through melodramatic iconography: totally emotionless, with ugly, blank faces and cold, dead eyes empty of anything except their contempt for others. Taken as a whole, the Nazis of *Holocaust* are among the most despicable of villains of the epic miniseries. They do not even seem to exist on the same plane of representation as the noble Jewish characters. There can be no doubt that these Nazis occupy the same televisual frame of reference as do the Jews, but clearly they are *not* the same. This doubtless accounts for the Nazis' insistence on displacing their own depravity onto the oppressed figure of the Jew. To do so, they rely upon the same type of historical-sexual memory the Whites used to define the Black man and woman in *Roots*. For the Nazis, the Jewish woman signifies the archetype of the Whore (in one scene, Karl is beaten senseless by the Nazis for refusing to refer to his mother as a "whore"). Similarly, the Jewish man, like the Black man, is associated with a powerless "emasculated" masculinity. Going further, the Jewish man and woman are connected to a totally abnormal, repellant sexuality. Through this characterization of the Jew as sexual "Other," the Nazis provoke more than enough fear and hatred to justify their plans for total annihilation. Just as in the paradigm of Wagnerian Myth, it is the small, dark, cunning Jew-Niebelung who defiles The Nordic god-race.

If this seems like more than enough abuse for the Nazis to heap upon the Jews of *Holocaust*, there is even more to come. Just as the pseudo-scientific concept of the sexual deviate is used to define the Jew under German authoritarianism, soon all other aspects of Jewish reality are equally distorted. Dorf's manipulation of language regarding the Holocaust resolutely erases the concepts of reason and meaning from the grammatical equation. And when Karl is first sent to the model concentration camp of Thersienstadt, he quickly realizes the whole of it is nothing more than a deception, an empty Hollywoodized façade, a nasty *trompe l'oeil* used to camouflage the Nazis' real intent against the Jews.

Music is also subjected to the same kind of fascistic erasure and distortion. For example, when the Weisses are sent to concentration camps, Dorf "appropriates" Anna's beloved grand piano for his own selfish purposes. Later, after the piano is destroyed in an air raid bombing, music itself is negated. Music can no longer be said to reflect the humanistic, civilized values it did at the start of the epic narrative. Now music signifies grave cosmic disharmony, death, doom, and total destruction: the destruction of Anna's beloved grand piano; of the members of her family; the destruction of the camp victims; of the Jews, Gypsies, Slavs, and homosexuals; the destruction of the continent of Europe, its people, its culture, and of all civilization.

For such reasons, composer Martin Gould found himself so overwhelmed by the force of the epic narrative and imagery of *Holocaust*, he chose to approach his scoring in a subtle, minimalist style. Apart from specific music source cues—the Nazis constantly play Wagnerian operas, Mozart is performed by musicians in the death camps (and in both cases, music reflects suffering, death and final solutions)—Gould's musical composition principally consists of the show's profoundly mournful main theme, the chilling, eerie music used in the many scenes of railroad transport to the death camps, and the full-scale finale, featuring the triumphant burst of pure sound signifying Rudi's journey to the promised land of Israel.

Similarly, *Holocaust* exhibits a rare, sparse, austere monumentality. Much of its overall evocativeness derives from this approach to the grave subject. Like a mythic tale out of the Old Testament, this technique allows for the message of the text to arise from a symphony of "pained voices ... which are allowed to clash even as the epic narrative plunges inexorably forward."[22] At times this results in an ironic avoidance of the epic style. Yet despite this approach, *Holocaust* is never in danger of deconstructing itself (as will happen with some of epic miniseries of the late 1980s). Instead, since the epic form is traditionally associated with classicism, paganism, and polytheism, a spurning of the mechanics of the epic only further reinforces the connection of *Holocaust* to the Biblical idea of the eternal struggle and suffering of the Jews.

A sense of the ironic is also reaffirmed by the extensive use of several black-and-white, "real-life" photographic montages all through the course of the epic narrative, depicting the horrors inflicted upon the Jews by the Nazis. On one level, such excruciating imagery "demonstrates the recognition of these now famous images as signs of historicity and as morally charged icons."[23] On another level, they work both to corroborate and subtly complicate the epic narrative, establishing a certain destabilization of the frame. The continuous stream of "real-life" Holocaust imagery (which, amazingly, the Nazis view for their own perverse pleasure) throws into question the slightly "unreal" quality of what is being viewed by both the Nazis and the audience. This throws out-of-focus such standard tropes of the epic miniseries as its often overblown rhetoric of melodrama, discontinuity of traditional plot construction, "false" happy endings, and distancing effects. For whether the rest of the world accepted it or not, the use of these images firmly establishes that what is at stake in *Holocaust* is nothing less than the heart and soul of Western civilization itself.

Along with the rippling effects created by the stripped-down visuals and extensive use of "real-life" Holocaust imagery, director Martin J. Chomsky provides a valuable object lesson in combining sight and sound to create a brilliant elliptical and contrapuntal effect. His sense of timing is consistently dramatic and assured throughout: as an extreme close-up of the Star of David burning in a synagogue fills the screen, the jarring sound of glass shattering in the distance is heard; as the hands of a young Jewish woman are shown stopping her playing the piano, the music she played is still heard; a shot of an old woman extinguishing Passover candles is accompanied by the discordant sound of gun shots, marking the start of the heroic Warsaw uprising. Such a contrapuntal effect sets up a surrealistic abstraction of texture, which symbolizes the events of the Holocaust. This approach is at a remove from the vast majority of the epic miniseries of American television of the time, only to find its way fruitfully back in those of the latter 1990s and 2000s.

Jews with Guns

We now return to the subject of Rudi, the only surviving member of the Weiss family, and his utopian dream of creating a new and better world for himself and his people in the earthly paradise, the new Zion — Israel. Early on, the rebellious Rudi, so titanic in his masculine athleticism, plays a rugged game of soccer. When a Nazi player on the opposing team calls him a "dirty Jew" and picks a fight, Rudi is more than happy to oblige him. It doesn't take long for him to get the better of the fascistic thug. While the other members of his family choose to ignore the threat of the Nazis, Rudi prepares himself for the worst. Taking matters into his own hands, he joins a group of rough-and-ready Russian partisans, whose goal is to wipe out every Nazi they can. Rudi becomes newly empowered. He is the prototype of the "Brave New Jew" bound for a new life of hopes and dreams, with a desire for spatiality and the pastoral idyll of Israel as opposed to the doom and gloom faced by the European Jews of the Diaspora.

Indeed, it is not overstating the matter to say *Holocaust* ultimately endorses a specifically Zionist point of view. When Rudi first connects with the Russian partisans, he admires their impressive arsenal of weapons, exclaiming, "Jews with guns!" Rather than allow himself to be "emasculated" by the Nazis, Rudi will reclaim his endangered masculinity through possessing the empowering phallic symbol of the gun to turn against his mortal "emasculating" enemy. After successfully completing his Zionist rite of passage (the killing of his very first Nazi), he can reclaim his rightful Jewish manhood for all to see and admire.

In his study of the depiction of the Jew in film, *From Hester Street to Hollywood*, Lawrence Langer severely criticizes *Holocaust* for ending on a positive note, rather than the negative note he felt the material necessitated.[24] Still, if the final hopeful image, depicting an exuberant, empowered Rudi playing a game of soccer with the group of beaming Jewish children he will take to Israel with him, does not fully mitigate all of the complex issues the epic narrative has raised, it nevertheless serves a crucial purpose. After all the sorrow and horror of the past 9½ hours of the epic narrative, the final image of *Holocaust* beautifully connects Rudi to the future utopian Jewish homeland of Israel, signifying "all that which makes survival a true possibility — hope."[25] Moreover, such a hopeful image establishes Rudi as the rightful predecessor of the mythic type of the Adventurer, who would come to dominate the epic miniseries of the 1980s.

In conclusion, Sally Bedell's remarks regarding the public's response to the airing of *Holocaust* deserve to be quoted in full:

> The odd makers all folded up their tents ... when *Holocaust* attracted masses of viewers. Over its four-night run, over 50 percent of the television audience tuned in.[26] Like *Roots*, *Holocaust* drew its phenomenal appeal from a compelling personal saga interwoven with melodramatic love stories and acts of heroism, featuring a collection of diverse characters to gain viewers' affection ... the epic miniseries also served as a painful reminder to the generation who witnessed the Holocaust, as well as the wrenching introduction to those born more recently. For that reason alone, it was airtime well used.[27]

Along with *Roots* and *Holocaust*, several other notable epic miniseries featured the mythic type of the Heroic Slave in the 1970s: *Moses—the Lawgiver* (CBS, 1975) featured Hollywood veteran Burt Lancaster as the founding father of monotheism; *A Woman Called Moses* (NBC, 1978) starred the extraordinary Cicely Tyson as the legendary Civil War–era slave Harriet Tubman; *Backstairs at the White House* (NBC, 1979) showcased many of the same iconic Black actors from *Roots* (Olivia Cole, Leslie Uggams, Louis Gossett Jr., Robert Hooks) in an *Upstairs, Downstairs*–like epic narrative focusing on an amazing mother (Cole) and daughter (Uggams) who serve for over fifty years as White House domestics for eight different First Families; and *Roots: The Next Generations* (ABC, 1979) continued Alex Haley's landmark familial saga, starting where *Roots* ended in 1882 and carrying the epic tale up to the present. James Earl Jones starred as Haley, and Hollywood heavyweight Marlon Brando contributed a riveting sequence as American Nazi leader George Lincoln Rockwell. This truly worthy sequel used the epic form with great assurance, and concluded powerfully with Haley returning to Africa, learning of his ancient "roots," and finally attaining Kunta Kinte's Great Dream of Africa at long last.

So persuasive does the Heroic Slave become during the 1970s, the archetype defines the attributes and associations of several of the other protagonists of the epic miniseries of the decade. As a consequence, aspects of the Heroic Slave, in both defeated and undefeated states, crop up in several likely and even unlikely places. Some of these include: Sybil Dorsett (Sally Field) fleeing into a multiplicity of different personalities to liberate herself from the unspeakable horrors of her traumatic childhood in *Sybil* (NBC, 1976); Howard Hughes (Tommy Lee Jones) descending into his own imprisoning madness in *The Amazing Howard Hughes* (CBS, 1977); Studs Lonigan (Harry Hamlin) struggling heroically against the oppressive forces of his Depression-era Chicago life in *Studs Lonigan* (NBC, 1979); and John Dean (Martin Sheen) fatally allowing his own ruthless ambition to entrap him in the political machinations of the Nixonian Watergate scandal in *Blind Ambition* (CBS, 1979).

What these characters and several others of the 1970s all have in common is a sense of a paradise being lost. Eden and doom, choice and destiny are the defining hallmarks of each. Despite the differences of their situations from those of the Blacks of *Roots* or the Jews of *Holocaust*, all are forced into the marginalized position of the Other, struggling against overwhelming odds in a heroic attempt to regain the privileged sense of a lost paradise, Edenic in its perfection.

Chapter 3

The Extraordinary Ordinary

The 1980s were a unique period for the epic miniseries of American television. The shift away from the archetype of the Heroic Slave of the 1970s, the conclusion of the manic mood swings of the 1960s, and the vague drift that characterized a good deal of the 1970s gradually evolved into a quite different cultural space in the new decade. The epic miniseries of the 1980s would be expressed much more lavishly than those of the 1970s, and with the ascendancy of Ronald Reagan to the presidency, to a certain extent more conservatively. This was also affected by the growing appeal of foreign ideas and more modernistic televisual techniques, as a result of the presence throughout the decade of such commanding texts by televisual artists like Sweden's Ingmar Bergman, Germany's Rainer Werner Fassbinder, Great Britain's Dennis Potter (all detailed in Chapter 5), and, to a somewhat lesser extent, two other epic miniseries that presented Germany's Nazi years in a new light: Wolfgang Peterson's *Das Boot* (1981) and Edgar Rentz's *Heimat: A Chronicle in Eleven Parts* (1984). It was these factors, as well as the emergence of the glorified archetype of the Adventurer—with all of his heroic energy, arrogance, incentive, fearlessness, and aggression of ambitiousness—that added up to a new type of epic miniseries for a new age.

The most popular of the five mythic types of the epic miniseries, the Adventurer is a bold sensualist, an ironist, a winning *bon vivant.* Essentially a Homeric or Virgilian figure, much like Odysseus of *The Odyssey* or even a demigod like Hercules, the Adventurer has the power to pursue an arduous struggle or journey to an extraordinary conclusion, no matter how great the cost to himself or others. The Adventurer shapes himself through epic action, as if the mythic quest were a thing separate from and more important than all else. The Adventurer *must* achieve his final goal at all costs. Like Odysseus, the Adventurer has the power to transform the ordinary into the extraordinary.

Since he possesses such heroic traits, it only stands to reason the women (and sometimes even the men) of the epic miniseries should be drawn to the charismatic figure of the Adventurer. The erotic dynamic that develops often takes the form of selfish male sexual desire directed at (and at times even *against*) the alluring type of the desirable woman. But what sort of relationships does the Adventurer have with women? Typically, such interactions form an eternal scenario of seduction and possession, of deviousness and indifference, of rejection and betrayal, and, on occasion, of ruthless abandonment. We see a good example of how this scenario operates in the epic miniseries *Cap-*

tains and the Kings (NBC, 1976). Based on the novel by Taylor Caldwell, the epic narrative contains one of the first and best early depictions of the mythic type of the Adventurer in the character of Joseph Armagh (Richard Jordan). In the America of the 1850s the young, orphaned and impoverished Joseph emigrates from Ireland in search of the American Dream. The epic narrative follows him on his harrowing journey to America, through his many extraordinary trials and tribulations, to his acquisition of wealth and power beyond even his own dreams of rapacity. We are given a vivid *Citizen Kane*–like portrait of a man who gains it all at an astronomical cost to himself and everyone else. Whereas the great trinitarian symbol of the epic miniseries (*Rich Man, Poor Man/Roots/Holocaust*) advocated an essentially traditional view of American humanism, celebrating a basic belief in the principles of the triumph of the individual and the virtues of an American system of values, *Captains and the Kings* takes a more jaundiced view of such matters.

This view is clearly reflected in Joseph's treatment of the women in his life. Although the female characters are depicted in the codified dyadic configuration of the Wife/Whore dialectic, the epic narrative modifies the two mythic types so that they are depicted even more transgressively. Wife and Whore form opposite sides of a scandalous triangular relationship with the wayward hero. (Diagram 3.1 graphs the triangle on which the epic action turns.)

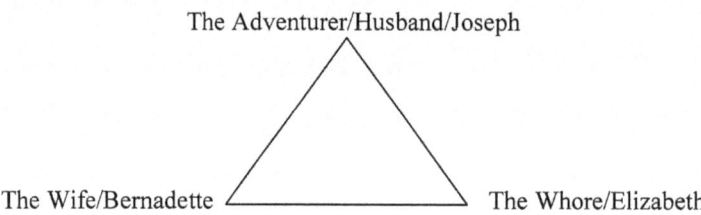

Diagram 3.1 — The triangular relationship of *Captain and the Kings.*

Matters are complicated even more by the fact that the younger, more beautiful, more desirable, and more comforting Whore, Elizabeth (Blair Brown), is also the widowed stepmother-in-law of the Wife, Bernadette (Patty Duke), whom Joseph only married for her wealth and prestige. The scene in which the two disparate women confront one another is one of the high points of the epic miniseries.

After Bernadette learns of her husband's scandalous affair, she pays a call on her rival. The scene takes place in the high-cultural space of Elizabeth's luxurious home (paid for by Joseph, of course). The predominant color scheme — red, white, and lavender — gives the room a vaginal mysteriousness. Initially, each of the women assumes a cool, detached air of civility. But as their words take on more stylized rhetorical formality, they become actresses attempting to upstage one another amidst the oppressive Victorian mise-en-scène. Their former dignified stances were, at best, a fraud. Each fueled by the determination of her own immovable will, the "civilized" encounter deteriorates into a bitter circle of betrayal, guilt, anger, and revenge. Although each seeks to overpower the other, poor Bernadette is no match for the more resourceful Elizabeth.

When all else fails, the deflated Bernadette sinks into a closed-off, interiorized space of drinking, bitter recrimination, and melodramatic despair. Her deepening self-pity and misery trigger explosive expressions of Ophelia-like hysteria, complete with florid monologues. Patty Duke (who was rightfully awarded an Emmy for her riveting performance) acts out these scenes with such mad intensity, *Captains and the Kings* attains the same sort Shakespearean ripeness achieved in the more harrowing parts of *Roots*.

Four years after the broadcast of *Captains and the Kings*, NBC scored a greater triumph with arguably the most popular mythic Adventurer in the character of John Blackthorne in *Shogun*. This chapter will examine how the philosophical themes and aesthetics explored in *Captains and the Kings* are further developed and evolved in four of the very best epic miniseries of the 1980s: *Shogun*, *Brideshead Revisited* (PBS, 1981), *The Thorn Birds* (ABC, 1983), and *Lonesome Dove* (CBS, 1989). In each case, we see instances of epic narrative patterning arranged and sustained to form a complex visual tapestry in which history and the idea of the ordinary becoming extraordinary are elevated to the ultimate epic televisual spectacle. Within the structure of the four texts, an additional epic narrative commentary develops using a series of eroticized motifs. The most significant of these takes the form of the transgressive and forbidden nature of the Adventurer's connection to the beloved or beloveds. So predominant does this motif become in the 1980s, it might even qualify as the sixth trope of the genre.

Shogun

Shogun is admired for the intricacy of its grand design, its elegant grandeur, and the excellence of its performances. Its appearance at the beginning of the decade signaled that the epic miniseries was moving into a new direction, constituting a new vision of high televisual style. The 1975 novel by James Clavell on which it was based sold over seven million copies in the hard-cover edition. When it was translated to the small screen, it provided Richard Chamberlain (cast as John Blackthorne) with the role of a lifetime and totally reinvented the contours of his previous star image.

The epic action begins with arrogant, mercenary Englishman Blackthorne, along with his crew of seven men, getting shipwrecked in Japan of the 1600s. Japanese warlord Yabu (Frankie Sakai) imprisons the Englishmen, feeds them rotten fish, and even boils one of the men alive. Thus begins Blackthorne's initiation into the inscrutable world of feudal Japan. Cunning and sly Lord Toranga (Toshirô Mifune) intervenes on Blackthorne's behalf. He sends rough-and-ready Portuguese seaman Vasco Rodriguez (John Rhys Davies) to bring the Englishmen to him. During a violent storm at sea, Blackthorne saves Rodriguez's life, indebting the Portuguese to him.

Later, Lord Toranga supplies Blackthorne with the beautiful Lady Mariko (Yoko Shimada) to teach him the customs and language of Japan. This act enrages powerful Jesuit priests Father Alvito (Damien Thomas) and Father dell 'Aqua (Alan Bladell). They view the presence of the Protestant Blackthorne as a threat to the ruthless Vatican plunder of the vast wealth of Japan. Over time Toranga and Blackthorne develop a close friendship, which leads to Toranga making the Englishman the first Occidental samurai.

As Mariko teaches Blackthorne the finer points of Japanese life and custom through a totally forbidden affair between Occident and Orient, he instructs her on the subtleties of Western love and devotion, which hardly endears him to Lord Buntaro (Hideo Takamatsu), Mariko's hot-tempered samurai husband.

The epic narrative goes on to chronicle the elaborate labyrinth of treachery and hard-fought battles Toranga must wage to become the all-powerful Shogun of Japan. Although Mariko is killed, Blackthorne becomes an honorable and courageous samurai in his own right. Unbeknownst to him, Toranga is the one responsible for the destruction of Blackthorne's ship the *Erasmus*. A final voiceover reveals Toranga will see to it that the invaluable Blackthorne never leaves Japan again.

Up until this point, all the epic miniseries we have considered presented the "Other" as a marginalized figure in contrast to the dominant White culture. *Shogun* and *Brideshead Revisited* reverse this configuration. Now the marginalized Other dominates the course of the epic action. Englishman John Blackthorne is forced to hold his arrogant Western ways in check. In *Brideshead Revisited*, bisexual artist Charles Ryder is in control of the commanding authorial voice. In both epic miniseries we see the use of history combined with superior production values, erotic plotlines of a forbidden nature, and the concept of the ordinary becoming extraordinary explored. Within the dimensions of the epic miniseries, history is hardly indeterminate. It is closely linked to a dazzling mix of desire for power, heightened stylization, ritualization, eroticism, exoticism, epic narrative, and a fetishization of visual spectacle. Since this connection of textual and contextual elements becomes so all encompassing, it deserves our close attention.

The phrase "World history from the keyhole perspective or backstairs view(s) of history"[1] best describes the epic miniseries of the 1980s. In the case of *Shogun*, this concept is articulated in the profusion of exotic and mysterious imagery. In his classic study *Orientalism*, Edward Said writes, "the Orient became known in the West as its great complementary opposite since antiquity." Out of this Western conceptualization of the East, a number of codified encapsulations developed, featuring such tropes as "the journey, the history, the fable, the stereotype, and the polemical confrontation. These are the lenses through which the Orient is experienced, and they shape the language, perception, and the form of the encounter between East and West."[2]

Along with its exemplification of Said's central thesis, another explanation for the singular achievement of *Shogun* grows out of teleplaywriter Eric Bercovici's decision to have all of the epic action perceived through Blackthorne's baffled Western sensibility. This risky concept involves having the action presented to us in the form of an unintelligible Japanese dialogical discourse without the benefit of English subtitles. Only the periodic voiceover narration of Orson Welles provides any explanation of what is taking place. This point is important. Since Western audiences are unfamiliar with Eastern codes and references, they are unable to de-codify the televisual code. Although Blackthorne does gradually gain greater understanding of the Japanese, it is the Eastern "Other" who is in control of the mystifying epic narrative.

It was playwright Bertolt Brecht who opened up the epic form to culturally didactic proportions. To a certain extent, *Shogun* exhibits a Brechtian influence. We see a preference for a relentless swath of history, with the more humanistic concerns toned down. There is a greater reliance upon Eastern concepts of mise-en-scène and a conspicuous dependence on epic narration in the form of Orson Welles's continuous voiceover narration. But above all else, *Shogun* depicts the idea of the ultimate power the strong exert over the weak. Rather than totally alienating audiences, this Brechtian influence has the opposite effect: the epic narrative becomes all the more mysterious and compelling. Clavell's complex literary structural patterning also helped make the epic miniseries a triumph of the spirit over time and place. The author provided the cohesion that interlocked the large cast of characters in place. This can be seen in the careful establishment of chronology, enabling us to follow all the complicated twists-and-turns as the epic narrative constantly moves forward in time. It can also be seen in the organizing pattern involving Blackthorne's personal development. More precisely, he undergoes four separate stages of culture shock: "(1) delight in his new culture; (2) horror, shock, revulsion, and resistance; (3) gradual accommodation; (4) immersion, and full acceptance."[3] Through this process, he is elevated from an ordinary character to an extraordinary one.

For the remainder of our discussion of *Shogun*, we will focus on the way mise-en-scène, music, stylized acting technique, and the idea of the ordinary becoming the extraordinary are combined to negotiate through and ease up on the inherent tensions of the dangerous encounter between East and West. Since much of the Japanese dialogue is unintelligible, we (along with Blackthorne) must struggle to make sense of matters. As a result, great emphasis is placed upon the enigmatic, sights, sounds, melodrama, poetry, décor, gesture, and movement that constitute the feudal Japan of the 17th century.

Concomitantly, *Shogun* becomes the polar opposite of *Holocaust*. There, the power of sound and the word dominated all; here, it is the image that dominates. This creates a realization of a metaphysics of the visual representation of the East. Said says this is the preferred aesthetic for the way the West has traditionally depicted the "Otherness" of the East. Indeed, the mise-en-scène of *Shogun* creates the effect of a series of exotic Japanese watercolored backdrops continually dissolving and reforming into an endless series of exotic patterns, sort of like a surreal, endless, lavender kimono unfolding through eternity. Within this fleeting, ephemeral world, the actors stand out, sharply delineated through their opulent, richly-hued costumes, histrionic gestures, and movements. Composer Maurice Jarre, who supplied the evocative musical score for *Shogun*, compared the cumulative effect of such imagery to viewing a sumptuous ballet. But he could just have easily compared it to the baroque, unnaturalistic style of grand opera and traditional historical pageantry. Accordingly, he saw his creative mission as providing music that would help audiences penetrate the obscurity of surface polish into the elegance of the epic narrative's exotic, erotic, esoteric beauty.

Relying upon the East-versus-West theme of the piece to its fullest, Jarre develops three distinct musical themes. The first signifies the harassed, world-weary West of John Blackthorne. The second represents the strident militarism and manipulations of Toranga's worldview. The third and most haunting theme reflects the sweeping Eastern Romanticism of the doomed Lady Mariko. For

The Noblest Englishman of All: John Blackthorne (Richard Chamberlain) is made the first Occidental Samurai in Japan 17th-century feudal Japan. *Shogun* (NBC, 1980).

her music, Jarre wed an unusual selection of traditional Japanese instruments to produce a lyrical, feminine sound. Mariko's theme conveys an intangible sense of the eternal, ageless beauty of both Woman and Japan in their combined timelessness, immortality, *lux perpetua*.

The sterling performances of Chamberlain, Mifune, and Shimada match Jarre's musical contribution. Chamberlain brings a subtle, larger-than-life-quality, combined with his matinee idol handsomeness and an emphatic acting style, to the role of John Blackthorne. Mifune's charismatic international star presence dominates every scene in which he appears as Toranga. Shimada plays Lady Mariko as an isolated, highly enigmatic figure imbued with a poignant beauty and grace. Although she lives out her days in a privileged world of luxurious royal palaces and secluded estates, Lady Mariko's is a cursed existence. For this reason, we fully understand her attraction to Blackthorne.

As in *Captains and the Kings*, the erotic dynamic of the sexes in *Shogun* is articulated as a triangular configuration. Here Mariko makes up the female component in a double-sided arrangement, consisting of the acceptable (public) triangle (Mariko, Toranga, Buntaro), and the forbidden (private) triangle (Mariko, Torango, Blackthorne). Diagram Example 3.2 illustrates the basic double triangular structure of *Shogun*:

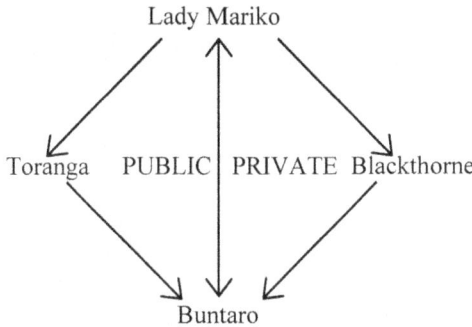

Diagram 3.2 — The double triangular relationship of *Shogun*.

This second, forbidden triangle raises the epic dramatic stakes of *Shogun* considerably. As a result of the dependency of the epic miniseries on the visual, a specific formal aesthetic comes into play in the way Mariko is depicted. She is the female as the forbidden, desirable Other. Her face a Kabuki white, her blue-black hair arranged in a confounding assortment of geometric configurations, her body clad in silk, satin, velvet, and damask, Mariko functions as a symbol of Japanese obsession with order, harmony, and tradition as beauty. When she speaks, her words have a haiku-like simplicity and purity. Their accumulative vision builds up into a concatenation perfectly in tune with the Japanese appreciation of beauty in the smallest and simplest of things. And because Mariko always expresses herself to Blackthorne with an incomparable delicacy of inner feeling, even during some of the most emotionally overwrought scenes, she is transformed into something deeper and more complicated than either of the mythic types of Wife or Whore. Like Dante's Beatrice, who inspires Dante toward Paradise, Mariko inspires and elevates Blackthorne. Here then the pastoral idyll of the West is shifted to Japan in general, and to Mariko in particular.

Conversely, while Mariko inspires Blackthorne, he creates within her a greater appreciation for the Western sense of the romantic, for justice and right. However, this idyllic symbiotic blending of East and West between the couple will not be the final image we carry away from *Shogun*. In an unexpected turn, the focus of the epic narrative is abruptly and irrevocably ruptured, moving from Blackthorne's point of view to the far more inscrutable point of view of Toranga. What had previously seemed only the manipulative game plan of a master powerbroker grows infinitely darker and more sinister. Thus, Toranga is revealed as an even more ruthless, controlling, and Godlike figure than either Axel or his brother, Harold, was to Tom in *Rich Man, Poor Man*. Like Axel and Harold, Toranga thinks nothing of using those around him as his pawns. Not only does he see to it Blackthorne will never experience the sort of joyous reunion Odysseus shared with his Penelope (after all, Toranga did have a hand in Mariko's death), he also sees to it that Blackthorne will never return home again when he orders the destruction of his ship the *Erasmus*. Thus, Paradise is never to be regained for Blackthorne.

In some ways, *Shogun* provides us with two different endings. The first, predictive ending depicts Blackthorne coming to terms with the loss of Mariko and experiencing a moment of self-contentment, of self-discovery, and personal epiphany while resurrecting the *Erasmus* to its former glory. But with the second ending, the prescriptive ending, we learn the full extent of Toranga's duplicity toward Blackthorne. Hence, in spite of Blackthorne's impressive personal development in *Shogun*, the last impression is one of an unequivocal nature. Blackthorne's destiny is to remain Toranga's prisoner in Japan until the end of his days, forever denied the joyous pleasures of both his beloved England and his beloved Lady Mariko.

Brideshead Revisited

Although a span of three hundred years separate the two, the Englishman Charles Ryder (Jeremy Irons) in *Brideshead Revisited* (PBS, 1981) finds himself in circumstances not all that different from those John Blackthorne faced in *Shogun*. Based on Evelyn Waugh's classic epic novel of upper-class English love, sorrow, and sensibility, *Brideshead Revisited* begins at Oxford University in the

1920s. It is there the ordinary-seeming Charles Ryder becomes romantically involved with spoiled, petulant aristocrat Sebastian Flyte (Anthony Andrews). When Sebastian takes Charles to meet his Catholic family at their lavish ancestral home, Brideshead Castle, Charles is bowled over by the great house and its occupants: the devout, possessive Lady Marchmain (Claire Bloom); her worldly husband Lord Marchmain (Laurence Olivier), who left his family to live in Venice with sexy, Italian mistress Cara (Stephane Audran); Brideshead, or Bridey (Simon Jones), the humorless elder son; beautiful daughter Julia (Diana Quick); and the pious youngest Flyte, Cordelia (Phoebe Nicholas). Clearly the Flytes are an utterly charming and utterly dysfunctional family at best, and their various dysfunctions follow their own Catholic idiosyncrasies. It should be also noted that Brideshead Castle assumes very much an enchanted aura and magical sort of being in the tale. In fact, the eldest son being named Brideshead signifies the family's total involvement with the castle and estate in which they so decorously live.

As Sebastian is gradually revealed to be a sadomasochistic alcoholic, Charles realizes the futility of their affair. The family eventually intervenes, sending Sebastian abroad to be cured, accompanied by Mr. Samgrass (John Grillo) and vulgar *nouveau riche* businessman Rex Mottram (Charles Keating), who later makes an unhappy marriage to Julia. While Sebastian gets involved with sadistic German Kurt (Jonathan Cox), and then takes refuge in a monastery, Charles receives little comfort from his acerbic father (John Gielgud).

As the 1920s progress, Lady Marchmain dies, and Charles drops out of Oxford to become a fairly successful if quite ordinary architectural painter. He also makes a loveless marriage to the unfaithful, ambitious Celia (Jane Asher), and has a son and daughter with her. But in 1936, when he meets Julia again, Charles's whole life changes. They fall madly in love and he moves in with her at Brideshead. They make plans to divorce their partners and marry. But when Lord Marchmain returns home to die, their plans are delayed. Before he dies, Lord Marchmain accepts absolution from a priest. So moved is Julia by her father's deathbed repentance, she leaves Charles. With the outbreak of World War II, the English army takes over Brideshead Castle, and Charles is powerfully drawn to Catholicism himself.

A great critical truism is that second and even third-rate novels make for first-rate epic miniseries. However, with the broadcast of *Brideshead Revisited* in 1981, we are given a spectacular exception to the rule. Teleplaywriter John Mortimer translates Evelyn Waugh's literary masterpiece brilliantly to the small screen. A large part of Mortimer's achievement derives from his utilization of a nondiegetic narrative voice-over (spoken impeccably by Jeremy Irons), which creates the same sort of Brechtian effect as in *Shogun*. Another part of his success takes the form of the delineation of the intricate relationships between Charles, Sebastian, and Julia, which along with the relationships of several other characters is articulated as an interlocking epic narrative synthesis consisting of two levels. The first outer synaesthetic level is made up of the complex connections Charles makes with the members of the Flyte family and with Brideshead Castle itself. However, while the outer synthesis is in constant motion, it is the inner workings (comprising each character's connection to the Church) that is most important, stamping the seal of Roman Catholicism on the grand epic design. This movement, outward and inward, makes it easier to understand how the principles of the secular (the outer structure) and the sacred (the inner structure) operate. This idea is schematized in Diagram 3.3:

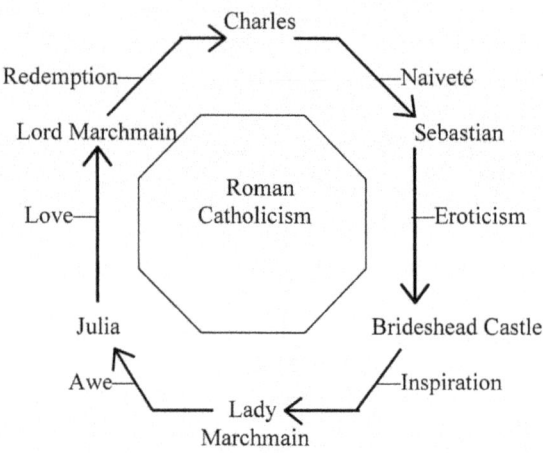

Diagram 3.3 — The foundational epic narrative of *Brideshead Revisited*.

Credit for helping us understand how this foundational structure of the epic plot operates goes to the excellence of all involved in the production: the superlative acting of the cast; the observant direction of Charles Sturridge and Michael Lindsay-Hogg; the opulent photography of Ray Goode; the meticulous attention to period detail of production designer Peter Phillips; the dream costumes of Jane Robinson; and the musical score of composer Geoffrey Burgon (his contribution is discussed below). In their combined hands, the sumptuous world of *Brideshead Revisited* takes full, exotic flight.

As fine as the achievements of these individual artists may be, there are two elements that predominate all else: the use of language and the presentation of rich architectural detail. The language of *Brideshead Revisited* is by turns epigrammatically concise, lyrically poetic, wittily Oscar Wildean, and rapier-like. For example, there is the witty use made of Bridey's intended wife, the indomitable but never once seen Beryl. Because she remains unconceptualized in both spatial and temporal terms, Beryl takes on a slippery extra-referentiality. We see this when Bridey expresses Beryl's moral indignation over the idea of Charles and Julia cohabitating in "sin" at Brideshead, *in medias res*. This function of the technique refers to an individual or event that happens outside of the frame, but helps to link together various segments or sequences of the epic narrative through the deployment of a mostly literary technique. With this, the language of the epic miniseries operates as both a narrative and dynamic element, evolving into witty and sophisticated repartee. In like manner, Lord Marchmain later evokes the comical figure of the farcical, unseen Beryl when he relates her vulgar behavior (quipping that Bridey is more the "virginal bride" than she in their relationship) at the time of her private audience with the Pope in Rome. With such verbal richness, it should come as no surprise that *Brideshead Revisited* is the connoisseur's epic miniseries.

Two of the most impressive examples of the use of architectural elements come with Oxford University in the early scenes and with Brideshead Castle throughout the epic narrative. While Oxford is a signifier of the youthful Dionysian love between Charles and Sebastian, Brideshead is a highly influential signifier all unto itself. It is a haunting emblem, which eventually becomes the heart and soul of the flow of the epic narrative, just as much a mythical symbol as any of its occupants. It is through these characters' connection to the great house of Brideshead that each of them makes his or her own journey to a state of personal grace. Waugh himself left little doubt of his final intent. He stated that *Brideshead Revisited* signaled his "attempt to trace the workings of the divine purpose in a pagan world in the lives of an English Catholic family," offering "a hope not, indeed that anything but disaster lies ahead, but that the human spirit, can survive all disasters."[4]

The mise-en-scène of this spiritualized agenda is provided with the perfect symbol in the somewhat incongruous, jewel-like chapel Lord Marchmain adds to Brideshead for the pious Lady Marchmain. Unfortunately, her piousness eventually gives way to her inherent destructiveness, making her something of "a saint spreading unhappiness all about her for everyone."[5] Much of Lady Marchmain's destructiveness gets directed at her neurotically poetic son Sebastian, who spreads quite enough unhappiness in his own right. And yet, while at Oxford, Charles is so overwhelmed with Sebastian's glamorous decadence and polymorphous perversity that he is blind to any such negativity. What he chooses to see instead is a god-like Golden Boy of impeccable breeding, exquisite sensibility, and strange enchantment. Sebastian even brings his large, stuffed Teddy-bear, Aloysius, to Oxford, which gives him an endearing Christopher Robin, little-boy-lost charm that proves irresistible to Charles. Although the love scenes between them are erotically intense, they are for the most part conveyed in a muted, diffused depiction. Still, there are those mythic scenes when the two men briefly kiss, dance together and sunbathe nude together, when the forbidden love that dare not speak its name unexpectedly rises more overtly to the surface of the epic narrative.

Much of this forbidden homoeroticism is set against the architectural magnificence of Oxford. These early, youthful scenes emphasize a certain paganistic classicism that is "defined in terms of space that is essentially static and centered upon the total indulgence of the self and the ego."⁶ The entire university is transformed into a fabulist façade, complete with the sinuous rhythms of *art nouveau* leaves and vines slithering up grand stone façades, hinting at all sorts of languid indolence and decadence within. Appropriately, it is in this setting Charles meets that mad travesty of a human being, Anthony Blanche (Nicholas Grace), who attends Oxford with Charles and Sebastian. Grace's Anthony Blanche is an altogether colorful creation. He usually spouts languid Wildean epigrams, drinks absinthe, dutifully worships the beautiful *Kritos Boy* of the ancient Greeks, and becomes a sort of mad, lurid figure out of Aubrey

The Love That Dare Not Speak Its Name: Lord Sebastian Flyte (Anthony Andrews, left), the golden object of Charles Ryder's (Jeremy Irons) youthful desire. *Brideshead Revisited* (PBS, 1998).

Beardsley, intertwined with the more modernistic overtones of Jean Genet. He's almost a caricature of the raving queen. And he dutifully appears at strategic points all throughout the tale, mostly at critical points to inform Charles of Sebastian's latest incident of personal disaster. With this, Sebastian slowly degenerates into a seething maelstrom of drunken debauchery, personal humiliation, and emotional deprivation.

When Sebastian exits the epic narrative, his sister, Julia, makes her grand entrance. Not without Dionysian tendencies of her own in her youth in the 1920s, the "New Woman" Charles becomes reacquainted with in 1936 is a very different Julia altogether. The change in her meaning and manner is conveyed in the visual terms of her sophisticated appearance and deportment, and in the streamlined mise-en-scène of the splendidly designed Art Deco ocean liner, the *Constantia*, onboard which she and Charles meet again. A marvel of strong, modern machinery with geometric, hard-edged cultural elegance forged by its lustrous planes and surfaces, the Art Deco ocean liner is no mere televisual folly. Dazzling in its modernist sense of time and space, it commands our full attention at once, as does the high-style glamour of the "new" Julia. Wearing diamond stars in her hair and a glittery silver lamé gown tightly fitted to her sleek, streamlined, Art Deco–ized body, Julia is suave, urbane, almost futuristic in appearance, a total triumph of Apollonian vision. A living, breathing symbol of spiritualized sexual illumination, she, much like the British Empire, is a radiant sun that never sets. At once Charles perceives her as the successor to his failed relationship with her brother. Thus the love/lust dynamic he once felt for Sebastian he now feels for Julia.

As the relationship between Charles and Julia deepens, the mise-en-scène moves into its third and final incarnation: the paradisiacal serenity and stately elegance of Brideshead Castle. With this movement, the epic narrative is defined in terms of a shifting away from separation toward reunion, from loss to recovery, from secular emptiness to spiritual fulfillment and the utopian. Like the condition of the Romantic Rousseauvian interlude Tom and Clothilde share in *Rich Man, Poor Man* and the idyllic African scenes of Kunta Kinte's boyhood in *Roots*, Charles and Julia cohabit in a benign state of nature in their archetypal paradise. But just as the domineering Uncle Harold and the White slave-catchers wreaked havoc on the utopian paradises of Tom and Kunta, in time the idyllic retreat of Charles and Julia is also intruded upon by forces totally out of their control.

As in the tradition of classic myth and fairy-tale, Charles and Julia have their happiness disturbed in three different ways on three different occasions: first with the news of various current events taking place in the outside world, such as the rise of Italian Fascism, the rise of Hitler in Nazi Germany, the pre-abdication rumors of King Edward and Mrs. Wallis Simpson; second through the disruptive appearances of the members of Julia's family, such as when Cordelia visits to report of Sebastian's total disintegration, or when Bridey announces his plans to marry Beryl and move into Brideshead with her; and third when Lord Marchmain returns to Brideshead to die. With his arrival, Marchmain seizes an absolutist control of the epic narrative and subjects Charles and Julia's relationship to the greatest threat of all. In other words, Lord Marchmain triggers Julia's own private, self-lacerating Catholic guilt.

With the devoted Cara by his side, Lord Marchmain returns to Brideshead. As is only befitting the return of the Lord to the manor, everyone must jump at his every command. From his luxurious Queen Anne "Death Bed," Lord Marchmain dictates that his surroundings be altered to his exact specifications. The excessively theatrical setting that results features heavy velvet drapery hung around the bed, burning incense, candles, a huge crucifix, and an imperial red-purple-gold color scheme, creating a perfect visual correlative for the turbulence of Lord Marchmain's melodramatic life and death.

Still, despite Lord Marchmain's efforts to immortalize himself, all of his hard work will be in vain if he should slip off of this mortal coil before attaining his redemption. As the hour of his death nears, the matter of the lapsed Catholic Lord Marchmain seeing the priest arises. Initially resistant, he finally relents, then accepts final absolution from the priest. Music plays a major part in his death scene. Composer Geoffrey Burgon's elegiac main theme, first heard at the opening credits, and then again and again in many variations, actually provides a clue as to the way the epic narrative must conclude for these characters.

Directly following Lord Marchmain's death and the ensuing events, both the inner and outer workings of the synaesthetic structure, which make up the flow of the epic narrative, are united, forming one integrated, organic structure. The spiritual dimension of Evelyn Waugh's full intent has now been realized. The model for this new narrative circuit is illustrated in Diagram 3.4:

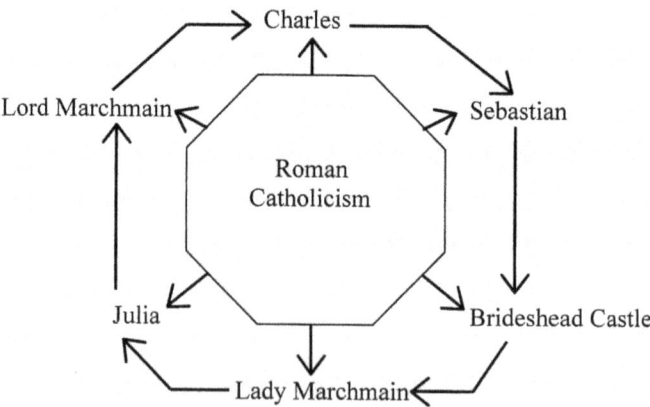

Diagram 3.4 — The foundational epic narrative of *Brideshead Revisited* fully integrated.

Through this mythopoeic process of integration, the romantic aspects of the epic narrative drop away. Eschatology and the divine take their place. So affected is Charles at witnessing Lord Marchmain's death and redemption, he even comes to understand Julia's reason for having to give him up. Charles also comes to understand that through the witnessing of another man's redemption, he is being given a vision of the ordinary being made sublimely extraordinary. This leaves the strong impression that Charles will one day seek redemption through the Church for himself.

The Thorn Birds

Roman Catholicism also looms large in *The Thorn Birds* (ABC, 1983), based on author Colleen McCullough's 1977 soap-operaesque literary blockbuster. Also prominent are the themes of the nature of forbidden love, guilt, and spiritual redemption. In *The Thorn Birds*, the lives of three women — three generations of the Cleary family — are detailed. The women are Fee/Fiona (Jean Simmons), her daughter Meggie (Rachel Ward), and Meggie's daughter Justine (Mare Winningham). The core of the epic narrative is the forbidden love between Meggie and Catholic priest Father Ralph de Bricassart (Richard Chamberlain).

A fourth woman, Mary Carson (Barbara Stanwyck), the wealthy, widowed, childless elder sister of Meggie's father, Paddy (Richard Kiley), also plays a crucial role in the epic narrative. Vain, embittered, and angry, the elderly Mary makes a spectacle of herself, flagrantly lusting after Father Ralph. His denial of her sexual advances leads to Mary's final act of vengeance. Knowing of his ruthless ambition to rise high in the Church, upon her death she forces him to choose between her vast estate being left to the Church or to Meggie and her family. By choosing his own selfish ambition over Meggie's well-being, he essentially cuts her off from her birthright. Thus, Mary Carson's will sets in motion the epic action that follows.

While Father Ralph goes on to a meteoric rise in the Church, Meggie marries the insensitive Luke O'Neil (Bryan Brown), who takes her from Australia to Queensland to hire her out as a maid. Weary after giving birth to her daughter Justine, Meggie is sent on a tropical vacation by her kindly employers, Luddie and Anne Mueller (Earl Holliman, Piper Laurie). Father Ralph joins her there. They consummate their love, resulting in the birth of Meggie's son Dane (Philip Anglim) and her decision to leave Luke. She returns to Drogheda to raise her children as a single parent.

The adult Justine becomes a stage actress in London, where she falls in love with Rainer Hartheim (Ken Howard). Under Father Ralph's guidance, Dane goes to Rome to become a priest. When he tragically drowns, Justine, blaming herself, refuses to marry Rainer. Meggie intercedes, urging Justine to accept Rainer's marriage proposal, thus not making the same mistakes Meggie made.

Although there are many similarities between *Brideshead Revisited* and *The Thorn Birds*, there are also important differences: (1) the depiction of the Catholic Church in *The Thorn Birds* is more negative; (2) the central focus is now on the four major female characters[7]; (3) there is much more of an emphasis placed on the televisual trappings of high romance and low melodrama. Since the actions of Mary Carson set the rest of the epic action into motion, she will be the first female character considered. With her vast wealth and power, Mary dominates the first three hours of the epic narrative. Her exclusive, privileged role in the text is most explicitly established by the huge, overpowering portrait of herself she keeps hanging over the mantelpiece of her palatial home Drogheda (which appropriately intimidates all who come into its forbidden presence).

Like the character of Richard Armagh in *Captains and the Kings*, both Mary and her brother Paddy leave their impoverished lives in Ireland behind them to seek their fame and fortune elsewhere. But it is only Mary, with her steely will and determination, who possesses the necessary wherewithal to claw her way to the top of Australian high society. Consequently Mary, rather than any of the males, is the real possessor of phallic power. Freud says the female's desire to possess the phallus can make such a woman harden "herself in her mistaken conviction that she truly does possess the penis, and may subsequently make her compelled to behave as if she were a man."[8] Mary proceeds to emasculate any man who gets in her way, including her deceased husband, her put-upon brother, and the handsome young priest Father Ralph de Bricassart. Flagrantly lusting after his muscular body, she continuously mocks him for being an unmanly, passive "virgin" in need of her aggressive sexual initiation. In one shockingly lurid scene of low melodrama and high camp, Mary voraciously fondles the priest's nude body, outrageously taunting him the whole time with bold promises of all she will do for him if he only surrenders to her aggressive sexual advances.

It is through the uncontrollable, inappropriate power of Mary's rampant sexuality that all hell breaks out in the epic narrative. Far too old and undesirable to assume the role of the object of desire, Mary is a comic-tragic carnal crone who is seen as unattractive, useless, and unloved. So defined, she is transformed into the intolerable and grotesque figure of the Aging Protofascist Dominatrix—complete with shiny leather thigh-boots, an unfurled leather whip in one hand, and a gun in the other.

Now Mary seems superhuman. On the surface, she appears to have it all: money, power, and a big gun—or does she really? After all, her condition negates her as a desirable woman and mythic type in the epic miniseries pantheon. Spurned and useless, all that is left for her to do is strike a series of outrageously over-the-top, sadomasochistic, tyrannical poses on the grand staircase of Drogheda. Her flamboyant behavior forces the epic action into moments of often striking *tableaux vivants* (in which dialectical elements of pain and pleasure, suffering and exultation, sex and love, life and death, all commingle in some unexpected new arrangements). Mary Carson becomes a towering project of Herbert Marcuse's view of the intermingling forces of totalitarianism and sadomasochism: "Pleasure in the abasement of others.... pleasure in the manifold surrogate for sexuality, in both meaningless sacrifice and false promises, because, the drives and needs that fulfill themselves in them make others less free, blinder, and more wretched than they have to be."[9]

Still, Barbara Stanwyck's imposing and complex performance[10] suggests that Mary is just as tormented a figure in her twisted passions as those she dominates. In preying upon the moral weakness of Father Ralph, she forces him to choose between his forbidden love for the beautiful, desirable Meggie and the future prospect of rising from an ordinary priest in the Australian Outback to the extraordinary Cardinal de Bricassart of the Holy Vatican in Rome. For her role in this act of cruelty, Mary knows she is destined to burn in Hell for eternity.

Fee Cleary, Meggie's dour, longsuffering mother, reminds us of Mary Jordache. Born into a prominent family, Fee is disowned after having an illicit love affair with an older, married man and giving birth to her beloved eldest son Frank (whom she favors as much as Mary did Rudy). To punish her transgression, the unwed Fee is married off to the socially and economically inferior Paddy Cleary. Although Paddy truly loves his wife, she cannot bring herself to show him or their children any genuine love or affection. Ironically, she can bring herself to show love only to her son Frank. But her husband Paddy has great difficulty with Frank, who looks upon him with Oedipal derision and scorn. Frank is abusive and very pugnacious. After a complete falling out with Paddy, he runs away and becomes a boxer. His brutal, combative nature surmounts his good sense, and the young man's death destroys his mother. Fee's youngest child and only daughter, Meggie, is the one who must bear the emotional brunt of her mother's cold elusiveness. Paradoxically, despite this profoundly dysfunctional atmosphere of emotional abuse, grief, and loss, Meggie still grows like a flower into a beautiful blossom of young womanhood.

As the immensely appealing heroine of *The Thorn Birds*, it is Meggie who will go on to make many of the same mistakes her mother made, as will she suffer the most from her Aunt Mary's vindictive nature. Feeling unloved and unwanted as a child, Meggie develops intense feelings for the only adult figure who ever shows her any real attention: Father Ralph de Bricassart. As Meggie grows into young womanhood, their feelings toward one another deepen into a forbidden love. Yet Meggie becomes neither a dour drudge like her mother nor a dominating woman like her aunt. Meggie becomes a highly desirable but dominated woman.

Meggie's desirability is first established as the central visual motif of the epic narrative on the same mythological grand staircase of Drogheda on which Mary demonstrated her own undesirability. Whereas we saw Mary make a most unpleasant spectacle of herself, unleashing her unwanted sexual hysteria everywhere, Meggie cancels out and balances the negative attitude. She is a pleasurable spectacle for the male eye to gaze upon. As she appears atop the grand staircase, looking like a fairy-tale heroine in her lovely ashes-of-roses gown (which her Aunt Mary gives her to wear to tempt Father Ralph) the epic narrative comes to an appreciative halt. A new momentum — a sea change, as it were — is affected. All eyes are now on Meggie. Father Ralph's gaze is especially transfixed on her. Shots of Meggie in close-up are followed by close-ups of Father Ralph, his eyes eloquently expressing his pride in her splendorous beauty and his desire to possess that beauty. Composer Henry Mancini's lilting, music box-like, romantic theme for Meggie adds yet another layer of meaning to the memorable scene's sense of timelessness.

Meggie's status as a dominated woman is established in the text through her subjugation to the power of the male over the female. This subjugation encompasses everything from the Draconian terms of her aunt's patriarchy favoring will, to her mother's preference for her eldest son Frank, to her loveless marriage to the manipulative Luke, to her unfulfilling love affair with Father Ralph, to the will of the patriarchal God the Father of her Church who deprives her of both the love of Father Ralph and of her beloved son Dane. Clearly, within the confines of the patriarchal world in which she lives, the course of Meggie's destiny is out of her control. If it had not been so, Meggie and not Father Ralph would have emerged as the real Adventurer of *The Thorn Birds*.

Temptation on the Grand Staircase of Drogheda: The young and beautiful Meggie Cleary (Rachel Ward) begins her forbidden love affair with priest Father Ralph de Bricassart (Richard Chamberlain). *The Thorn Birds* (ABC, 1982).

This idea of Meggie as the real Adventurer is further suggested by the mise-en-scène that surrounds her. Like Tom in *Rich Man, Poor Man*, Meggie inhabits a world of elemental Dionysian force and cosmic reality: earth, sky, sun, water, blood, sweat, tears, birth, death — these signify the details of her instinctive, natural woman's space. She never once loses sight of the Edenic promise and pastoral idyll. To reinforce the spatial dynamics of this idea, scenes of Meggie in her world are frequently juxtaposed against scenes of Father Ralph going from one self-aggrandizing career highlight to another in the privileged, monumentalized, Apollonian power spaces of the Vatican. As in *Brideshead Revisited*, the specifications of lavish set design combined with contrasting light effects and props provide the historicized stage upon which the epic narrative is enacted. Fueled by the cruel terms of Mary's will, surrounded by colossal marble columns, vaulted ceilings dotted with glittery golden stars and medallions of images of Christ, Mary, and the Saints, lit with the hallucinatory glow of vibrating colors from the grandeur of visionary stain glass windows, Father Ralph goes about the duplicitous business of selling off Meggie's birthright one piece at a time in his self-centered quest to become the esteemed Cardinal de Bricassart, a true prince of the Roman Catholic Church.

In this epic tale of male desire and female domination, Meggie gets projected into a dream-like space in which the themes of forbidden love, unfullfilment, and the idea of the ordinary becoming extraordinary predominate. One reason for this is found in Freud's theory of the "Family Romance," in which he accounts for the necessity of the unloved child to deny the miserable reality of her "real" life and "true" parentage and project herself into a more noble, imaginary life and family.[11] Meggie's first attempts to do this occur when she turns to Father Ralph to provide her with her "family romance." When this proves unsuccessful, she turns to Luke for the same purpose, to disastrous effect. At least their union does lead to the birth of her daughter Justine, the fourth major female in the epic miniseries.

Justifiably, critics have complained about the badly flawed last three hours of *The Thorn Birds*. Much of this critique centers around the abrupt way the leisurely pace of the epic narrative is suddenly sped up to encompass a time frame of over thirty years. So confusing does the epic action become, with its incessant jumping about from time frame to time frame, it becomes necessary to superimpose captions announcing each new scene. Without such a questionable technique, it is doubtful audiences would be able to follow the abrupt twists-and-turns of the jumpy, almost incoherent plotline. Although such a structural configuration still attempts to embody a coherent teleology, at times the epic narrative seems in danger of being disrupted to the point of deconstruction. Before this happens, it is put back on track in the way the television-makers utilize the text's many strong set pieces to insure that the epic story does not loose its inherent followability.

As previously stated, the dialectical nature of these elaborate set pieces is initially set off by the destructive nature of Mary's sexual hysteria. In concluding our discussion of *The Thorn Birds*, we will look at two scenes in which the device is spatially and temporally contextualized to striking effect. In both cases the spatial and temporal contextualization draws upon the epic narrative tropes first enunciated in *QB VII* and *Rich Man, Poor Man*, in the form of stylized and eroticized mise-en-scène and the application of the compelling musical score by Henry Mancini.

In the first scene, Mancini's music takes on a classical Greek-flavored style, connoting Justine and Dane's joyous holiday in sun-drenched Greece. As Justine experiences her first orgasm with Rainer, her lovemaking is criss-crossed with scenes of Dane drowning in the deep blue sea outside of her bedroom window. While Justine emits moans of ecstatic sexual pleasure and Dane lets out his final gasps of life, the two scenes are depicted in a montage that unites the arbitrary nature of pleasure and pain — life and death — in a disquieting way.

Even more unforgettable is the consummate way mise-en-scène, Mancini's music, and the physiognomy and gestures of Chamberlain and Ward are combined in the final moments of the epic narrative. In the natural splendor of Meggie's Edenic rose garden at Drogheda (in which the roses are the same color as the gown she wore the night Father Ralph became most fully aware of her extraordinary beauty), Meggie forgives Father Ralph for his treatment of her through the years. Profoundly moved by her generosity, he tearfully acknowledges that she was closer to God in her selfless love than he in his selfish ambition. A look of sad knowledge engulfs Meggie's still-beautiful face (like images of the Virgin Mary, Meggie's natural beauty is projected through the idealization of an eternal youth untouched by the ravages of age), signifying her deep awareness she has spent a lifetime giving all that she ever was or had or could have been to a man who could not respond to her in kind. Meggie lovingly cradles his head in her lap and forgives Father Ralph. Father Ralph dies at peace, knowing the woman he loves has forgiven him. As the camera tilts upward, it slowly ascends from the moving tableau in the rose garden to the airplane that is carrying Justine off to a more hopeful future through the mastering of her chosen art (the theater) and the man she loves (Rainer). The following diagram provides a visualization of the progression of the epic narrative's trajectory 3.5:

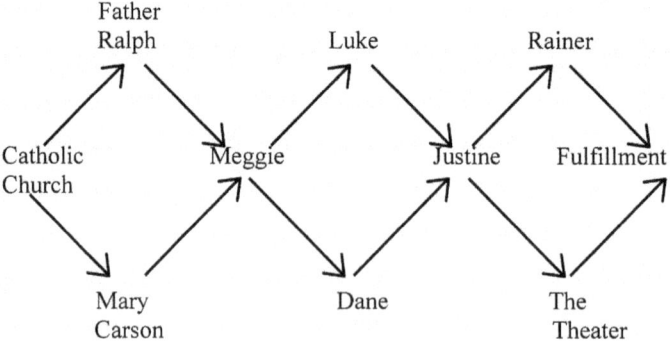

Diagram 3.5 — The connections between the characters of *The Thorn Birds*.

But if this conclusion strongly suggests that Justine will finally escape the curse of the Cleary women, a more ambiguous interpretation is also hinted at. Although we perceive that both Meggie and her world are morally and spatially continuous, the palpable sadness of her tear-stained face provides its own distinct range of reference. True, Meggie has survived and Justine will go on to thrive, but since the dead Dane leaves no heirs behind (nor do any of Meggie's brothers) Drogheda is virtually finished as a Cleary empire. The name of Cleary will be lost forever in the annals of historical time and the expanse of space. It is only through Justine that the bloodline of the Clearys will continue, though not the name. Thus in its own way the promise of the female will triumph over the patriarchal male forces in the end.

Lonesome Dove

After the exotic locations (Japan, England, Italy, Australia, Rome) and the emphasis of European high-style and distinctive Old World sensibility of *Shogun*, *Brideshead Revisited*, and *The Thorn Birds*, *Lonesome Dove* (CBS, 1989) provided audiences of the 1980s with a more streamlined and pastoral, but still elemental and monumental vision of the American epic miniseries. There is no overwhelming sense of European dread, historical dimensionality, entropy, and spiritual decline. However, *Lonesome Dove* will explore some of the same values and thematic concerns of those three other canonical texts. Arriving as it did at a point when the epic miniseries as a viable television art form was believed to be on its final legs, *Lonesome Dove* proved the genre still had considerable life left. Moreover, the prospects for the genre of the televisual Western were not all that promising at the time, although the fate of the Western in the cinematic realm was becoming more hopeful. With the box-office success of films like Clint Eastwood's *Pale Rider* (1985) and director Christopher Cain's Brat Pack Western *Young Guns* (1988), the time looked right for a full-blown Western epic miniseries for television. *Lonesome Dove* fit the bill perfectly. *Lonesome Dove* had originally been conceived as a motion picture in the early 1970s.[12] As it turned out, the big screen's loss was to be the small screen's gain.

In the American West of the 1870s, ex–Texas Ranger Augustus (Gus) McCrae (Robert Duvall) and Captain Woodrow Call (Tommy Lee Jones) have settled comfortably into retired life outside Lonesome Dove, Texas. Fellow ex–Ranger Jake Spoon (Robert Urich), who like Gus, is a heavy-drinking, womanizing, gambling man, unexpectedly re-enters the pair's complacent lives only to shake things up again. Wanted for killing Sheriff July Johnson's (Chris Cooper) brother, Jake convinces Gus and Call to gather up a crew of men (consisting of Joshua Deets [Danny Glover], Pea Eye Parker [Timothy Scott], and Newt Dobbs [Rick Schroder], the illegitimate son of a prostitute), round up a herd of cattle, and join him on what he promises will be the grand finale of their careers. Jake also brings along his sweet-tempered, prostitute girlfriend Lorena Wood (Diane Lane), who at one time or another has sold her services to most of the men on the cattle drive.

While July heads off to capture Jake, accompanied by young stepson Joe (Adam Faraize), his very pregnant wife Elmira (Glenne Headly) runs off to find her first husband, Dee Boot (Michael Tylo), with Sheriff Roscoe Brown (Barry Corbin) in hot pursuit of her. Meanwhile, Call, Gus, and Jake push on to Montana with their cattle. Along the way they encounter numerous challenges, those

The Final Round-Up: Augustus "Gus" McCrae (Robert Duvall, left) and Woodrow Call (Tommy Lee Jones) embark on their last great cattle drive. *Lonesome Dove* (CBS, 1989). (Photofest).

of nature (sun, wind, snow, rain) and those of man (vengeful outlaws, bloodthirsty Indians, mercenary horse thieves, and assorted cold-blooded killers).

Growing restless on the cattle drive, Jake goes off on a gambling-drinking-whoring spree, leaving Lorena unprotected. When she is abducted by violent half-breed Blue Duck (Frederic Forest), Gus's longtime arch-enemy, Gus convinces July to help him rescue Lorena from the sadistic, lusty Indian tribe to whom Blue Duck has given her. Although they rescue Lorena, Blue Duck viciously murders Roscoe and young Joe, and Jake takes up with a notorious gang of bank robbers and cutthroat murderers.

As the action of *Lonesome Dove* winds down, the epic narrative overflows with an abundance of incidents: Gus is reunited with his long-lost love Clara Allen (Angelica Houston); he and Call capture Jake and his outlaw gang and hang them; Elmira gives birth to a son, Martin, whom she leaves with Clara, and goes off again to find Dee; Dee is executed for murder, and Elmira is later killed in an Indian ambush; both July and Lorena stay on with the widowed Clara and her daughters; and after being ambushed by Indians, Gus loses a leg and dies. Before dying, he makes Call promise to bury him back in Texas. Call carries out Gus's final wish at an incredible cost to himself.

The fabled Wild West is a mythic space of boozy saloons, arduous cattle-drives, cutthroat outlaws, bloodthirsty Indians, warm-hearted "good" women, and gold-hearted "bad" women. Its radiantly beautiful archetypes resonated fully in the collective psyche of an older generation that grew up with episodes of *Rawhide* (CBS, 1959–66) and *Bonanza* (1959–73), which provided mythic, larger-than-life heroes and villains and American gods and goddesses. The Western mythos was further articulated in such popular mythic epic mini-series as *Centennial* (NBC, 1978), *Wild Times* (Syndicated, 1980), and *Dream West* (CBS, 1986), as it is in *Lonesome Dove*. When we meet the heroes of the epic narrative, Gus and Call, their glory days are far behind them. All that is left for them to do is what old men typically do best — re-live their former glory, get lost in the past, and repeat all the old stories until no one wants to hear them anymore. However, after Jake Spoon re-enters their lives, he regales them with tall tales of the excitement, fulfillment, and personal wealth that will be theirs if they lead a cattle drive to Montana. Hardly able to contain himself, Call jumps at Jake's proposal. Gus's response is considerably more ambivalent. Like the aging Westerners played by Gregory Peck in *The Gunfighter* (Henry King, 1950) and Gary Cooper in *High Noon* (Fred Zinnemann, 1952), Gus prefers to leave the past to the past. He revels in his place out of the limelight. But knowing Gus even better than Gus knows himself, Call reminds him that the cattle-drive will pass through Nebraska, the home of Gus's great love Clara Allen. With the mention of Clara's name, Gus changes his mind in an instant. The long cattle drive East commences.

If Gus recalls the heroic characters from *The Gunfighter* and *High Noon*, that is only the beginning of the complex way *Lonesome Dove* references several classic Western texts. Even though the epic narrative is informed by the same principles of mythic archetype and dialectic binary as distinguishes many other epic miniseries, there is also a high level of referentiality and self-consciousness at work, encapsulating much of the American Wild West of fact and fantasy, myth and legend, film, literature, and television. Thus we are presented with a densely textured mise-en-scène resonating with mythic echoes of a whole cluster of references to many canonical Westerns. For example, the overall conceptualization of Gus's amiable personality pays tribute to all those easy-going, charming Western heroes played by such actors as James Stewart, Henry Fonda, Clark Gable, Joel McCrea, and Paul Newman, all so fortunate with a gun and even more fortunate when it comes to bedding beautiful women. In fact, the relationship of Gus to the mythic Whore figure, Lorena, and the mythic Wife (Mother) figure, Clara, forms the triangular romantic structure that determines a good part of the epic action.

In dramatic juxtaposition to Gus is the figure of his partner Call. Like Rudy and Tom in *Rich Man, Poor Man*, Gus and Call are as unalike as night and day. Call is essentially a brooding loner with little to say to anyone. The Apollonian Call has little use for the Dionysian antics of men like Gus and Jake. In terms of style and temperament, the characterization of Call can be traced back to some of the more famous dark-tempered, brooding, iconic loners such as those played by Western megastar John Wayne in *Red River* (Howard Hawks, 1948) and director John Ford's sublime Western masterpiece *The Searchers* (1956). Yet another element that plays an important role here is the complicated, ambiguous relationship between Call and Newt Dobbs. A thematic motif of the epic narrative is Newt's transformation from boy to young Texas man and the crucial role Call plays in it by granting or withholding his acknowledgment of Newt as his son.

While Call never acknowledges Newt as his son, he does defend Newt from a vicious whipping in a town where the Army tries to requisition their horses. He also gives Newt an excellent young horse, which he tells an angry Clara (angry because he won't verbally acknowledge that he is Newt's father) is even better than giving him his name.

Newt's transformation from hard-scrabble child to rugged young man by the rigors he endures on the trail of the mythic cattle drive also underscores a significant motif of *Lonesome Dove*, one present in several other great epic miniseries. This motif concerns the elaborate process by which the boy becomes a man in the epic narrative. Traditionally, it is only other men who must say the boy is a man, making the process a mythic quest fraught with anxiety as the boy is usually made to go through a series of ritualistic endeavors and prodigious feats to prove his manhood. More often than not, this involves a dialectic of power and control, and acts of manipulation, cruelty, and, sometimes even physical abuse and violence against women. Thus, on a surface level, we witness Newt learn to shoot guns and seek out whores with the best of the young cowboys. But on a more subtle level, Newt also earns his manhood by adhering in his heart and in his actions to the unwritten heroic code of honor of the cowboys of the Western. It is a code that Jake Spoon violates when he joins up with that gang of bank-robbers and murderers, and it is that same code of honor that impels Gus and Call to hang Jake, much as they don't want to.

As for the female characters of *Lonesome Dove*, they do not ultimately have the same sort of pressing ritualistic need to prove they are women. Each month a woman's menstrual period reaffirms that irrefutable fact. Therefore, in her heart of hearts, a woman *knows* she is a woman no matter what any man may have to say on the matter. That said, we do still see the two central female characters—Lorena and Clara—conceptualized in the codified configuration of the Whore/Wife (Mother) dyad. On the one hand, Lorena descends from a long line of memorable Western whores-with-hearts-of-gold, such as Claire Trevor's lovely *Boule de Suif*-like prostitute in *Stagecoach* (John Ford, 1939), and Marlene Dietrich's spirited, worldly saloon singer in *Destry Rides Again* (George Marshall, 1939), who willingly takes a bullet to save the life of the man she loves. On the other hand, Clara pays homage to such devoted, unconditionally loving Western wives and mothers as those Jean Arthur plays in *Shane* (George Stevens, 1953) and Vera Miles in *The Searchers* and *The Man Who Shot Liberty Valance* (John Ford, 1962). But Anjelica Huston also infuses the role of Clara with an all-knowing, sensuous, womanly warmth that is all her own and most appealing.

Much like its characterization, the mise-en-scène of *Lonesome Dove* is made up of a compendium of visual symbols and motifs that pay tribute to several classic Westerns, forming a complex system of heroic visual codes and nostalgia-inducing homages. Although it is tempting to cite all of these references, for our purposes three will suffice. The overall evocation of time and place brings to mind the strong visual style of numerous classic John Ford Westerns based on the work of American primitive painters. Particularly wonderful are the many exterior scenes of Gus, Call, and their crew, out on the arduous cross-country cattle drive, evoking the stark pictorial simplicity of similar scenes in *Red River*. The depiction of Clara's vast estate, which signifies a civilizing, feminine force in contrast to the desolation of the surrounding masculinized wilderness, makes it an Edenic, maternal, pastoral paradise set against an arid masculinist wasteland. In such a context, the great house pays homage to the Victorian mansion of Rock Hudson and Elizabeth Taylor in *Giant* (George Stevens, 1956), and the great Ponderosa Ranch in the amazingly long-running television series *Bonanza*.

Lastly, the iconic visual design of *Lonesome Dove* recalls the stripped-down, Spartan visual style of *Holocaust*. This sets it off from much of the stylistic excess that is one of the major hallmarks of the epic miniseries of the 1980s. For this reason the text presents much of its frontier melodrama in so restrained a manner that it eventually achieves a full-blooded expression of pure emotion.

But while *Lonesome Dove* draws upon the attributes of numerous classic Westerns for inspiration, it also repeats some of the worst stereotypes that characterize those texts. These characterizations are indicative of the classic Western's privileged standing as a "totalizing system with its iconic representation of America in the cowboy, and its heroic celebration of masculinist individualism (often to the obliteration of the female) and a racist Manifest Destiny."[13] Such racist tendencies are articulated in the negative stereotypical depiction of the torture-loving, property-vandalizing, White-woman-raping, child-murdering figure of the un-noble savage Indian Blue Duck (played by Frederic Forrest in a huge, false nose, which recalls the arch-fiend character Fagin played by Alec Guinness in *Oliver Twist* [David Lean, 1948], a long, shaggy wig that makes him look like a 1970s acid-rock star gone to pot). Particularly offensive in this regard is the excruciating misogynistic scene in which Blue Duck kidnaps Lorena, followed by another equally problematic scene in which he and his drunken tribe of Indians subject her to the maximum level of sadistic sex and violence the televisual censors would permit.

While such racist and sexist attitudes undoubtedly mar the trajectory of the epic narrative, they also help open it up to the same sort of post-modern tendency expressed in antimythic Westerns like *Little Big Man* (Arthur Penn, 1970) and the iconoclastic *McCabe & Mrs. Miller* (Robert Altman, 1971). This sets in motion a process of critique that can subvert and challenge the more negative attitudes of the traditional Western in ways that are unusual and unexpected. Mainly we see this process in terms of the delineation of Clara, who does for *Lonesome Dove* what Lady Mariko did for *Shogun*. Although she is determinedly identified as the mythic type of the Wife (Mother), her awesome presence dominates. John M. Reilly says of her characterization:

> Clara alone furnishes a total world of her own. She is a capable horsewoman and dealer, a self-determining woman ... a caring mother, the executive of a large farm household, a counselor, and a woman who has selected, rather than fallen into, her life. If Gus and Call are the normative men in *Lonesome Dove*, then Clara is the normative woman, a remarkable person audiences can identify with when they have tired of all the limitations set up by the rigid patriarchal world of the Old West.[14]

Accordingly, Clara's femaleness takes on a more layered multi-dimensionality. Like the depiction of her stately home, offering an Edenic feminine refuge to all those seeking shelter, Clara assumes an equally significant role in the text. Eventually all the threads of the epic narrative must lead back to her; the completion of much of the epic action circles back to her time and time again, until Clara comes to symbolize the very womb-tomb of Mother Nature in which all must begin and end.

For example, in the scene in which the now-widowed Clara resolutely informs Gus she has no intention of ever marrying him or any other man, she displays the full paradox of her emblematic simplicity and sex-surpassing power.

Like a generative Western Earth Mother, she has the power to restore order to the chaos in her own life and in the lives of others. Therefore, for all those who reject her there is loneliness, anguish, uncertainty, and even death. An interesting dichotomy and even paradox is the path that Elmira chooses as contrasted to that of Earth Mother Clara. Elmira may be a wife and mother, but she scorns and negates the responsibilities of her role.

She is of the archetypal Medea of Greek myth. She sends her young son Joe on what she knows will be a dangerous journey with her husband July to capture Jake. She does this so she will not be burdened with young Joe as she runs off on her crazy quest to find her first husband Dee Boot. She also seems to have no regard for her pregnancy in her perilous escape, and when she ultimately gives birth at Clara's house, she absconds with her two male friends and leaves the baby with Clara. Naturally Clara nurses and loves the baby, and will help raise him with July. Later Elmira is killed by ferocious Indians along with her two male friends.

In contrast, Lorena finds a whole new way of life at and through Clara, and makes one of Gus's young friends most anxious to forget her whore past and honorably marry her. This transformation is only possible with Clara's bigheartedness and truly Demeter-like redemptive quality for those who will accept her kind guidance and advice. The Old Wild West is finally usurped and civilized by Clara and other women like her. For those who accept Clara there is much to be gained: for Lorena, Clara offers hope and the possibility of a new life; for Newt, she offers stability and the unconditional love of the mother he never had; for July, she becomes the possibility of healing and a reason to go on living. The following diagram provides a model of Clara's centrality to the epic narrative and her connection to the other characters. 3.6.

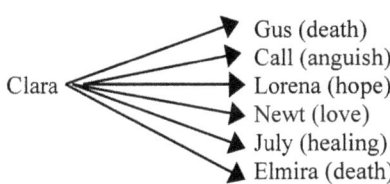

Diagram 3.6 — Clara's connection to the other characters in *Lonesome Dove*.

The music Basil Poledouris composed for *Lonesome Dove* cannot possibly be over-praised. He rightfully took home an Emmy for his folk idiom-inspired Western score. Providing over three hours of music, Poledouris uses specialty folk instruments appropriate to time and place. His memorable theme music is "at once elegant and bittersweet, capturing the essence of the epic story in a memorable way ... reflecting both the intimacy and the grandeur of the epic work."[15]

All in all, despite its problematical depictions of Native Americans and certain aspects of Lorena's character, *Lonesome Dove* is a true television milestone. Universally praised, it would score one of the largest audiences for an epic miniseries in several years. It also rejuvenated the epic Western as a viable television genre for the 1990s, and it would spawn several sequels: *Return to Lonesome Dove* (CBS, 1993), *Larry McMurtry's "Streets of Laredo"* (CBS, 1995), *Dead Man's Walk* (ABC, 1996), and *Comanche Moon* (CBS, 2007). Yet the triumph of *Lonesome Dove* did not necessarily mean there would be a bright, shining future for the epic miniseries. But before we consider the full implications of this matter, the next two chapters will examine how various other epic miniseries of the 1980s exerted their own influences on those of the 1990s and 2000s. These influences, we will argue, are most relevant to our project.[16]

Chapter 4

Visions, Values and the Void

War has been a staple of the epic miniseries since its inception. One can understand how war stories, with their emphasis on the dialectical and didactical presentation of Good vs. Evil, offer many rich opportunities to glorify and make visible such topics as carnage, cowardice, intolerance, victimization, exultation, courage, and human triumph. This emphasis can be seen in abundance in such epic miniseries as *Once an Eagle* (NBC, 1976), *Holocaust, The Rhineman Exchange* (NBC, 1977), *From Here to Eternity* (NBC, 1979), *Ike: The War Years* (ABC, 1979), and *Inside the Third Reich* (ABC, 1982), reaching its grand televisual apotheosis in the 1980s with the presentations of *The Winds of War* (ABC, 1983) and *War and Remembrance* (ABC, 1988–89). It is especially with *War and Remembrance* that we have this extreme contrast between the Light Bearers of relative Good (i.e., Western Civilization and all the good it represents) and the Dark Bearers of complete bestial depravity and moral perversion (i.e., Nazi Germany and the Axis Powers). Clearly, then, War as a grand subject has attracted a wide range of televisionmakers. And perhaps first and foremost among them we would have to place the name of Dan Curtis.[1]

The Winds of War

When ABC first announced that producer/director Dan Curtis would be taking on the Promethean task of transforming Herman Wouk's sprawling bestsellers *The Winds of War* (1971) and *War and Remembrance* (1978) into a pair of mega-epic miniseries of unprecedented proportions, many critics believed both ABC and Curtis were setting themselves up for dismal failure. However, with the broadcast of *The Winds of War* Curtis proved all those naysayers wrong. He succeeded on an epic scale. Rather than the dismal failure anticipated, *The Winds of War* went on to draw an enormous televisual audience of 125 million viewers. So extraordinary was this response by the public, *The Winds of War* now stands as the third-highest rated epic miniseries of all time (only *Roots* and *The Thorn Birds* have commanded larger audiences). Naturally, attaining a televisual hit of such magnificent breadth, the executives of ABC quickly put into operation plans for Curtis to transform *War and Remembrance* into an even bigger, more expensive, more expansive, and infinitely greater epic miniseries than its illustrious predecessor had been.

Understandably, Curtis was ecstatic at being offered this once-in-a-lifetime opportunity for the creation of a "total epic miniseries." This is similar to writer Garcia Marquez's phrase "total novel," and it suggests a complete, totally self-contained world made possible through the very highest level of televisual artifice, expressing a complete visual, aural, imagined reality: a total televisual space of its own. Since the "total epic miniseries" thrives on heightened dialectical and didactical adversity, war and human struggle are watersheds in its development. Such "total epic miniseries" include, of course, the great 1970s triumvirate of *Rich Man, Poor Man, Roots* (along with its sequel *Roots: The Next Generations*), and *Holocaust*; most certainly *Shogun, Brideshead Revisited, Berlin Alexanderplatz, The Singing Detective, Lonesome Dove,* and *From the Earth to the Moon*; with some minor reservations, the flawed but still ambitious and far-reaching texts of *Amerika* (ABC, 1987), *Wild Palms* (ABC, 1993), and *Band of Brothers* (HBO, 2001), all of which, unfortunately, are outside the scope of this present volume; and without any hesitation, *Angels in America*, which as its title indicates develops a total epic narrative out of the whole of America as a totality of theatrical and televisual experience. To this select list, we also unequivocally add *The Winds of War* and *War and Remembrance*. In order to gain a full appreciation of Curtis's ultimate achievement with these two texts, we shall next examine *The Winds of War*.

The epic narrative focuses on the upper-middle class, stereotypically WASP American family the Henrys: father Victor "Pug" Henry (Robert Mitchum) is a career naval officer, while wife Rhoda (Polly Bergen), having grown bored in her marriage to the stalwart Pug, turns to alcohol and adultery to alleviate her boredom. Pug and Rhoda have three grown-up children: eldest son Warren (Ben Murphy) attends flight school, becomes a naval pilot, and marries Janice La Couture (Deborah Winters), the daughter of an isolationist Senator; daughter Madeline (Lisa Elibacher), rather than attend college, moves to New York and takes up with married, vulgar radio host Hugh Cleveland (Tom McFadden); youngest son Byron (Jan-Michael Vincent) goes to Italy to work as a researcher for brilliant Jewish-American scholar Aaron Jastrow (John Houseman), and becomes romantically involved with Aaron's niece, Natalie (Ali MacGraw). Through Byron's connection to Aaron and Natalie, the major theme of the Holocaust enters the epic narrative.

In 1938, believing his career is all but over, Pug accepts an assignment to go to Berlin as a naval attaché. While in Germany, he and Rhoda meet several high-level Nazis, including Hitler (Günter Meisner). After Pug makes astute observations about Nazi Germany's total readiness to wage war, he comes to the attention of President Franklin Roosevelt (Ralph Bellamy). From then on, the President enlists Pug as an unofficial observer. His son Byron falls in love with Natalie, who, though engaged to American diplomat Leslie Slote (David Dukes), returns Byron's affections. She and Byron go to Poland to visit relative Berel Jastrow (Topol) and attend a wedding. The Germans invade Poland in a

Wagnerian storm of brutal Nazi force. Suddenly, hellishly realistic scenes of Nazi bombing and Blitzkrieg are shown; children are blown up and mangled in the bombed-out streets, and Natalie tells Byron and Slote she's seen pregnant women bombed and burning at a bombed maternity hospital. But these brutal waves of bombing are just foreshadowing of the genocidal nightmare to come. Although Byron and Natalie do make it out of war-torn Poland, his family responds badly to Bryon's involvement with a Jewish woman.

Over the next two years, the turbulent course of world events affects each member of the Henry family differently. Rhoda continues to drink heavily and has an indiscreet affair with government engineer Palmer Kirby (Peter Graves). Pug is stationed in England, meets Winston Churchill (Howard Lang), and becomes attracted to the much younger Pamela Tudsbury (Victoria Tennant), the daughter of eccentric war correspondent Alistair "Talky" Tudsbury (Michael Logan). Byron attends submarine school and marries Natalie, who remains in Italy attempting to get her Uncle Aaron back to America. While still in Italy, Natalie gives birth to son Louis. Pug and Pamela's relationship deepens in Russia, where they meet Stalin (Anatoly Chaguinian). Rhoda sends Pug a "Dear John" letter, confessing her love for Palmer Kirby.

On December 7, 1941, the Japanese bomb Pearl Harbor, resulting in America's entry into World War II. With the war's outbreak, the lives of the characters grow even more complicated: Pug and Rhoda attempt a shaky reconciliation; Italy declares war on America, forcing Aaron and Natalie to set sail illegally for Israel; Madeline continues her relationship with Hugh Cleveland; Byron, now stationed on a submarine, grows increasingly worried about Natalie and son Louis; and Warren is stationed at Pearl Harbor. The epic action concludes with Pug attaining his lifelong dream of commanding a battleship.

The Visionary Televisual

With *The Winds of War* and *War and Remembrance*, Herman Wouk strove to create a powerful literary statement honoring all "the brave men and women of America who serve it at a time of great crisis."[2] To achieve this, Wouk turned to several canonical literary texts for inspiration. Pearl Bell acknowledges that the author's grand design was to create "a genuine American epic on the visionary scale and scope of Homer's *The Iliad* and Virgil's *The Aeneid*: the story of an entire nation struggling for its very life, and the tale of the hero (or as in Wouk's case the hero and heroine) whose noble actions bring glory to themselves and their people."[3] Along with *The Iliad* and *The Aeneid*, the third text to have the greatest influence on Wouk was *War and Peace* by Leo Tolstoy.

Therefore, as with *War and Peace*, it is sometimes difficult to clearly identify the hero of the epic narrative in Wouk's novels. The case could even be made that an entire nation assumes the role of the hero collectively. But in translating Wouk's literary vision into an epic miniseries, Curtis has streamlined and contained the author's sometimes unwieldy epic narrative: Pug and Natalie are now clearly the epic tale's hero and heroine. Not surprisingly, there is a greater emphasis placed upon the similarities between them for television, the most obvious being their readiness to act. If Pug appears to do this out of a deep sense of duty, Natalie comes by the quality most naturally. For example, by staying on in Italy to help her uncle, she puts herself at tremendous risk. When viewed against the explosive backdrop of World War II, the similarities between Natalie and Pug are thrown into even greater relief. This suggests that they share a special bond. In fact, when Pug first meets Natalie in person, he accepts and fully approves of her romance with Byron without reservation, being concerned only with Byron's callow age to be so deeply involved with such a remarkable older woman. And despite the obvious differences between them, Pug and Natalie hold one another in high esteem. Indeed, one magnificent hero immediately recognizes another.

Connections (Private)

The theme of the triangular relationship, detailed in Chapter 3, informs the epic narrative of *The Winds of War* in four distinct configurations: first, there is the triangular relationship involving Pug, Rhoda, and Palmer Kirby, which is later reconfigured into the second triangle of Pug, Rhoda, and Pamela; a third involves Byron, Natalie, and Slote, while a fourth encompasses Madeline, Hugh Cleveland, and his love-suffering wife, who like the figure of Beryl in *Brideshead Revisited* remains an unseen absenting presence. Within these four triangular arrangements, the epic matrix is additionally organized according to parallel paradigms of varying levels of complexity.

Examples of this structure include both Natalie and Pamela devoting themselves to an eccentric, elderly man (Natalie's Uncle Aaron, Pamela's father "Talky"), and the striking similarities between the cool, business-like efficiency of Palmer Kirby and Slote. This results in Slote being posted to diplomatic positions in Germany, Russia, and Switzerland, where he becomes an early witness to Hitler's devastating destruction of European Jewry. Likewise, Palmer Kirby's connection to the U.S. government leads to his assuming a key role in the Manhattan Project, resulting in the creation of the atomic bomb, which concludes the war.

Yet another crucial parallel paradigm exists between Aaron and Berel Jastrow. As an internationally acclaimed scholar and the best-selling author of *A Jew's Jesus*, Aaron is a signifier for the fully assimilated, cultural Jew, like Berta Weiss. The type is carried to even greater extremes when Aaron reveals to Natalie he is a convert to Catholicism, which he firmly believes will somehow place him in good standing with the Nazis. Completely oblivious to his surroundings, he spends his days deeply immersed in his study of Pope Constantine, despite the signs of the gathering storm clouds on all sides. His cousin

The Ultimate Adventurer: Victor "Pug" Henry (Robert Mitchum) commands his battleship during World War II. *The Winds of War* (ABC, 1983).

Berel, on the other hand, is a signifier for the poor, hard-working Jew who remained behind in the Old World, as opposed to the Jew who emigrated to the New. The simple, able-bodied, manly charismatic Topol (so superb as the hearty Tevye in *Fiddler on the Roof* [Norman Jewison, 1971]) plays Berel as a pious Jew, resourcefully adept at handling whatever might come his way. His quick-witted responsiveness (as when he delivers his wife and children out of Poland after the Nazis savagely invade the country) and his ability to act present us with a model for the way Jewish targets of Hitler reacted to the escalating Nazi brutality against them.

Connections (Public)

Moving from the private to the public level of representation, there is the matter of Pug's unique connection to the triangular configuration of the three Allied leaders— Roosevelt, Churchill, and Stalin — which provides the epic narrative with its underlining superstructure. The meaning of this formal technique involves both the interconnectedness of Pug to the text's other characters on the private level, and on the public level his encounters with the three great world leaders. Additionally, Pug experiences two separate encounters with Hitler while he and Rhoda are in Germany. In each scene, we witness Hitler's megalomanical demagoguery act as the transmitter, which sets all other aspects of the epic historical narrative into motion. In each scene, the entire frame takes on a cold, mannered grandiosity, establishing Hitler's fascistic mannerisms in theatricalized spaces, heavy with excess and artifice. Hitler's scenes are further heightened throughout by the use of offbeat camera angles, which transform the Nazi mise-en-scène into an ostentatious sphere of baroque stylization and decadence. The final effect is absolute: Hitler is viewed striking rigid, puppet-like poses while pronouncing the fascistic, Aryanized glorification of his unique brand of ruthless individualism. In such scenes we fully see Hitler as a towering Satanic figure of ruthless evil who will destroy the world to create a new one — one in which the Aryan master race is in total fascistic control and is also completely free of Jews. In fact, Hitler and company are a gestalt of pure evil. It is through this epic narrative strategy that the figure of Hitler comes to emanate the perversity of some deadly, ravenous, mythical beast, which triggers off the collective powerful heroic response of the Allied leaders.

It is through the response of the Roosevelt/Churchill/Stalin trinity to Hitler's excesses that the ideological position and political zeitgeist of the epic narrative is finalized and concretized. In like fashion, as Pug bears witness to the response of the Big Three, he believes he is reading the historical tablet that matters most. This puts him in the center of momentous historical events. Moving along the contours of power, he is reassured in the view that history and epic narrative are driven by a handful of wise and powerful men in total control of everything. The view espoused by the epic narrative of *The Winds of War* doubtlessly accounts for the text's popular reception and the way that initial reception later affected the one given to *War and Remembrance*. A model for the epic narrative circuit of *The Winds of War* is illustrated in Diagram 4.1:

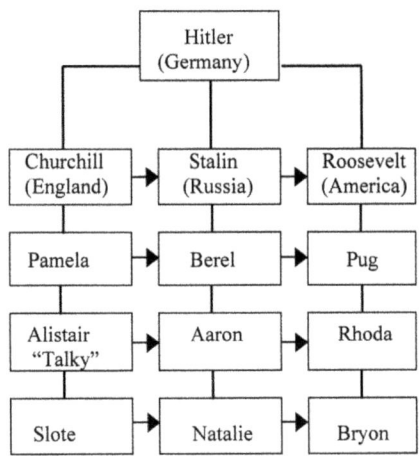

Diagram 4.1 — The epic narrative circuit of ***The Winds of War***.

When Pug shares encounters with Churchill and Roosevelt, the narrational and visual codes are in dialectical opposition to the ones used to depict Hitler and his Nazi excesses. With the depiction of the places and spaces the Allies occupy, the epic frame is tempered with a democratized aesthetic. The cold, harsh tones associated with the Nazis are muted, softened, and transmuted with an atmospheric glow, which gives the mise-en-scène an inviting warmth. Although an exalted, dramatic sense of pomp and circumstance is still in evidence, we have no trouble accepting Pug's ability to feel at ease while he is in the presence of such powerful and noble personages. In this regard, even the problematic, fascistic ramifications of Stalin's iconic image are smoothed out and unified both thematically and visually in the prescribed system of pictorialization. At times, the way in which Stalin is depicted in *The Winds of War* borders on becoming almost a visual apologia. But space does not permit us to explore the full political and ideological implications of this representation. Instead, what such an epic visual presentation of character conveys on a visceral level is considerable formal sweep and maximal dramatic impact.

Three Women

Before turning to an exploration of *War and Remembrance*, the terms in which the three major female characters of *The Winds of War*—Rhoda (The Wife), Pamela (The Whore), and Natalie (The Untyped Heroine)—are presented deserves our attention since all three will also go on to play even greater, more important roles in the second miniseries. The figure of The Wife (the middle-aged Rhoda) is unflatteringly depicted as a neurotic, obsessive, self-absorbed, alcohol-abusing social climber. Often vain and snobbishly trivial in her interests and pursuits, Rhoda will even reveal an unattractive anti–Semitism toward Natalie—though this is not the rabid anti–Semitism of the Nazis, probably stemming from Rhoda's being quite a snob and not accepting others not of her esteemed class, despite Natalie's wonderful charm, beauty, and brains. And later, after Byron marries Natalie and has Louis, whenever Rhoda hears any family member talking about the Nazi threat to Natalie and little Louis in Europe, she just pooh-poohs such concerns away, as legitimate as they are. Rhoda will also reveal a predatory side when she sets out on her endless quest to find a new man to replace Pug, whom she believes cannot give her the love or romance she so compulsively craves. Although as the epic action unfolds, Rhoda's definition of love looks more and more like a matter of calculated manipulation. In one memorable scene, Rhoda is prepared to tell Pug that she wants a divorce. But before she gets the chance, he informs her they have been extended an invitation to a private dinner at the White House with the President and First Lady. Hardly one to allow such a brilliant social opportunity to slip through her fingers, Rhoda promptly puts her romantic quest on hold, at least until after she has had dinner with the Roosevelts.

The argument could easily be made that with the creation of Rhoda, Wouk was not being particularly charitable toward her character. Of course there are those who say Tolstoy was equally harsh with some of his female characters in *War and Peace.* As a rule, Tolstoy's heroes are depicted as Adventurers on a quest for some form of moral purity, which is constantly threatened by "woman's selfish interests and particularly her problematic sexuality."[4] Although *The Winds of War* does attempt to depict the total absorption in marriage and family as being perhaps the best bet for disarming and containing the dangerous side of female sexuality, this solution works about as well for Rhoda in this context as it did for Julie in the context of *Rich Man, Poor Man.*

Still, just as Curtis has taken certain liberties with Wouk's epic narrative, so too does he take understandable liberties with the televisual depiction of Rhoda, toning down some of her harsher aspects. Curtis accomplishes this in two ways. First, he imbues Rhoda with a greater sense of the immediacy of a middle-aged woman who gets caught up in and "pulled apart by the War, forever changed by a course of life-altering events that will force her to take on a new, totally unanticipated role."[5] Second, Curtis elicits a nuanced, multifaceted performance from Polly Bergen. While Bergen supplies all of the requisite vanity and neurotic self-absorbtion required, she can be just as touching as she is tough. Like some naïve heroine from the pages of an excessively romantic novel, Bergen's Rhoda conveys a certain pathos that affects and moves us in surprising ways. And this even despite such scenes as the one in which she flagrantly suck-ups to her unctuous Nazi host and hostess in Berlin, or another in which she plots one of her clandestine interludes with Palmer Kirby behind Pug's back.[6]

Pamela and Natalie are each depicted in binary opposition to Rhoda. Much less calculating, each young woman exhibits a more spontaneous spiritedness. This aspect of their personalities cannot help but affect others. For example, there is the transcendent scene when Pamela travels to the Russian front and sings for the soldiers. The scene begins, as Curtis begins several others, with a long, gliding track-in shot. Pamela is revealed in long shot standing at a piano, singing with a forlorn pathos. As she continues singing her heart out, the camera moves in closer to her. It then slowly glides around the room revealing the faces of the war-weary, melancholy soldiers all gathered around her. She delivers her moving rendition of "The White Cliffs of Dover," while they bask in the irresistible warmth of her enigmatic womanliness.

Of all the females in *The Winds of War*, it is Natalie who will become the undeniable heroine of the epic narrative. For several reasons, as will be revealed in far greater detail in *War and Remembrance* (where her role becomes greater), she is the most complex and appealing female character. Much like the "new" Julia of the Art-Deco 1930s in *Brideshead Revisited,* Natalie is a virtual female delta, an approachable Venus always in motion, a Mythic Woman for the modern age. Exquisitely balanced, fluid in her grace and beauty, Natalie is a nurturing, sensuous presence. She also ushers in a new kind of heroine into the Epic Miniseries Pantheon: the Contemporary Untyped Woman. She makes the idea of being a beautiful woman with brains immensely sexy.

When Natalie and Byron are on their honeymoon in Portugal, she leaves him to change. When she returns to him, her body is clad in a luminous, white silk robe. She is love and sex, pure and simple, and she is every bridegroom's honeymoon fantasy. As she makes her way toward her husband, she is also a dream vision moving in dreamy slow motion. While Curtis times her sensuous movements to the music, composer Bob Cobert's popular, lyrical standard "Love theme from *The Winds of War*" soars to full crescendo. With the couple's passionate embrace, photographer Charles Correll's velvety, romanticizing camera swirls fully around them. This technique imbues them with a hypnotic richness that is evocative of the unforgettable, lyrical love scenes between James Stewart and Kim Novak in Alfred Hitchcock's cinematic masterpiece *Vertigo* (1958).

War and Remembrance

In his revelatory autobiography *Shattered Love*, King of the Epic Miniseries Richard Chamberlain views both the fate of the epic miniseries as a televisual art form and the decline of his own career as being linked:

> The glory days of the mammoth epic miniseries like *Centennial, Shogun, Wallenberg, The Bourne Identity, Dream West,* and *The Thorn Birds* that dominated earthly television and my career in the 1980s were rendered extinct by the disastrous (for the three major networks) collision with the hurtling meteor of Cable Television. The proliferation of many cable channels divided and scattered our viewing audience and thus starved the network of the abundant greenbacks needed to feed those spectacular dinosaurs of epic television ... both the Golden Age of the Epic Miniseries and my long career would fade away with the 1980s.[7]

What Chamberlain fails to point out is that the summa of the whole dizzy, fantastic, prodigal Golden Age of the Epic Miniseries, its coming to full perfect bloom and its too rapid decline, can all be traced directly to one truly glorious televisual offering: *War and Remembrance*. Considered a ratings disaster when it first aired during the 1988–89 television season, the text has never really had much of a popular reputation. Far more complex, more expansive, grander, richer, and infinitely more symbolic and visionary than its predecessor, *War and Remembrance* is to *The Winds of War* what *The Godfather, Part II* is to *The Godfather*. It broadens the scope and enriches the full meaning of the earlier work. And even though Curtis has succeeded in accomplishing the same monumental feat that Coppola did, neither he nor his magisterial achievement have ever received due credit. For our purposes, the question comes down to this: Did

Curtis and his artistic collaborators create a televisual artifact so totally integrated into the dynamics of its time and place that it is now forever locked in some sort of televisual time warp? Is it even credible to speak of it as a bona fide work of televisual art still relevant for us today?

These and other questions suggest that there are still many unanswered paradoxes in need of further exploration. For it is our belief that *War and Remembrance* is, in many ways, the ultimate epic miniseries of American television. Indeed, it is so much more than it initially appeared to be, and repeated viewings reveal even more of its matter and manner, its constructs and ambiguities, its self-consciousness and reflectivity, and even its flaws and final triumph. Within *War and Remembrance*, Curtis tells what are essentially four epic stories (all organized around the favored epic miniseries archetypal systems of the female and the male), which all take place at around the same time. Throughout, Curtis masterfully crisscrosses back-and-forth, forth-and-back. The male variant of this back-forth epic narrative technique concerns Pug's experiences in war-torn Europe (encompassing his intensifying love affair with Pamela), and Byron's in the Pacific. The female variant follows Rhoda's romantic adventures and misadventures in America, and Natalie's persecution by the Nazis in Europe. In each variant, the protagonist is made to undergo a traumatic alienation, or expatriation, from the idyllic matrix of the harmonious established order into a more chaotic, abstracting, new symbolic order. Because Curtis charges the entire production with so much visionary excitement and visceral immediacy, the viewing of the epic narrative is often an emotionally overpowering experience for its audience.

The epic action of *War and Remembrance* picks up where *The Winds of War* concluded — one week after the Japanese bombing of Pearl Harbor. Finally, Pug is made commander of a Navy cruiser. Remaining true to form, Rhoda continues with her drinking and carrying on with Palmer Kirby. While Warren (Michael Woods) is stationed in Honolulu, his increasingly anxious wife, Janice (a very young Sharon Stone), constantly awaits his return home. Souring on her on-off relationship with married Hugh Cleveland, daughter Madeline (Leslie Hope) begins seeing eligible naval officer Simon Anderson (William R. Moses). Byron serves with stunning success as a submariner in the Pacific. Pamela, for her part in the war effort, traverses the globe with her ever more eccentric father Talky (Robert Morley). Also, through an ongoing set of complicated bureaucratic circumstances and despite the gallant efforts of Byron and Slote to help, Natalie (Jane Seymour), young Louis (Hunter Schlesinger), and the stubborn Aaron (John Gielgud) all remain trapped in Italy.

At his wit's end, Aaron turns to his former student and fawning Nazi SS official Werner Beck (Bill Wallis) for help. But after Beck arranges for Aaron to make a series of anti–Ally radio broadcasts from Rome, he and Natalie plan to escape to the new Zion — Israel. Tragically, Warren's airplane is shot down at the Battle of Midway. While Pug responds to his loss by breaking off with

Pamela, Rhoda drinks even more excessively and begins a new scandalous affair with suave ladies' man Harrison "Hack" Peters (Mike Connors), who works on the top-secret Manhattan Project. After Aaron and Natalie's attempt to escape to Israel fails, they are stranded in Nazi occupied Vichy France with a group of other American detainees.

When her father is killed in a landmine accident, Pamela makes plans to marry a neurasthenic English nobleman. Simultaneously, Pug and Rhoda attempt another reconciliation, the widowed Janice gets involved with Byron's commander Carter "Lady" Aster (Barry Bostwick), and Slote continues his fight to assist the Jews of Europe. Aaron is sent to Paris for surgery, where the ubiquitous Beck reenters his and Natalie's lives. Despite the efforts of Comtesse de Chambrun (Nina Foch), a fashionable American expatriate and collaborationist chatelaine, Beck has Aaron and Natalie sent to Thersienstadt, the same model concentration camp where Karl was sent in *Holocaust*. However, Berel makes a heroic escape from Auschwitz.

Pug reunites with Pamela in Russia and they rekindle their romance and make plans for the future. At Thersienstadt, Eichmann beats Aaron into submission for refusing to join the Jewish Council of Elders. For her part in organizing a series of anti–Nazi performances, SS Major Karl Rahm (Robert Stephens) threatens to have Natalie and Louis sent to Auschwitz. Natalie quickly arranges for Berel to rescue Louis from the camp. When it becomes apparent to the upper Nazi echelon that Hitler (Steven Berkoff) has doomed Germany to failure, orders are given to exterminate all remaining Jews. The inmates of Thersienstadt are sent to Auschwitz. Arriving on the last train to the death camp, Aaron and Natalie meet different fates. While her life is spared, he is gassed to death.

Later, Natalie is among the surviving prisoners to evacuate Auschwitz as the Allies advance. When the Nazis slaughter Berel's entire village, he saves the life of young Louis. Although Natalie survives, she requires a long hospitalization. Upon her request, Byron goes off on a somber mythic quest throughout war-torn Europe searching for Louis. After their divorce, Pug marries Pamela and Rhoda weds Hack Peters. The epic narrative concludes with Byron finally finding his lost son and taking him to Natalie.

Critic John Simon speaks of two different kinds of greatness in works of art. One type transcends "all previously known boundaries ... defying all norms," while the other, is characterized by "perfect taste ... exquisite tact."[8] Artists such as Wagner, Mahler, Michelangelo, Picasso, Dostoyevsky, and James Joyce possessed the Promethean artistic temperament to execute creations of artistic grandiosity on a massive scale, which Simon says defy all artistic norms. In our interpretive history of the epic miniseries, Curtis is this same sort of protean artist. With *War and Remembrance*, he reaches for a more visionary epic miniseries experience: one that fuses the high-pitched melodramatics of *Rich Man, Poor Man* and *Roots* with a grander design and historical sweep, and an epic narrative drive to top even his own prior achievement of *The Winds of War*.

In a similar context, Pauline Kael claims that certain great movie directors, after achieving an enormous popular success (such as Curtis had with *The Winds of War*), next go mad on the limitless potential of the medium. This can lead to these artists hoping to make a huge visionary epic as their cinematic magnum opus by which they might even alter the perceptions of people around the world and literally "bring mankind the Word."[9] Kael believes this is the same sort of creative impulse that led Tolstoy to write *War and Peace*. We believe it is this same sort of impulse that led to Wouk's writing of *War and Remembrance*, and Curtis's attempt to transform the book into the grandest epic miniseries of them all.

Tolstoy's Curtis

In our reading of *The Winds of War*, we pointed out the way Pug's connection to the power triumvirate of Roosevelt/Churchill/Stalin led him to believe he acquired a privileged understanding of the mysterious forces undergirding both history and epic narrative. However, with *War and Remembrance*, that understanding changes. As the epic narrative unfolds, a more persuasive voice begins to make itself heard. Eventually, this voice makes it difficult to embrace the idea that it is only those in power who always drive the course of history and epic narrative. That voice belongs to the Leo Tolstoy of *War and Peace*.

There is a point in *War and Peace* when Tolstoy likens Napoleon to a carved figure on the bow of a ship, which the ignorant believe powers and directs the vessel — and to a small child, grasping at the ribbons and braids that decorate the inside of a carriage, mistakenly believing he is driving it. For Tolstoy, the theory that the powerful alone always drive and control the forces of destiny is erroneous. Rather, he believed it was the everyday experiences of millions upon millions of people that shaped, organically and chaotically, the true course of history and epic narrative. In Tolstoy's theory of determinism, societies are infinitely complex entities, moving and breathing through the constant jostling of multitudes of mentalities and habits. In this bottom-up rather than top-down theory, politics can suddenly become a thin crust on the surface of culture, and political leaders end up playing a smaller role in the ultimate transformation of a people than they would perhaps like to believe they do. This process is especially accelerated when the integral fabric of the world is being torn apart as it is in *War and Remembrance*.

There is a defining moment that comes near the end of *The Winds of War* when Pug describes the way the forces of history and epic narrative are pushing the members of his family in many different directions at once. Like so many tumbleweeds, they are being driven far apart by "the Winds of War." Yet at the conclusion of *The Winds of War*, the nuclear American family still weathers the storm. Neither the forces of history nor epic narrative have succeeded in bringing about its disintegration. The family and its traditional values appear to remain intact.

But as we will see, just as the theory of history and epic narrative shifts dramatically in *War and Remembrance*, so too does the fate and preservation of the nuclear family and its value structure. Hence, it is through the idea of depicting the process of the disintegration of the nuclear family (signified by the collective fate of the Henry family) and the ideals of Western Civilization (signified by the fates of Natalie and Aaron) that the epic miniseries is pushed to its fullest and greatest potential. But here some unexpected difficulties arise. We next turn to what, for many members of the audience, turned out to be the biggest difficulty of all.

Brecht's Curtis

In Chapter 3 we saw how certain Brechtian elements—the use of elaborate pageantry and excessive spectacle—entered the epic narrative through *Shogun*, establishing specific formal and thematic effects. With *War and Remembrance*, those Brechtian elements are carried to their logical conclusion. Brecht believed there was an out-worn "reactionary" side to the traditional dramatic model that created a false sense of dramatic unity and undesirable feelings of identification and fascination in audiences. He considered such feelings as politically detrimental and in response called for new techniques to purposely disrupt and alienate his audiences from experiencing such self-satisfying complacency. Brecht disrupts the smooth, soothing flow of the epic narrative with the use of dreams, fantasies, musical segments, satire, parody, camp, extreme violence, and excessive spectacle.[10]

Although *War and Remembrance* contains some of the most lavish use of spectacle ever presented in any televisual epic miniseries,[11] these are not the scenes that have a truly disruptive effect on the epic narrative, creating a negative viewing experience for some audiences. We wish to posit the idea that this occurs mostly through the obsessively detailed depiction of the horrific details of the fates of Natalie and Aaron at the hands of the Nazis in Europe. For example, Nazi-controlled Vichy France is a place utterly vile and mortally dangerous to the Jews, French and Americans alike. Auschwitz shows evil collusion between German civilian life and complete genocide with its slave-labor component. There is a sharp juxtaposition of lush, civilized Nazi officers' family settings and diabolic crematorial fires for innocent millions. Could such an advanced culture produce Schiller, Brahms, Mozart, and Beethoven? But it also produced Kant, Nietzsche and Wagner. The poet Heine once wrote that a society that could burn books would end by burning people, too. Perhaps because these excruciating scenes are juxtaposed against others of a far less disruptive nature, they stand out all the more in their horrific detail. As they accumulate over the course of the 30-hour running time in their brutal force, they hit the members of the audience in the face with a seemingly unending series of jolts of brutal reality. The final result so disrupts the complacent immersion of the epic narrative flow that for many, the schism was too fatal to repair.

The first example we get of how this diegetic effect operates comes in the form of the extended sequence when a group of high-ranking Nazi officials are given a guided tour of a "special action" against a trainload of unsuspecting Jews at Auschwitz. In a very real sense, Curtis reassembles the process of the Final Solution in such painstaking detail that a good part of *War and Remembrance* becomes more a spectacle of harsh reality and less one of absorbing epic duration. The scene at Auschwitz begins with images of a train carrying freight cars of Jewish men, women, and children into the camp. After a process of selection, those condemned to die are told to undress and are herded into showers and gassed to death, their lifeless bodies hurled into a huge mass grave. While this horrific event takes place, the Nazi officials look on with the perverse, distant amusement of a group of petty bureaucrats, discussing possible ways the extermination process can be made even more efficient and cost-effective.

In fact, it is with this ghoulish, horrific scene that a good example of German/Nazi doubling-doppelganger occurs. Emerging from the trainload of Jews is a pretty young mother with a lovely little girl who is terrified by the shouting Nazi guards and the seemingly devouring barking dogs. To calm the child before the guards intervene, the mother picks a beautiful flower from a bush near the gas chambers. The beauty of the flower calms the child. Then they're herded with the others Jews into the gas chambers, the doors are sealed and the canisters of Zyklon B are dropped. There next emerges horrible screaming and the sounds of hellish struggles, which are observed clinically and scientifically by leading SS Officer Himmler through a glass hole in the door of the gas chamber. When the bodies are covered over in a pit with lime (the Nazis hadn't brought crematoria into the process yet), one can see the gassed, lifeless form of the little girl in her mother's arms, still holding the crushed flower. Later at the Commandant's house near the camp, Himmler behaves most affectionately with the Commandant's young children, embraces the young daughter and gives the girl a pretty flower from a bouquet on the dining room table. The flower becomes a symbol of chilling Nazi evil and doubling/doppelganger.[12]

Another scene that pushes the envelope from the absurdity of German cruelty to the sadistic Nazi nadir point is the one in which a bestial SS officer is shown urinating on the desiccated corpses of slain Jewish men, women, and children. A Jewish prisoner is so revolted at the final indignity shown to the dead that he somehow grabs a gun and shoots the SS guard and several others before being shot in turn. Berel and a compatriot make a break for it in the

Final Solutions: Natalie Jastrow Henry (Jane Seymour) faces the cruel brutality of Nazi Death Camps. *War and Remembrance* (ABC, 1988–89).

chaos and confusion; though Berel's friend is violently shot in a river, Berel escapes and joins the Prague Underground. Then there is the scene in Thersienstadt when Natalie is taken to SS Major Karl Rahm's office along with little Louis. Louis is taken from her by an SS officer and Rahm tells the officer, who is dangling Louis by the legs, to tear the child in half and have Natalie mop up the blood and guts and send it to the crematoria. Natalie hysterically says she'll do anything they ask. The commandant says, "Anything," and the SS officer dangling Louis fumbles with his zipper and has a very crude joke at Natalie's expense. Fortunately Natalie is able to rescue Louis from their clutches but such an episode convinces her that Louis is much better off away from the camp. So she and Aaron fake the boy's death and give him to Berel to be taken to the Czech farm village.

In the mounting up of such disturbing scenes as these, the power to disrupt becomes so overwhelming that these scenes can no longer be absorbed into or adequately contained within the fabric of the televisual epic narrative. In the end, it is this effect more than anything else that wears down all the earlier feelings of pleasurable fulfillment experienced by the audience of *The Winds of War*. Rather than the final sense of harmonic unity, the promise of a new paradise that typically occurs through the classical tradition of *coincidental opprobrium* (the careful juxtaposing of binary opposites) in the epic miniseries of the past, a good deal of the epic narrative is subjected to erasure. This leads to the ultimate rupture and total fragmentation of the canonical achievement, the ratings debacle of *War and Remembrance*, and the discontinuation of the long-form epic miniseries as a viable future televisual art form.[13]

The Aaron Question

In the last ten hours of *War and Remembrance*, the story of Aaron and Natalie dominates the sweep of the epic narrative. Although he is an overly secular, fastidious scholar of impeccable (if not downright fussy) taste and refinement, Aaron's behavior can frequently impress the viewer as irritating. At times he seems an insufferable egoist, utterly out of touch with any sense of reality. Transcending his humble Polish roots, he is an aristocratic symbol of hierarchical high-culture aestheticism. The personification of Apollonian above-it-allness, he has refashioned himself into the Assimilated Jew as Sophisticated Citizen of the World. Despite Natalie's repeated efforts to persuade her uncle to return to America with her, he refuses to budge an inch on the matter.

When the insidious Nazi Werner Beck reenters her uncle's life, Natalie cannot help but suspect the worst. Of course her worst fears are soon realized when Beck attempts to pressure Aaron into the reductionist role of a Nazi collaborator. It is only then that Aaron finally realizes the full *gravitas* of their predicament. Curtis uses these scenes of the shifty-eyed Beck's harassment of his illustrious mentor to a chillingly wicked effect. Bill Wallis, the actor playing Beck, has a quivering, piggish-looking quality, which Curtis counterpoints against all of his vapid philosophizing of a Nazified world to a comic-horrific grotesquerie.

In one scene, while Aaron and Beck converse over dinner in the hushed tones of cultivated abstraction, Natalie looks on appalled. She simply cannot believe her uncle's complete lack of common sense. The expression on her face grows so intense it burns like fire. Then again, Natalie understands what her hopelessly hierarchical uncle cannot: Beck and his kind mean to make over all of Europe into a Nazi madhouse. And for her and her uncle, it will become something even worse: a massive Nazi death camp. Thankfully, when he realizes something so very momentous is unfolding, Aaron snaps to full attention. He applies the whole of his intellect and sensibility into plotting Natalie's and his escape. If all of his efforts prove too little, too late, at least they make us realize he is nothing if not a man of many contradictions. He is a Jew in love with Christian culture; a Polish-American who prefers *la dolce vita* of Italy over either his native or adopted lands; and a man of thought who can spring into action with the very best of them.

Aaron's contradictions provide Curtis with an excellent opportunity to combine the word-oriented approach of *Holocaust* with one of the most sumptuous displays of mise-en-scène technique ever seen in any epic miniseries. With this, the most ancient conflict of Western Civilization — between Jew and non–Jew, between "Hebrew word-worship versus pagan image, of the great unseen versus the glorified thing"[14] — is united in a Judeo-Christian visual harmony. This pictorial strategy derives from Aaron's life-long admiration for pagan antiquity and Catholicism expressed in the Humanist thought implicit in the rebirth of pagan form and image that is Renaissance Italy. However, despite Aaron's profound admiration for such Renaissance visual daring, he turns ironically to the impermeable foundation of his Judaic origins against the crushing oppression of Nazism. Like Kunta Kinte in *Roots* and Rudi in *Holocaust*, Aaron looks to the ancient wisdom of his forebears in his hour of greatest need. He is even shown tearing up his old conversion papers and donning the robes of a Rabbi intoning his faith. The full scope and complexity of this word-image dyad is stunningly articulated in the flawless photography of Dietrich Lohmann.

Lohmann Assoluta

Long associated with several of the greatest directors of the New German Cinema of the 1970s and 1980s,[15] Lohmann's dazzling use of color in *War and Remembrance* is praised in *Variety* for the way color is made to glow with so much emotion that it dominates the eye: "rich, golden brown woods are used for many impressive interiors, icy, cool gray marble for Hitler's Nazi excesses, deceptively cheerful bright tones for Thersienstadt. While Natalie and son Louis are anxiously awaiting dread news, they sit alone in a room washed with blue. The mushroom cloud (in the aftermath of the dropping of the Atomic Bomb on Hiroshima) is bathed in a malignant red" (*Variety*, May 5, 1989).

Such high praise notwithstanding, we are still not prepared for the full-scale brilliance of Lohmann's achievement in *War and Remembrance*. The mise-en-scène of the epic miniseries operates on a more complex mythic and operatic level than did that of *The Winds of War*. Very often, Lohmann's magic-seeming camera is transformed into a mobile eye documenting and aestheticizing the places and spaces of Western civilization, visually sublimating them until they take on the tragic beauty and mystery of Paradise being annihilated.

Hence, the interior scenes featuring Hitler and the Nazis signify the cold, gray allure and hard severity of marble, and exude the unwholesome, unholy grimness of death and human extinction. In contrast, the interiors of the Allies have a burnished, bronze tone, which visually endows them with the sublimity of life. The Allied scenes look like they are lit with the diffusion of golden candlelight. Equally impressive are several interior compositions in which Lohmann employs this same interplay of light and dark to create a Leonardo Da Vinci–like chiaroscuro effect. This is most evident in the scenes that take place at Aaron's palatial home in Italy. A sense of forbidden gloom and certain Old World coziness alternate accordingly. It is in these iconic Italian scenes that

Natalie's maternal Jewish beauty grows in dignity and intensity. As Natalie shelters her young son from the endless Nazi threats, Lohmann depicts her in the central image of Catholicism: Mary and the Christ Child (another iconic Jewish mother and baby). This connection universalizes their plight in much the same way the characters of *Roots* and *Holocaust* were universalized to appeal to the broadest possible international audience.

There are many other instances of Lohmann's visual mastery worthy of attention. Take the amazing extended sequence when Beck brings Natalie to the opulent Paris Opera to attend a performance of Mozart's *The Marriage of Figaro*. As the unlikely couple take their seats in a private balcony, the camera moves from a long shot of the conductor leading the opera's overture to a close-up of Natalie's startlingly beautiful, enigmatic face. Lohmann uses the codified technique of the worshipful Hollywood glamour close-up of the Golden Age in his visual idealization of Natalie. Her eyes are liquid and luminous, her lips shiny and full, her hair splendid and luxurious. As the French sociologist Edgar Morin states, Hollywood reaches for the ideal in the heart of the real. So too does Lohmann use Natalie's beauty to show us the extraordinary within the ordinary, the metaphysical within the physical, the unknowable within the known.

Or take the way Lohmann can make the sunset resplendent with oranges and golds, yet still muted and earthy. There are other times when he uses combinations of different colors (especially in all the sumptuous scenes shot in Paris, Rome, London, Moscow, New York, and Washington) creating a viridescent play of yellows, reds, blues, and purples. Or there is the scene of a kind-hearted farmer giving the Jews on the transport train to Auschwitz a large bagful of succulent red apples. Natalie's stark, beauteous face is shown devouring the apple in ravenous ecstasy as if it were a seven-course gourmet meal. Her face is contorted with starvation as she devours the apple. And there are the somber scenes of the metallic, silver-gray severity and gleaming hardness of great battleships and sleek submarines engaged in ferocious battles on tumultuous high seas, which give way to the eerie, shadowy blackness of the dark-toned, ascetically stark scenes of Auschwitz, which suddenly dissolve into the visionary materialism of a handful of priceless diamonds against deep black velvet that Aaron offers the Nazis in a last-ditch effort to save the lives of Natalie and Louis. It is in such a scene that Aaron fully and finally redeems himself as a man and as an agent of the Light. He is cunning enough to have concealed the dazzling diamonds all this time from the Nazis and he realizes, with the lives of Natalie and Louis at stake, he must now exchange them for their very lives. If it is his fault Natalie and Louis are in the camp with him by his being so arrogant and stubborn about not fleeing to America when he had the chance, he redeems himself completely in this one stark, magnificent visionary scene.

The Longest Shadow

The history of the epic miniseries is filled with an unforgettable televisual gallery of memorable characters. From Kunta Kinte, Kizzy, and Chicken George to Karl, Rudi, and Inga Weiss, to Father Ralph de Bricassart and Meggie Cleary, to Charles Ryder, Sebastian and Julia Flyte, these and several other unforgettable characters have impressed themselves upon our collective memory with an indelible collection of mythic heroes and heroines. And even villainous characters such as the slave-abusing Master Moore, the twisted Nazi couple Erik and Marta Dorf, the vindictive Mary Carson, and renegade Blue Duck have taken hold of our imagination and are not so easily shaken off.

While discussing the subject of not-so-easily shaken-off villains, we must now speak of the most elusive and determined villain of them all: Death. Indeed, we have seen Death assume many different forms and guises in the past. Yet Death has never before assumed quite the all-consuming role he does in *War and Remembrance*. The first victim to fall prey to Death is Warren Henry when the Japanese shoot down his plane at the Battle of Midway. As his bomber is engulfed in flames, Warren prays before plunging into the watery vastness of the Pacific Ocean. His heroic death signifies the destruction of the brightest and best. Talky Tudsbury, like Warren, also meets Death in a fiery blast of immolation when the military vehicle he is riding in hits a land mine planted by the Nazis. No less violent are the deaths of Slote and Berel, both of whom are viciously gunned down while they are in the midst of taking heroic stands against the Nazi aggressors.

We believe, however, that in our history of the epic miniseries, arguably the most astonishing portrayal of Death is that depicting the demise of Aaron Jastrow at Auschwitz. Beginning with a fiery close-up of the engine furnace of the last train to Auschwitz being stoked with coal, the rising flames engulf the entire screen with a hellish light. An alternating series of close-ups and long shots of the moving train rambling down the railroad tracks follow. (Repeatedly, Curtis uses images of moving trains as a signifier for approaching doom.) As the lumbering sound of the train fills the soundtrack, Lohmann's camera makes it look like a heavy, mindless mechanical beast, making it a symbol of the tormenting Nazi nightmare. Such an attitude toward the visual is different from the traditional attitude we have seen in other epic miniseries. It's more along the lines of the illogical demonological darkness of surrealistic dream logic. Upon the train's arrival into the staging area, Nazi stormtroopers and their growling dogs are lined up on either side of the railroad tracks.

Now the real Nazi horror begins and the epic narrative reimagines the abyss. To the overwhelming strains of composer Bob Cobert's affecting, dirge-like death march, Aaron and the other Jews selected to die are forcibly led to the showers. After undressing, the naked, confused men, women, and children are brutally shoved into the showers. Even the regal Sir John Gielgud is not exempt from the brutality. Once again Lohmann uses color for heightened dramatic impact. The lighting inside the showers turns part yellow, part blue, like the color in an Expressionist painting. While being gassed to death, Aaron recites the Lord's Prayer. He directs his eyes toward Heaven in the universal visual language of supplication. Aaron's death is depicted in the philosophical language of stoicism, whereby all bodily impulses and passions are made no longer worthy of rational reflection. As such, these impulses and passions are erased and a kind of idealized temperament of serenity and the divine is attained. Finally, at Auschwitz, Aaron finds his God. Most shockingly, after he is dead, Aaron's body is then shown being brutally shoveled into the blazing furnace. As when the engine of the train was stoked with coal, the entire screen fills once again with an extreme close-up of the raging flames, engulfing his earthly remains. The sequence concludes with a moving final image of Aaron's ashes being dumped into the river, from which they float past the place of his boyhood home. Ashes to ashes, dust to dust, the Prodigal Son has returned.

Although Aaron perishes into the abyss, Natalie survives. We interpret this as her becoming a signifier for Walter Benjamin's famous thesis of the philosophy of history seen through the melancholic eyes of the Angel of History. Benjamin describes the Angel of History as staring fixedly, contemplatively, with mouth open, wings spread, and face turned toward the past: where we might perceive only a baffling chain of disconnected events,

> The Angel of History sees one single catastrophe which keeps piling wreckage upon wreckage and hurls it in front of his/her feet. The Angel would like to stay, awake the dead and make whole what has been smashed. But a storm is blowing from Paradise; it has caught in her/his wings with such violence that the poor Angel can no longer close them: This storm irresistibly propels the Angel into the future to which his/her back is turned, while the pile of debris before the Angel of History grows ever skyward.[16]

But if Natalie is a signifier for Walter Benjamin's Angel of History, she is also a signifier for the Victim of History. As such, she is the defiant Victim of History staring straight into the face of a world that did little to save her and her people from almost total annihilation. Like Alberecht Dürer's allegorical, androgynous figure of Melancholia, at the end of *War and Remembrance*, young Louis cannot speak, and his mother sits alone on the deserted railroad tracks. All of her beautiful hair has been shorn, making her look like Falconetti as St. Joan in *The Passion of Joan of Arc* (Carl Theodor Dreyer, 1928). Natalie has been beaten, tortured, and thoroughly violated. Her eyes are sunken in, burning, her face worn and shadowed, her body gaunt and broken. The stranded props and remains of Western civilization are hurled, shattered, and smashed at her feet. On one level, we could say Natalie has become the universal symbol for all divine aspirations ever brought down and defeated by the shortcomings of human evil and indifference. But on another level, Natalie can be perceived as a great deal more: she is a tragic tableau of humanity, driven from Eden after the Fall; and, paradoxically, while all of the men lie broken and defeated, Natalie alone is the Spirit of Woman, Defiant, Undefeated, and Triumphant.

Chapter 5

Transitional Places

A great filmmaker is an artist with the ability to express a total world view. The whole point of the text the filmmaker creates is to illuminate for us the human condition. In the end, this singular, deeply personal vision is all that matters. The filmmaker's unique vision of our world is the picture's real subject. The three epic miniseries we will discuss in the first part of this chapter were made for European, not American, television. The first two texts, *Scenes from a Marriage* (PBS, 1974) from Sweden, and *Berlin Alexanderplatz* (PBS, 1980) from Germany, were directed by two of the greatest filmmakers in the history of cinema — Ingmar Bergman and Rainer Werner Fassbinder, respectively. The third, *The Singing Detective* (PBS, 1989) from England, was written by Dennis Potter, arguably the greatest writer ever to have worked in the medium of television.

Because these three epic miniseries were made for European television, they were created under a completely different set of circumstances than if they had been made for American television. In other words, these artists were not pressured into coming up with works with a strong emphasis on entertainment value for the purpose of capturing the highest Nielsen ratings possible. No, Bergman, Fassbinder, and Potter were all permitted to reach for the highest level of their artistic daring. And they could do this with an obsessive, personal concentration on detail, a not-always-easy-to-read symbolism, and a deep sense of profound personal self-revelation. Accordingly, these epic miniseries demand an openminded attitude from an audience. But, if they ask for much, they also give much in return.

Along with bringing attention to these three superlative foreign epic miniseries, this chapter will conclude with a survey of a diverse group of American televisual texts of the latter 1980s that were to serve a transitional function, moving the epic miniseries from the 1980s into the 1990s. Whereas the creative mission of those epic miniseries made for American television in the 1970s and early 1980s was to develop and refine the formal and thematic strategies of the form as a means of negotiating for itself a commanding position as a high-profile, special televisual event, those of the latter 1980s were about televisual places of a more transitional nature. While these texts do not negate the past completely, we believe they exhibit less of an essentialist view and make for a more daring, experimental and extratextual viewing experience for the television audience.

Scenes from a Marriage

When Ingmar Bergman, the most famous Swedish director in the history of film, turned his genius to creating an epic miniseries for television, expectations ran high. Bergman did not and does not disappoint. A meticulous cinematic perfectionist with a supreme command of film technique, the director takes a microcosmic rather than a macrocosmic approach to the long-form televisual drama. This approach results in a unique production that has the intimacy and immediacy of a chamber piece. It is the most intimate of epic miniseries, but its intimacy has epic depth. Although Bergman relies upon the same episodic soap operaesque structure the artists of American television favored in such epic miniseries as *Rich Man, Poor Man*, *Captains and the Kings*, *Roots*, and *Holocaust*, he also takes their panoramic view and narrows its focus considerably. The focus now becomes more obsessive, claustrophobic, constantly reaching inward and downward, providing an indepth exploration into the 10-year marriage of Marianne (Liv Ullmann), a divorce lawyer, and her husband Johan (Erland Josephson), a university professor.

On the surface theirs is an idyllic marriage, an Edenic existence. They have a lovely home, two beautiful daughters, money, health, and happiness. But beneath that placid surface, much unrest stirs. Johan can be cruel and overbearing, Marianne too eager to please others. When they witness their married friends, Katarina (Bibi Andersson) and Peter (Jan Malmsjö), viciously attack one another, they vow never to let their marriage descend to such an abject level.

Still, when Johan pressures Marianne into having an abortion and continues to find faults with her, she grows resentful of his authority over her. While Marianne is shaken up at work by an unhappy older woman seeking to divorce her cruel husband, Johan is equally shaken by his colleague and on-off mistress, Eva (Gunnel Lindblom), criticizing his lack of originality. His irritation leads to his telling Marianne of his unhappiness with their life together and his intention to leave her for Paula, a 23-year-old college student he has fallen hopelessly in love with. Some months after walking out, Johan visits Marianne. After she complains of his neglect, Johan confesses that Paula forbids him from seeing either her or their girls. To escape Paula's dominance, he intends to leave her and take a job in America. Marianne reads to Johan from her journal (which only puts him to sleep), and confesses she has taken a lover for herself, but still prefers Johan. She also tells him Paula has sent her a letter promising to let Johan see his family in the future.

A year later, Marianne, smartly dressed and looking more secure within herself, brings Johan their divorce papers to sign. In between consuming large quantities of alcohol, they discuss their lives. Johan tells of his bitterness over Paula and his not getting the job he wanted in America. Marianne tells of her intent to remarry and travel extensively with her new husband. Johan and Marianne make love and haggle bitterly over the details of their divorce agreement.

After a violent physical confrontation, the exhausted couple sign their divorce papers.

Considerable time passes. Both Johan and Marianne have remarried other partners, yet they have become lovers once again. With their spouses away, they decide to spend a romantic weekend at a friend's cottage by the sea. While Marianne tells of her new husband's sexual prowess, Johan confesses he wishes he had become a small-town bookstore owner and lived a simple life with Marianne and their daughters. During the night, Marianne awakens from a nightmare. After she and Johan talk, Marianne returns to bed. They peacefully fall asleep, lovingly locked in one another's arms

In filming *Scenes from a Marriage*, Ingmar Bergman instructed cinematographer Sven Nykvist to provide him with an austere, stripped-down, cinema vérité–like visual style for the epic miniseries. Nykvist relied upon many of the same techniques pioneered by the early BBC serial television dramas of the 1950s. Emphasis is placed on extremely tight close-ups and rather claustrophobically composed interiors, which convey an enclosed feeling over more expansive exterior scenes and the continuous cutting back-and-forth from one speaking character to another.[1] Mainly what differentiates *Scenes from a Marriage* from the early BBC serials is the way Nykvist juxtaposes bold colors, and the probing intensity of his riveting close-ups. In his expert hands, the camera takes on a source of power. It becomes a viewer, absorbing every minute detail of the actors' facial expressions, concentrating so relentlessly, so closely on stars Liv Ullman and Erland Josephson, that as a result we become deeply involved with them and their lives.

As we become deeply engrossed in the couple's relationship, we also begin to experience the disorientation of the Freudian concept of the uncanny. There is something so disturbing, yet so intensely familiar about the characters and their situation, initially we might not want to name it or recall it. This is similar to the psychological process Freud called "parapraxis." It is a key element of classic art and literature, and is also found in the Morality plays of the Middle Ages. John Simon says these plays were intended to provide allegories for people to use as a personal model for the attainment of the knowledge and wisdom needed to live a good, moral life, and hopefully to experience a peaceful death. In a similar way, Simon believes "Bergman's epic miniseries sums up for us ... all there is to know about love, sex, marriage, divorce — of life together and life apart."[2] Thus, Bergman creates a male and female protagonist who are so prototypically Everyman and Everywoman that we cannot help but recognize ourselves in them, whether we care to do so or not.

Bergman achieves this effect in three ways: (1) through the simple, direct style of the mise-en-scène; (2) in the rendering of Johan and Marianne as recognizable, universal mythic archetypes; (3) by the use of a detailed, highly theatrical, always-probing approach to the dialogue. Since we have already addressed Nykvist's accomplishment (and will return to the matter later), we will next consider Bergman's rendering of Johan and Marianne as the two most uniquely universalized male and female characters of the epic miniseries pantheon, bar none. Yet they have not been universalized in the standard way the characters of epic miniseries have traditionally been. Although they do signify the mythic archetypes of Husband and Wife,[3] they also signify those types with considerably more psychological complexity added. While the mise-en-scène may be stripped-down and claustrophobic, the same cannot be said of either Marianne or Johan.

Because Bergman eschews the use of such standard tropes of the epic miniseries as the alteration of complex plotlines involving several characters and the reliance upon a glittery gallery of revolving guest stars (except for an electrifying appearance by the incomparable Bibi Andersson), the trials and tribulations of Marianne and Johan dominate the epic narrative completely. This necessitates Bergman making them one of the most fascinating and complex couples of the Epic Miniseries. This need is further exacerbated by the fact that except for a few brief scenes, they are the only two characters ever to appear on screen. Therefore, while Bergman makes them two great mythic archetypes, he also makes them highly articulate archetypes. As the visual style pays homage to the BBC serial dramas of the 1950s, so too does Bergman's use of theatrically flavored dialogue. Yet if Bergman's dialogue seems overly mundane, trivial, and commonplace at one moment, in the next moment, something is said or done to elevate the epic narrative onto a highly poetic, cosmological level.

An example of this occurs in the opening scene when Marianne and Johan are being interviewed by a reporter for a women's magazine as the "ideal" married couple. While Johan goes on and on about himself, as is his fashion, Marianne quietly looks on with a mysterious, ironic, Mona Lisa–like smile on her face. When asked to describe herself, Marianne simply replies that she is content to be the wife of Johan and the mother of two lovely little daughters.

In a later scene, some months after he has walked out on her, Johan visits Marianne and encourages her to read to him from her private journal. While Johan relaxes on the green sofa (the luxurious and almost penetrating emerald greenness of which Nykvist makes look like an Arcadian meadow), Marianne reads to him. At first her words are almost embarrassingly flowery and trite as she reads of her early girlhood experiences. But then there is an abrupt shift in tone, and she speaks of feeling like a stranger even to herself. Although she blames her marriage to Johan for contributing to her negative self-image, she also reveals that her father also tried to dominate all aspects of her life. Like Ibsen's Nora in *A Doll's House*, Marianne trades one tyrant for another.

Throughout the revelatory sequence, Bergman uses a montage of black-and-white "real-life" photographs of Ullmann from various periods of her life to ironic effect.[4] Much of this irony stems from the fact that in several of the photographs, Ullmann smiles in the same mysterious Mona Lisa–like way she smiled in the opening scene when she was interviewed for being one part of the "ideal" married couple.

If there are many aspects of *Scenes from a Marriage* that set it apart from other epic miniseries, there are also other aspects that connect it back to those works. For example, Bergman concludes each weekly serialized episode with a powerful blast of drama. This creates an effect similar to, but much more subtle than, the "cliffhanger" melodramatic endings that traditionally conclude each installment of the epic miniseries. At the end of the first episode, Johan visits Marianne in her cold, sterile white hospital room after she has had an abortion. After avoiding any talk about what Marianne has just been through, Johan rather abruptly leaves her. With his departure, Marianne, sobbing uncontrollably, pulls the covers up over her head and hides under them, concluding the episode.

The third episode ends just as powerfully and devastatingly. The morning after Johan has informed her he is leaving her and the children for Paula, Marianne helps him pack his suitcase. After eating their breakfast and discussing the details of their various social obligations, Johan prepares to leave. Then, through a doorway, which Nykvist backs with a lacerating splash of blood-red drapery, Marianne frantically throws her arms around Johan's neck, pleading that he not leave his family. She seems to clutch on to him with the desperation of the damned reaching out of Hell for salvation. In doing so she is trying to hold on not just to Johan but to her own identity, her psyche-soul, if you will. The fear of losing who and what she is, her very being, makes her cling to him so desperately now. But Johan, totally ignoring her desperate pleas, pushes free of her, walks out, and loudly slams the door behind him.[5] Gripped by existential dread, Marianne, as in the first episode, climbs back into bed. After some time passes and she is more composed, she telephones a close friend. But when he tells her that he and several others already know of Johan's affair with Paula, the betrayed Marianne takes refuge under the bed covers and the episode concludes the same way as did the first. But in hiding under the bed covers this time, and in giving way to her deepest tears and terror, Marianne is doing more than hiding beneath the covers as a little girl would from a nightmare. She is trying to shield herself from a life transformed into total black existential nightmare. Still the theme hinted at here is also that of transformation — and transformation can become positive as well as negative. In fact, in this epic drama, transformation can be a magical event, almost as in a fairy-tale.

It seems that in the beginning, Marianne and Johan were living both in the bubble and the illusion of an ideal marriage. But beneath the surface, there were the demons of Johan's infidelities and Marianne's traumatic childhood. Then thesis, antithesis and synthesis — the bubble bursts and the demons come out with Johan's duplicitous betrayal and Marianne's emotional collapse. It is an existential abyss and dark night of the soul that they then go through with their separation and divorce, especially Marianne. But in finding others to love, they eventually find themselves and the ability to truly love each other free of illusion or protective bubbles.

If such emotionally charged, unresolved concluding scenes owe a certain debt to the narrative patterning of the BBC serials, like much else about the text they also have a distinct uniqueness that is all their own. This grows directly out of Bergman's personal conception of drama. For Bergman, drama is worthless if it refuses to deal with imperative metaphysical questions. The greatest expression of this credo comes in the hauntingly profound final scene of *Scenes from a Marriage*.

The scene begins with a long-shot of the deserted-looking cottage in which Marianne and Johan are spending the weekend. Nykvist floods the frame with an eerie deep-purple light. After the sound of a foghorn is heard wailing in the distance, Marianne awakens from a nightmare, sobbing uncontrollably. She tells Johan of her bad dream: while out walking on a dangerous roadway with her family, she suddenly begins to sink into a deep hole. In an attempt to save herself, she reaches out for her family to pull her out, but they cannot, for she no longer has arms left. The couple then discuss the feelings of despair and hopelessness her dream has stirred within her. After she has calmed down, Johan comforts her. He says that despite all they have been through together, he believes they truly do love one another, but in an imperfect world and in altogether imperfect, human way.

The power and strength of this concluding scene derives from the way Bergman's deceptively simple dialogue begins seeming so ordinary and prosaic, only to then bloom into a metaphysically sublime form of poetic expression. For Marsha Kinder, such a conclusion has deep meaning for us all in that it implies "if we only have the strength to take a relationship as far as it will go ... to live through all the outbursts of hatred and violence, to confront honestly and openly our full range of human feelings we might discover an emotional capacity that is much deeper and richer than we ever expected."[6] Thus, pain mired through the most bitter experience becomes the catharsis for the transforming power of love for both Johan and Marianne.

Berlin Alexanderplatz

The flamboyant theatricality and camp overadornment of the cinematic world of Rainer Werner Fassbinder is, in many ways, the dialectical opposite of Ingmar Bergman's austere universe. Grisly slaughterhouses, crumbling tenements, decadent brothels, seedy bathhouses, and creepy bunkers—these are just some of the many dark, moody spaces at which Fassbinder pointed his compulsive, unrelenting camera. Yet despite his infamous, drug, alcohol and sex-fueled impatience, Fassbinder, the Enfant Terrible of the New German Cinema, is one of the great artists of the film world. Having first read author Alfred Döblin's great novel *Berlin Alexanderplatz* when he was a teenager, Fassbinder had long dreamed of turning it into a great film. His dream would come true when he got the chance to transform Döblin's literary masterpiece into a 15½ hour epic miniseries for German television.

Berlin Alexanderplatz begins in 1927 in the city of Berlin. The burly and violent Franz Biberkopf (Günter Lamprecht) is released from prison for murdering Ida (Barbara Valentin), the young prostitute he pimped out. Although he has resolved to redeem himself by leading an exemplary life, the sadistic side of his nature soon resurfaces. He visits Ida's married sister Minna (Karin Baal), and beats and rapes her. Later he even flirts with the nascent Nazi party. While working at a series of marginal jobs, he gets involved with the loyal Lina (Elisabeth Trissenaar) only to desert her. Franz next gets involved with the evil Reinhold Hoffmann (Gottfried John), who soon pulls him back into a full-time life of crime and gives him his various discarded mistresses.

Through Reinhold, Franz gets embroiled with Pums (Ivan Desny), the crime boss of a ruthless gang of Berlin cutthroats and thieves. Although Franz is a valuable asset to the gang, Reinhold causes him to have an automobile accident, in which he loses an arm. Undaunted and determined, Franz tries to push on. But when his efforts come to nothing, he falls into a severe depression. His good friend and former lover, Eva (Hanna Schygulla), and her new lover, Herbert (Roger Fritz), intervene. They introduce Franz to Mieze (Barbara Sukowa), a young, naïve prostitute, with whom Franz falls deeply in love. Still not finding gainful employment, he resorts to pimping out Mieze as he did Ida. The couple achieves a state of romantic blissfulness.

Reinhold, out of his mind with jealously over Franz's happiness, attempts to steal Mieze away. When she refuses him, Reinhold lures her to a forest and murders her. Realizing what Reinhold has done, Franz suffers a total breakdown and is committed to an insane asylum. There he experiences a series of dreams, delusions, and hallucinations concerning grief, pain, and death. In time, he is deemed "cured" and released. Now he is finally a respectable member of German society.

As is apparent, Franz Biberkopf is a hard man to like. In the first episode of *Berlin Alexanderplatz* alone, he is released from prison for killing Ida (displaying little, if any, remorse for his crime), then he visits her sister Minna and beats and rapes her. With this act of sexual and physical violation, the central theme of the epic miniseries is established: Life is a Darwinian struggle between the victimizer (male) and his victim (female).

Although Franz pays lip-service to being redeemed and becoming a model German citizen, his actions make such claims difficult to believe. As he exploits woman after woman and involves himself with the Nazis, his behavior takes on the strident, demented perversity typically associated with German Expressionism. Fassbinder and his cinematographer, Xaver Schwarzenberger, create a nightmarish mise-en-scène, evoking extreme psychological stress, tension, and a stifling sense of claustrophobia. This is further emphasized by Fassbinder's filming of *Berlin Alexanderplatz* in the same classical studio-style, on stage-like interior sets, favored during Hollywood's Golden Age.[7] Thus German history is aligned with the claustrophobia-inducing films made by Hollywood in the 1930s and 1940s. And because so much of the epic action is played out in Franz's shabby rooms, which are lit by a continuously flashing hot pink neon sign out on the street, the sense of theatricality and Hollywood artificiality is further intensified.

In taking all of this stylistic excess into account, we fully realize just how perfectly it suits Fassbinder's melodramatic vision of his protagonist. A crude, hulky, surly peasant, Franz is the embodiment of out-of-control male brutality, which once again brings us to the matter of his basic unlikeability. Why should we care about a man who behaves the way Franz does, especially toward women? Whenever the female characters speak, Franz never seems to hear them, like the characters in Virginia Woolf's *The Waves*. But even worse, we must repeatedly watch his brutal murder of Ida — Fassbinder returns again and again to a devastating close-up of her bloodied face, as she attempts to speak her last words before dying. Then there is Franz's beating and raping of Ida's sister Minna, his heartless abandonment of Lina, and his exploitation and beatings of the childlike Mieze. Actually, the women in *Berlin Alexanderplatz* are so badly treated it borders on the demonological.

To keep Franz from descending to such depths of dislikeability, Fassbinder shrewdly casts Günter Lamprecht in the role. Even when Franz is at his most despicable, Lamprecht amazingly allows us to see the sentimental, childlike side of his nature. Also, Fassbinder tempers the negativity of Franz's character by constantly contrasting him to the totally despicable Reinhold, to whom Franz always remains so perversely devoted. Even after Reinhold is the cause of the loss of his arm, Franz remains loyal to his treacherous friend.

When Eva first introduces Franz to Mieze, Franz is enchanted by the alluring child-woman. Even though she sells her body to men on the mean streets of Berlin, she is paradoxically as pure and as fresh and appealing as a day in springtime. Mieze is a baby-whore with a heart of pure gold. She gives off a golden glow. Franz is totally enraptured by her. He compares her to a golden sunset. Like Julia on the Art Deco ocean liner in *Brideshead Revisited*, she offers the hero a second chance at life. Like Bell and Kizzy were to Kunta Kinte in *Roots*, Mieze is a reason for Franz to go on living. She is the dialectical opposite of Reinhold. If her mission is to give life, his is to take it away. Soon after Mieze enters Franz's life, she so sublimates the power of the text that she becomes the active agent of the epic narrative. The only problem with this is Reinhold has already staked his claim to that privileged position. This, combined with Reinhold being unable to stand seeing Franz so happy in love, seals Mieze's fate. Being a man hard-wired for destruction, Reinhold plots out the destruction of Mieze.

His plot begins with his first encounter with her in a darkened stairwell, and ends with his brutal assault of her in the woods. Because the act occurs in a beautiful, sun-drenched natural setting rather than a closed-off stage-like interior set, Fassbinder magnifies its horror. When Reinhold leads Mieze deeper in the enchanting setting, a piece of pure visual poetry is achieved. As golden rays of sunlight beat down through the lush overhanging foliage, a mythic, holy space is evoked for Reinhold to commit his most unholy deed.

With her soft pink dress, pink satin ribbon in her golden blonde hair, and pale white skin, Mieze is frail and defenseless looking, the heroine of the epic miniseries as feminine weakness personified: a dreamy child-woman about to be hurled into the abyss, a fairy-tale heroine in a dark, tragic fable. When Reinhold forces himself on Mieze, the scene takes on a sensuously sadomasochis-

Beauty and the Beast I: After brutally beating her, Franz Biberkopf (Günter Lamprecht) comforts child-woman Mieze (Barbara Sukowa). ***Berlin Alexanderplatz*** (PBS, 1980).

tic edge, leaving us to cringe in horror. For here is the great Epic Miniseries battle of good versus evil, male versus female, innocence versus corruption, encapsulated in one astonishing televisual image. Before she is murdered, Mieze attempts to protect herself against Reinhold. She calls out in desperation for Franz. But in the end neither Franz nor anyone else hears her desperate pleas. Reinhold's murder of Mieze recalls what Ayn Rand said about Marilyn Monroe at the time of her death: "Anyone who has ever felt resentment against the good for being good ... is the murderer of Marilyn Monroe."[8]

Following Mieze's murder, Franz descends into a Dantesque *Totentanz*. With this turn of events, Fassbinder breaks with the classical Hollywood narrative style and melodramatic technique he has used in the preceding 13½ hours of *Berlin Alexanderplatz*. In the controversial 2-hour epilogue, Fassbinder employs a more frenzied mise-en-scène consisting of a combination of surrealistic nightmare imagery, assorted mythic and religious symbolism, jarring historical anachronisms, political critique, and overall Freudian excess.[9] Although the words we hear on the soundtrack, delivered in an incantatory, hypnotic style, are from Döblin, the heightened imagery (flaming out, as it were, in a visual vortex fueled by the director's private excess) is pure Fassbinder. When the series premiered in Germany, Fassbinder declared he *was* Franz Biberkopf.[10] This deep identification with his protagonist results in Fassbinder imbuing the epilogue with the attitude of a shocking private confession.

For many, Fassbinder's approach to the concluding episode proved a baffling assault on the senses. Indeed, a large percentage of the initial German television audience stopped watching the epic miniseries altogether at this point. Whereas Fassbinder had exhibited a (for him) surprising objectivity in the preceding 13½ hours, in the concluding episode all bets are off; all Hell breaks out. So much of his private torment is unleashed, there are times when Fassbinder appears to hem himself in. Not only does he thrust his always-unrelenting camera into his customary seedy bars, brothels, and slaughterhouses, he also appears to be on a mission to rival even the Marquis de Sade with his depiction of scenes of flagellation, violation, rape, castration, and human beings being ground down, devoured, and vaporized. In such scenes, as they are to Reinhold and to a lesser degree Franz, the tropes of sex and violence are one and the same.

Shocking image after shocking image flow into one another at an alarming rate: Franz is seen having his arm crushed by a car repeatedly; Nazi storm troopers goosestep in and out; a straitjacketed Franz is forced to eat out of a bowl on the floor surrounded by hordes of rats; naked human beings are tortured, beaten, raped, killed in grisly slaughterhouses, and hung upside down on meat hooks; Franz is stripped, whipped, nailed to a giant cross like Jesus and hoisted aloft for all to see.

While the sheer boldness of such scenes is pure, unadulterated Fassbinder, the director so primitivizes the mise-en-scène that it becomes unbearably brutal. As in late Freud, the sex instinct becomes totally amoral and destructive. As Sade says of sex in his problematic masterpiece of sexual depravity, *Juliette*, "It demands, it militates, it tyrannizes." But just as it appears that *Berlin Alexanderplatz* is in real danger of being derailed by Fassbinder's erotic self-consciousness and stylistic excesses, he switches gears once again. He interjects various elements of dark humor, historical anachronisms, and mythic imagery of surprising prescience into the epic narrative. For instance, Frau Bast (Brigitte Mira), Franz's frumpy and ubiquitous landlady, who witnesses Franz's murder of Ida and his beating of Mieze, is depicted as the Virgin Mary, holding a plastic Baby Jesus doll with Franz's face. Reinhold appears dressed in full drag to whip Franz with a feather boa; then he and Franz transform into boxers, fighting one another to the death in a boxing ring. Anachronisms abound in the numerous references made to Hitler and the Nazis; the Youth Culture of the 1960s and 1970s is signified by visions of naked young couples copulating wildly in orgies of druggy, Dionysian excess; characters drink bottles of Coca-Cola; the Atomic Bomb explodes, engulfing everything in a giant mushroom cloud; assorted pop music is heard sung by the likes of Janis Joplin ("Me and Bobby McGee"), Elvis Presley ("Santa Lucia"), the Velvet Underground ("Chelsea Hotel"), and Donovan ("Atlantis"), mixed with an eclectic assortment of classical composers such as Beethoven, Strauss, Schubert, and Wagner.

Fassbinder's prescience is seen in the way he uses two androgynous-looking angels to act as Franz's guide through the densely textured dreamscape. With their long, flowing, pre–Raphaelite golden hair, glistening golden breastplates, and lurid display of piquant pink flesh around sexy black lace panties and black garters, these Apollonian angels are as forceful and alluring to behold as the fully armed Amazons, Belphoebe and Britomart, in Edmund Spenser's epic poem *The Faerie Queene*. By using these otherworldly figures in this way, Fassbinder prefigures the ferocious women of Dennis Potter's *The Singing Detective* and paves the way for the fifth mythic type of the epic miniseries, The Avenging Angel, of the 1990s and 2000s.

The Singing Detective

Although he is principally known as a writer of teleplays and not as a director, Dennis Potter is the auteur of his televisual texts as much as Bergman and Fassbinder are of theirs. *The Singing Detective* is Potter's "*Hamlet*, his *Ulysses*, his *Remembrance of Things Past* ... his *Seven Pillars of Wisdom*, his *Life and Opinions of Tristram Shandy*, his *White Album*. And so it is a *vade mecum* of all his major themes and concerns and characters and obsessions and techniques."[11] It is also an unbelievably rich, complex, endlessly watchable visionary work of art that stands as one of the greatest works ever created for television. *The Singing Detective* both summarizes and expands upon the possibilities of the epic miniseries when it is in the hands of a supreme artist.

Potter's eponymous hero, Philip Marlow (Michael Gambon) is a British writer of cheap detective novels. Plagued by psoriatic athropathy, a crippling skin and bone disease (which Potter himself suffered from), Marlow is bedridden in a hospital in the London of 1985. Estranged from his wife, Nicola (Janet Suzman), the embittered Marlow undergoes a variety of treatments, ranging from the pharmacological (hallucinatory drugs) to the psychological (his psychiatrist, Dr. Gibbon [Bill Paterson], forces him to confront his traumatic past). To escape, Marlow projects himself into a realm of fantasy, hallucinations, dreams, and memories. In the dark, film-noiresque fantasy London of 1945, Marlow is the fictional alter ego from his novel *The Singing Detective*, a wisecracking, debonair lounge singer at the Art Deco nightclub Skinscape. There he encounters all sorts of spies, counter-spies, Nazi agents, drug-addicted prostitutes, and luscious and lethal femme fatales. Marlow goes about his business of tracking down the mystery men out to kill client Mark Binney (Patrick Malahide), until he kills Binney's murderers as well as his "real" self.

Marlow's childhood memories also take place in 1945. He is the unhappy only child of his unhappily married parents (Jim Carter, Alison Steadman). When his unfaithful mother takes up with Raymond Binney (also Patrick Malahide), young Marlow catches them *in flagrante delicto*. He gets his revenge by accusing Binney's slow-witted son of defecating on the desk of an enraged spinster teacher (Janet Henfrey). After his mother drowns herself, young Marlow goes back to live with his father.

In the London of 1985, the bedridden Marlow rails against officious Nurse White (Imelda Staunton) and idolizes beauteous Nurse Mills (Joanne Whalley), who tenderly greases his scaly, flaking skin. He fantasizes that the doctors, nurses, and other patients periodically burst into elaborate song-and-dance routines. He also hallucinates that Nicola is out to steal the screenplay adaptation he has written of *The Singing Detective* to benefit her lover Finney (again Patrick Malahide). After a final hallucination in which Nicola kills Finney then drowns herself as his mother did, Marlow reconciles with her and she takes him home to recuperate.

For many, the first exposure to *The Singing Detective* is an off-putting experience. They are put off by Potter's use of extensive fantasy, his non-linear, free-floating, stream-of-consciousness approach to epic narrative, and his designed incoherency. For example, there is a curious recurring memory-fantasy of a scarecrow waving in a huge, desolate field that turns out to be both the sadistic schoolteacher from the defecation episode of Marlow's youth and a *Sieg Heiling* Hitler being shot up by British soldiers. While Fassbinder uses a similar stylistic approach in the two-hour epilogue of *Berlin Alexanderplatz*, Potter makes it a totalizing experience. But if *The Singing Detective* recalls the epilogue of *Berlin Alexanderplatz*, in many ways it rewrites Fassbinder's text, reversing its movement and meaning. Furthermore, Marlow ultimately achieves a harmonious balance with his traumatic past. This leaves both him and us feeling mercifully more elated than depleted.

This point is simple, but also complex, due mainly to the utter monstrousness of Marlow's medical condition. So limited and confined does he become, he must use his imagination to set himself free. He becomes a visionary who fantasizes life as one great big 1940s Hollywood musical. Sometimes Marlow's fantasies project elements of the fantastic, the elaborate, and the grandiose onto the proceedings. This occurs when he imagines the wholesome Nurse Mills as a scantily-clad, exotic chanteuse, belting out a sultry rendition of "Blues in the Night" in the 1940s nightclub Skinscape. But at other times, these musical segments are used more self-consciously and ironically, creating a Brechtian disruptive effect. This happens when a character suddenly breaks into song during scenes of a more somber, negative variety. An example of this occurs in the scene when Mr. Marlow croons a mellow version of "Do I Worry," accompanied by a shot of lounge lizard Raymond Binney gazing at his wife with lascivious intent. Peter Stead believes the use of songs in *The Singing Detective* has a deeply psychological effect in the ambiguous way they often act as "painful reminders for Marlow of all the bad moments from his life that have contributed to his total wreckage."[12]

Ambiguity is also carried over into the way we respond to Marlow. Belligerent, sarcastic, and vengefully malicious, he is made a monster because of his disfiguring skin disease, and he is the Artist as Sacred Monster because of his talent. This is especially true when he taunts the other pathetic patients in the hospital with him, or he is all riled up about what he imagines his wife has done against him. Like Franz Biberkopf, Marlow is not an easy character to like. He is saved from becoming totally reprehensible through the combined power of Michael Gambon's sterling acting and Potter's terse, witty dialogue, which Gambon delivers with consummate skill. The actor's voice caresses each Raymond Chandleresque syllable with an acrid terseness.

Of course, it is Marlow's sarcastic terseness that leads to Dr. Gibbon accusing him of disliking women, which strikes us as a bit too glib. Rather than disliking them, Marlow simply cannot understand women: they're just too complicated for him to understand. This, along with the fact that his physical condition has rendered him totally passive and inactive, opens up another kind of ambiguity in the text concerning the depiction of the passive, inactive male body (object) and active female body (subject). In a sense, Marlow's physical limitations emasculate him. He must look to all the complicated women in his life for his most basic human needs. In *The Singing Detective*, Woman is active, Man is passive. It is only within the confines of Marlow's imagination that he can fantasize he is able to assert his passive self over the active Woman. But actually, even Marlow's imagined containment of the female is highly debatable. Taken on their own terms, the women of *The Singing Detective* are some of the most imperious and volatile women to have ever appeared in an epic miniseries. Amazons, angels, and she-devils, Potter's women are some real fierce females. They throw off a strange, blinding aura. Like Earth Mothers, they find exultation in the male's masochistic vulnerability. They harken back to the mysterious, naked Daughters of Albion in the poetry of the English Romantic poet William Blake who "glowed with strange beauty and cruelty" and could "obscure the sun and moon" so that no male eye could ever "look upon them." Their influence would be felt in many of the later women of the epic miniseries who follow them.

One of these is Marlow's narcissistically glamorous mother, who disdains her weak, emasculated husband and thinks nothing of carrying on an illicit affair with Raymond Binney. When she makes love to him in the Arcadian forest, she is an Apollonian goddess taking her Dionysian pleasure where she will. Freud said the child witnessing the primal scene of parental intercourse is traumatized, believing the male is wounding the female. Young Marlow's response to witnessing his mother having intercourse with a man not his father, therefore, doubles that trauma. Still, this does not stop the grownup Marlow from marrying a woman as psychologically and sexually complex as his mother. Nicola asserts herself early on, and she is not above making an eroticized spectacle of herself, à la Julie in *Rich Man, Poor Man*. Janet Suzman plays Nicola with the same world-weary hierarchal glamour and grave elegance she brought

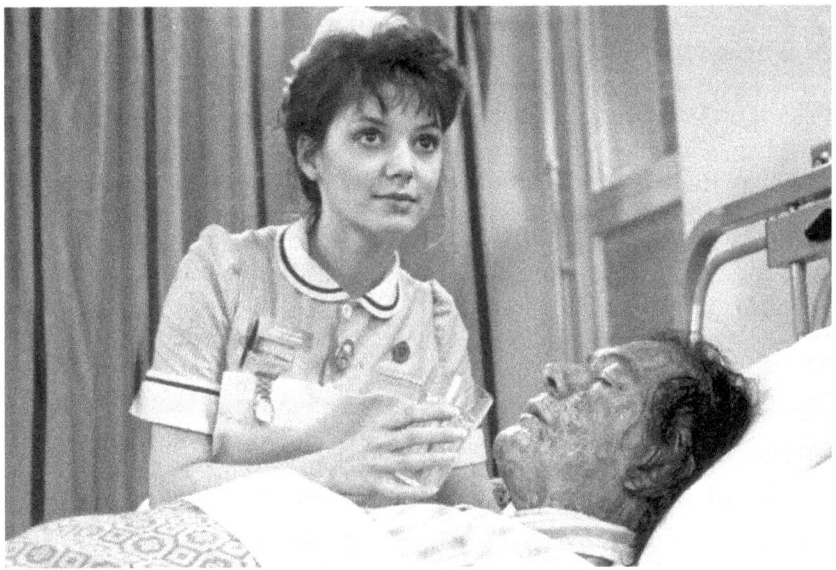

Beauty and the Beast II: Angel of Mercy, Nurse Mills (Joanne Whalley), comforts stricken mystery writer Philip Marlow (Michael Gambon). *The Singing Detective* (PBS, 1989).

to her Czarina Alexandra in *Nicholas and Alexandra* (Franklin Schaffener, 1971). This is not to say Nicola is completely devoid of feminine vulnerability and affection. On the contrary, she can express both of these traits, but only after she has a man where she wants him. Actually, the role of Nicola in *The Singing Detective* is especially interesting. She is, without question, the must complicated woman of the epic narrative diegesis. While she does share obvious qualities with Marlow's beautiful, adulterous mother who later drowns herself, Nicola only drowns in the realm of her husband's fevered imagination. Unlike Marlow's tragic and duplicitous mother, Nicola returns Lazarus-like from the watery grave to reclaim Marlow. As the reunited couple leave, and he's seen healing in her regenerative love, the dark, dank hospital corridors suddenly shimmer with a burst of pure, warm sunlight.

The only female character in *The Singing Detective* who seems free of any sort of female guile is the delicious Nurse Mills, played by Joanne Whalley. A pure Angel of Sex and Love, Nurse Mills is like a magic elixir transmuting all of a man's pain and suffering into comfort and joy. As she makes her rounds through the hospital wards, all in white, she is a dialectical and delectable love goddess giving off a warm, sensual glow amidst the sepulchral male gloom. Like the beautiful Muse Claudia Cardinale plays in *8½* (Federico Fellini, 1963), who excites the fevered imagination of Marcello Mastroianni, Nurse Mills is "young yet old," "a child, yet ancient," and unbelievably and unimaginably beautiful in her purity and purpose. Even when she has to reprimand Marlow for getting too sexually excited when she greases him, Nurse Mills does so with the style and grace of a true Angel of Mercy.

There is also much to value in the uncanny make-up design of Frances Hannon and the evocative photography of Ken Westbury. Relying upon the autobiographical medical details of Potter's own illness,[13] Hannon transforms Gambon's entire body into an exact replica of the writer's, right down to the last explicit, horrific detail. And Westbury's photography effortlessly creates the livid-lurid physical environment of Marlow's world to visual perfection. The scenes taking place in the fantasy London of 1945 are appositely dark and dank and filled with fear and anger. Westbury's fantasy London is a dead night-world of lust, deceit, violence, and murder that takes on a certain sinister beauty all its own.

For the various musical segments, Westbury relies on the use of a surrealistic mise-en-scène that is artificial, exotic, and nostalgically fantastic, as when a team of medical interns suddenly breaks into an ecstatic Busby Berkeley–like extravaganza to the tune of "Dry Bones," complete with doctors using parts of a skeleton as musical instruments and a leg-kicking chorus line of sexy dancing nurses. Or else they can take on a more muted somberness, elegiacally washed in sepia, when songs are meant to be more meditative and introspective.

No less fine is the way Westbury's camera introduces certain mythic and sublime images (the nude body of a woman floating facedown in the Thames; Mrs. Marlow alone on the bridge from which she will soon plunge to her death; young Marlow at the top of a tree exclaiming he will grow up to be a famous detective), then drops them, only to return to them again and again, creating a musical feeling and iconic leitmotif that is constantly unfolding, endlessly, ritualistically, hypnotically mesmerizing, until an obsessively spiraling vortex of visualized emotion pulls us in just as relentlessly as it does Philip Marlow.

Style Is Its Own Reward

In a number of the epic miniseries of the latter 1980s, we see an artistic pathway being cleared that makes for a televisual construct considerably different from what had previously been expected of the genre. In other words, the genre will be altered in imaginative new ways to create new meanings. But despite such alterations, the genre still has the right to the label of epic miniseries. Along with this occurrence, elements of ambiguity and self-consciousness enter into the text. As we shall see, this will go on to take many different thematic and stylistic forms.

From roughly 1985 on, the epic miniseries seems less concerned with achieving the sort of classical balance and authoritative clarity we saw in such canonical texts as *Roots*, *Holocaust*, *Shogun*, and *Brideshead Revisited*. Although the epic miniseries of this period do still reveal traces of the dialectical synthesis of binary oppositions, the subtle interplay of the real and mythic, and the rational justification of the symbolic order (even if not always believable), they are now more diffused and no longer seem as relevant as they once were. Instead, there is a greater push on the part of those ever-anxious television executives and producers to chase down those increasingly hard-won Nielsen points. Naturally, mass-culture in the late 1980s was still consumed by both ruling and subordinate classes alike, but a significant development of the Reagan 1980s was the new reality of many aspects of American culture being more radically controlled by powerful corporate entities than ever before. The style and substance of the epic miniseries of these years reflect this reality. For the most part, it is style over substance, much like the presidency of Reagan, that becomes the great thesis and genesis of the American epic miniseries examined here.

We will argue first that both the emphasis on style and the de-emphasis on substance give voice to some of the political social tensions of the time, and second that the stylistic exigencies of these texts are like the artworks produced in the late 16th century. Unlike the artists of the Renaissance, who developed their characteristic styles out of a close study and observation of nature to create and generate their unique conceptualization of pictorial space, the Mannerist artists of the late 16th century "turned to the masters of the High Renaissance (especially the work of Michelangelo) and to Roman sculpture"[14] for their creative inspiration. Whereas earlier artists looked to reality to find style, the Mannerists looked to style and re-created reality. Although the artworks of Mannerism often display a greater level of stylistic flamboyance and virtuosity, these were achieved by placing aesthetic form over all else: Style became its own reward.

Likewise, we see something similar occurring with several of the epic miniseries of the latter part of the 1980s. It will be noticed that as style is looked to to create a more "stylish" reality, various forms of thematic deconstruction quickly aggregate. In Chapter 4 we discussed the way certain Brechtian "distancing" techniques could lead to both the disruption of the epic narrative and the alienation of audiences from experiencing the deeper feelings of identification and fascination once created by the traditional dramatic epic model. In this chapter, we will see how such aspects as Musical Segments, Fantasy, Camp, Parody and Satire, and Excessive Spectacle are employed both to attract and sometimes to alienate the gradually dwindling television audience for the epic miniseries as the 1980s progress.

Musical Segments

The saga of European immigrants coming to turn-of-the-century America to forge new lives and identities for themselves in a new land is a natural subject for the epic miniseries. With *Ellis Island* (CBS, 1984), the epic narrative sets out to achieve just that. But another, equally sizable part of the text relies a little too much on the mechanics of a promising but usually uneven form of soap opera–laden melodrama to tell the sprawling epic story. An internal conflict is released. To resolve this variance, a reliance upon elaborate musical production numbers, conceived by the character of Broadway composer Jake Rubin (Peter Riegert), is used. Based on legendary Broadway composer Irving Berlin, Jake (born impoverished Russian Jew Jacob Rubinstein) leaves his oppressive Russian homeland to seek fame and fortune in a new land. In *Ellis Island* this is signified by America's fabled Broadway in the form of two different beautiful, desirable women: voluptuous and ruthlessly ambitious white actress Nellie Byfield (Ann Jillian) and sleek, black soulful Harlem torch singer Flora Mitchum (Melba Moore).

Since Jake is inspired by Berlin, he composes six Irving Berlin–style songs.[15] Although we have seen the ambiguous and selfconcious aspects of the epic miniseries resolved through a diverse system of codified tropes, a reliance almost totally on music and song to do so displays rare poetic and stylistic elegance. Typically, music is only one of a series of tropes used to help organize the teleology and epic narrative into a harmonized vision. *Ellis Island* uses the trope of music, in the form of Broadway song, in a new way. Signified by two desirable women, the Dionysian Nellie Byfield and the Apollonian Flora Mitchum, the lavish Broadway production number is made a means of integrating both the internal conflicts of the epic American saga of the immigrant experience and the excessive melodramatics of the epic action into a cohesive, narrational system.

Although it is true that the sparkling use of song goes a long way toward revealing the essential humanity of the immigrant and black characters as they define themselves in the baffling, sometimes cruel social order of America, and despite the excellence in the ironic pastiche technique, the songs are not fully integrated into the epic narrative matrix, and so are in danger of appearing as a succession of dazzling star turns for Jillian and Moore to strut their not-unimpressive musical stuff in a fantasy America that is the stuff of purest myth and legend.

Music and Song can also be used as a trope for human existence itself. In this mode, music is meant to express a deeper philosophical and metaphoric dimension. It can even be equated with humankind's mortal quest for immortal meaning. Music is used in this way in the epic miniseries *Mario Puzo's "The Fortunate Pilgrim"* (NBC, 1988) and *Onassis: The Richest Man in the World* (ABC, 1988). In the former, immortal Italian superstar Sophia Loren plays Lucia Angeluzzi, a strong-willed Italian immigrant who comes to America in search of the elusive American Dream for herself and her family. In the latter, Raul Julia plays peripatetic shipping magnate Aristotle Onassis involved in a torrid romantic triangle with two immortal women: opera diva Maria Callas (Jane Seymour) and ex–First Lady Jacqueline Kennedy (Frances Annis).

With the casting of the legendary Sophia Loren in *Mario Puzo's "The Fortunate Pilgrim,"* all of the florid over-the-top melodramatic excess is instantly elevated by her majestic presence. Her immortal big-screen star-image is so monumental, the confines of the small-screen can barely contain her. Immortality is further reinforced by the operatic-sounding music of composers Lucio Dalla and Mauro Malavasi, and the use of Lucio Pavarotti's singing of Caruso-style songs on the soundtrack. In this mode, music, combined with Loren's star power, lift Lucia's ordinary dream of America up to the extraordinary heights of ancient Roman myth and Italian grand opera.

Ancient myth and grand opera also play a large part in *Onassis: The Richest Man in the World*. While ancient Greek myth enters the epic narrative through the nationality and given names of both Onassis and his sternly authoritative father, Socrates (Anthony Quinn), it is left to the immortal Maria Callas to signify the symbolic embodiment of grand opera. Whether on-stage or off, Seymour (in an Emmy Award–winning performance) portrays the volcanic Callas as an immortal prima donna with more than her share of hierarchical, classic hauteur.

Fantasy

The reimaging of Lewis Carroll's well-bred, imperialistic Victorian heroine in *Alice in Wonderland* (CBS, 1985) as something of a shape-and-size-shifting, Time-and-Space-defying Adventuress on a great mythic quest makes perfect sense in the context of the epic miniseries of the 1980s. Teleplaywriter Paul Zindel and director Harry Harris rely more on the visually experimental approach taken in Walt Disney's *Alice in Wonderland* (Clyde Geronimi, Hamilton Lushe, Wilfred Jackson, 1951) rather than the witty, literate one Carroll takes on the page. This sets up a peculiar duality that lies in the tension between a close observation and genuine affection for the original source, and the desire to broaden its appeal to reach the largest possible televisual audience.

Here, Alice (Natalie Gregory) is the lead character in an asymmetrical, idiosyncratic world of music (Steve Allen composed 19 songs for the production) and fantasy combining a surrealistic, kaleidoscopic explosion of psychedelic images and bright, fluorescent colors, which for some became an exhausting bombardment of sight, sound, color, and hyperkinetic movement. For example, the visibly threatening, fire-breathing, red-eyed-flashing presence of the ubiquitous Jabberwocky (uncannily designed by special effects wizard John Dykstra) is used as a visual manifestation of Alice's repressed Victorian Id run amuck in a nihilistic frenzy. And Paul Zastupnevich's costumes look like an eclectic collage between John Tenniel's original iconic drawings and the Flower-Power fashions of the incendiary 1960s. None of this, by the way, went down all that well with either the critics or public in 1985. It would not be until the latter part of the 1990s that the use of fantasy as a solid and viable stylistic trope of the epic miniseries would be more advantageously explored and appreciated.[16]

Camp

In her famous 1964 essay "Notes on 'Camp,'" Susan Sontag describes the camp style as one that exalts "artifice, exaggeration, and the unnatural" and satisfies a taste for extravagance of "art that may propose itself seriously, but cannot be taken altogether seriously because it is too much."[17] To a certain extent, one could argue certain elements of camp have always been a significant part of several epic miniseries from the beginning. However, we believe the epic miniseries of real high-camp style did not receive its fullest aesthetic expression until the 1980s with the broadcast of such outrageous texts as *Lace* (ABC, 1984), *Hollywood Wives* (ABC, 1985), *Sins* (CBS, 1986), and in an altogether different sort of camp idiom, *Small Sacrifices* (ABC, 1989).

Lace, *Hollywood Wives*, and *Sins* are three in a long series of epic miniseries which are perhaps best described in order of their campy trashiness. Hav-

Chapter 5 • Transitional Places 121

Venus in Spurs: The Mythic Whore, International Sex Goddess Lili (Phoebe Cates), lights out on a mythic quest to find (and possibly destroy) the "Bitch" Mother who abandoned her. *Lace* (ABC, 1984).

ing spent the greater part of her Dionysian life on an obsessive, single-minded mythic quest to find (and perhaps destroy) the mother who abandoned her as an infant, the mythic type of the Whore is magnified to *uber*-proportions in the tantalizing form of an internationally famous (infamous?) sex goddess— the much desired exotic/erotic/neurotic figure of Lili (Phoebe Cates). After luring the three female protagonists of *Lace* (Bess Armstrong, Brooke Adams, and Arielle Dombasle) to a private audience with her, she demands to know which one of the "bitches" is her real mother. Although the rest of the epic narrative never attains the supreme campiness of that classic scene, the baby-faced Cates, all dressed-up in her trashy Frederick's of Hollywood lingerie, is such a polymorphous, perverse femme fatale, she commands our full attention whether we like it or not.

One truly enters the universe of full-scale televisual camp with *Hollywood Wives* and *Sins*. *Hollywood Wives*, in particular, is a sado-masochistic wet-dream of Hollywoodized self-laceration. Both Tinseltown itself and its glamorous but vapid glitterati are made the butt-end of some very dirty jokes. According to *Hollywood Wives*, the entire movie industry is driven by a pack of totally corrupt, capricious, ruthless, unholy fools, all pumped up on drugs, drink, debauchery, deceit, and sexual deviance of every shape and form. But of course we already know most of this. Just as we also know the only real reason *Hollywood Wives* exists is to provide Hollywood actresses of a certain age (Candice Bergen, Joanna Cassidy, Angie Dickinson, Stefanie Powers, and Suzanne Somers) a chance to find work and look fabulous wearing all those gowns designed by Nolan Miller (of *Dynasty* fame), with wit and amusing insight.

Much the same can be said of Joan Collins and her leading-lady role in *Sins*. Riding sky-high on the wild surge of popularity for her career comeback as super-vixen Alexis Carrington in the mega-hit, primetime soap *Dynasty* (CBS, 1981–89), Collins begins her one-diva demolition course to systematically deconstruct the epic miniseries of the latter 1980s. Essentially, *Sins* is the epic miniseries as epic vanity production. It was designed for the sole purpose of showing off the well-seasoned charms of its famous executive producer and leading lady, Joan Collins. Elaborately wigged-out, bejeweled, false-eyelashed, with tons of make-up on her face, and luxuriously clad in a seemingly unending series of high-fashion creations designed exclusively for her by Valentino, Collins plays a superhuman version of the sort of tough-as-tacks heroine Joan Crawford use to play in her Hollywood heyday. Among other things, we see Collins become an accomplished seamstress, resurrect the flagging virility of a pre–*Viagra* Frenchman (Jean-Pierre Aumont), kill Nazis, claw her way to the top of a powerful French publishing house, marry a good-natured American composer (Gene Kelly), commit various forms of adultery, get blackmailed, kill more Nazis, gain a fortune, lose a fortune, regain another fortune, and never look the worse for wear from any of it. With *Monte Carlo* (CBS, 1986), Collins would continue with her one-diva course of deconstruction.

In contrast, high camp of another sort entirely is found in Farrah Fawcett's amazing performance in *Small Sacrifices* (ABC, 1989). Fawcett plays real-life murderous mother Diane Downs, a small town mail carrier who carries on an illicit affair with married co-worker Lew Lewiston (Ryan O'Neil). But when the idea pops into her head that O'Neil might just leave his wife for her if she were *sans* her children, Fawcett summons a ferocious female energy. "Like Eve, Circe, and Salome, she is a black-widow spider of female sexuality" (with the energy of murderous Mother Nature, or Medea in the final act), and her poor, innocent babes haven't a chance against her. In fact, with "her hoarse cracked voice and torn blonde hair, her miniskirts and mythomania,"[18] Fawcett is so over-the-top and flamboyantly operatic in her unleashed maternal wrath, she signifies the high camp idiom of over-adornment and elaborate theatricality within a most incongruous, lurid, low-rent context, achieving finally the mantle of High Art.[19]

Parody and Satire

A variation of the formalistic experimentalism of *Alice in Wonderland* gets carried over into *Fresno* (CBS, 1986), a spoof of both the epic miniseries and the enormously popular primetime soap operas of the 1980s such as *Dallas* and *Dynasty*. The storyline of *Fresno*, such as it is, concerns a no-holds-barred fight for water rights by two highly competitive raisin-growing families in Fresno— America's 64th largest city.

Comic genius Carol Burnett, arguably the most inventively comical woman ever to appear on American television, plays Charlotte Kensington, the haughty matriarch of one of the families. Clad in an outrageously witty, Bob Mackie–designed high-glamour wardrobe, Burnett perfectly captures the correct balance between high camp aesthetic and low melodramatic turmoil (as does also the sparkly garishness of the tawdry mise-en-scéne). Clearly the reason for the failure of *Fresno* with critics and audiences at the time of its broadcast had nothing at all to do with Burnett. Rather, there was a sense that the epic tale being told was hardly all that epic or that much of a tale to begin with. What would have probably made a solid two to three-hour comedy has been bloated and stretched so thread-thin that even the comedic genius of the divine Burnett could not totally save the day.

Excessive Spectacle

We see a completely different set of problems arise with many of the historical epic miniseries of the latter part of 1980s. This is due mainly to the tremendous emphasis now placed upon excessive spectacle above all else. Enormous epic sweep and spectacular largess are presented with a seemingly unrestrained application over such other matters as character development, emotional intimacy, and dramatic intensity. Gradually epic narrative is drained of the passion for good, clear storytelling. The beginnings of the process can be traced back to the epic miniseries *Marco Polo* (NBC, 1982). Marco Polo (played by Ken Marshall in a generally lackluster performance) is depicted as the mythic type of the Adventurer, lighting out on his legendary twenty-year, ten-thousand-mile odyssey from Venice to Cathay. Although the epic narrative does feature several strong performances (unlike Marshall in the lead) from its all-star international cast (stand-outs include: Burt Lancaster [Pope Gregory X], Denholm Elliot [Niccolo Polo], Leonard Nimoy [Achmet], and Ying Ruo Cheng [Kublai Khan]), its true pleasures are manifested principally in the codified tropes of mise-en-scéne, costume design, and music. The history of the 13th century explorer becomes not so much the vision of writers David Butler, Guliano Montaldo (who also directs), and Vicenzo Labella as it does that of production designer Enrico Sabbatino, photographer Pasqualino De Santis, and composer Ennio Morricone. The collective achievement of these artists is the real raison d'être for the existence of *Marco Polo*. Their combined forces usher in a total convergence of epic narrative and history, subjugating them to the overwhelming thrust and monumental scope that would become the televisual spectacle of many epic miniseries of the 1980s.

The logical outgrowth of this formalistic agenda is seen in *Christopher Columbus* (CBS, 1985) and *Peter the Great* (NBC, 1986). With *Christopher Columbus*, the story of the explorer's great voyages and discovery of America in 1492 is projected onto the Apollonian Western space of grandiose televisual fantasy. Once again, as with *Marco Polo*, it is the combined artistry of production designer Mario Chiari, costume designer Maria De Mattheis, and the lush photography of Franco Di Giacome that dominate. Only here the formalistic dominance is total. Style is substance, history an excuse for opulent historical pageantry, mise-en-scéne a frozen, crystalline tableau against which the huge cast of international stars (among them: from Italy, Rossano Brazzi, Virna Lisi, and Raf Vallone; from England, Oliver Reed and Nicol Williamson; from Ireland, Gabriel Byrne; from Sweden, Max Von Sydow; from America, Faye Dunaway and Eli Wallach) strike hierarchic poses in costumes of fetishistic detail. Even the fact that *Christopher Columbus* features such an international all-star cast does not help matters any. With the predominately Italian cast speaking Italian (the production originally appeared on Italian television months before its broadcast in America), and all the other cast members speaking either in English or their native languages, there was no "original language" version of the epic miniseries created. Therefore, all of the dialogue had to be dubbed in at a later point. Because of this method, there is a flat deadness to the soundtrack. The televisonmakers unsuccessfully attempt to camouflage this fatal flaw by relying on an overabundance of music, image, grand gestures, and over-the-top melodramatics, until historical epic is in grave danger of becoming a gaudy epic parade.

Peter the Great presents another variation on the same theme, albeit for a whole different set of circumstances. Based on the critically acclaimed book by

Robert K. Massie, which is adapted into an uncompromisingly literate and balanced teleplay by Edward Anhalt, the power of the word is treated with considerable respect this time. Instead, the main problem with *Peter the Great* derives from the fact that superb actor Maximilian Schell (who plays Peter) had to leave the delayed production midway through the filming. Although refilming Schell's extended scenes with another actor in the role was considered, the cost of doing so proved prohibitive.[20] Instead, a compromise of sorts was reached. Much younger and fitter-looking actor Denis De Marne (dubiously billed as "the adult Peter in selected scenes" in the credits) was brought in and quite literally thrust deeply back into the farthest shadows of the background throughout the last crucial hours of the epic action. Making matters even worse, Schell's later dubbing of De Marne's dialogue creates the effect of the same sort of flat deadness that happened in *Christopher Columbus*. (There are times when the words Schell speaks don't even match up with the movements of De Marne's mouth).

Nevertheless, and even with Peter lurking much too far back in the murky shadows and too far out of the panoramic epic frame, when the epic action demands that he be center stage, there is still much to admire in *Peter the Great*. Relationships are searchingly explored and many in the all-star cast make strong impressions indeed. Among these are Vanessa Redgrave (Peter's imperious sister Sophia), Omar Sharif (Peter's canny political ally Feodor Romodanovsky), Trevor Howard (Isaac Newton), Laurence Olivier (King William III of England), Mel Ferrer (King Frederick of Germany), Elke Sommer (Charlotte, his queen), and Hanna Schygulla (as the love of Peter's life, Catherine Skevronskaya).

Also excellent are the unmatchable photography of Vittorio Storaro and the musical score of Laurence Rosenthal. Storaro shoots the interior scenes so that the light becomes a subtle play of sepias, soft yellows and the rich, burnished golden tones of Byzantine icons, while his exteriors do poetically for the snow of *Peter the Great*'s Russia much of what Fred Young's camera did for the snow of *Doctor Zhivago*. "From blue, through white, to shimmery silver—baleful in storms, pristine in the moonlight, brooding in time of war, the snow waltzes like an intoxicated *corps de ballet*, cowers submissively under the sibilant sleighs ... and when shored up against windowpanes, it frames and isolates the faces behind them more broodingly than mere glass ever could."[21] Storaro, like Young, gives the snows of Russia the crystalline beauty of a visionary historical dreamscape.

For the masterful musical score, Rosenthal draws deeply upon a rich source of Russian musical history. From the liturgical music of the Orthodox Church to the idiom of Russian folk song and his own extensive knowledge of canonical Russian composers from Glinka and Tchaikovsky to Prokofiev and Shostakovich, Rosenthal has created a musical score of consummate artistry and enormous richness.

At this point in our epic story, it is perhaps rather difficult to imagine how the experimentalism of canonical foreign televisual masterpieces like *Scenes from a Marriage*, *Berlin Alexanderplatz*, and *The Singing Detective*, along with the excellences and excesses of the golden age of the epic miniseries, can somehow fuse together to weather the enormous changes of the coming decades. To understand how these contradictory ideas get conflated is the subject of the next chapter with the very different sort of epic miniseries of the 1990s. The process of how the exaggerated and affected adherence to a Mannerist formula, and a more experimental approach, shifted toward a formula that becomes more self-conscious and trenchantly satirical in style will be examined in detail, as will the establishing of a new aesthetic in which the ever-so anxious male tries desperately to hold onto his dominant role of the Adventurer in a televisual cosmos of ever-dwindling possibilities. Paradoxically, at the same time the role of the female expands exponentially. From queens to temptresses, to mothers to lovers, to entrepreneurs to glamorous stars, to sinners to saints, to the mythic type of the Avenging Angel, Woman in the Epic Miniseries of the 1990s comes into her own once and for all.

Chapter 6

The Lady Is a Champ

As the 1980s came to a close, so too did the Golden Age of the Epic Miniseries. Many of the contradictions and dynamics found in the genre during the 1990s stem from this fact. With the number of cable channels rising, the demographics and economic dominance of the three super-networks continued their steady decline. As the once all-consuming power of the "Big Three" dissipated, both the form and content of the epic miniseries were much affected. As one might expect, the ratings and financial failure of "the Ultimate Epic Miniseries," *War and Remembrance*, did little to alleviate this general atmosphere of negativity. To counter some of this, we witness the genre undergo several significant changes in an attempt to maintain and recapture some of its former glory. This is evident in the various alterations performed on the form and content of the epic narrative: length shortens, epic narrative narrows and grows more compressed in its focus, and there is a noticeable toning down of the stronger emphasis once placed on weightier issues (i.e. war, religion, slavery, the Holocaust) in favor of subject matter that makes for quite a different sort of viewing experience (i.e., true crime stories, fantasy, the supernatural, feminist concerns).

We have demonstrated how certain innovative Brechtian techniques in the latter 1980s created a certain discrepancy between teleological and histrionic display. The principles of this discrepancy will continue in the 1990s and well into the New Millennium. It will also be recalled that during the 1980s the epic miniseries displayed a bolder virtuosity of style and Manneristic flamboyance than did those of the 1970s. However, while some of the epic miniseries of the 1990s continue in this aesthetic mode, many others are no longer strictly defined by such a stylistic agenda. Instead, they are organized more self-consciously, and at times even more paradoxically than in the past. This creative activity leads to the continued creation of a sense of contextual displacement, often engendering a more ironic viewing experience. Moreover, there is a more experimental approach to narrative and characterization than in the past.

Symbolic of this process, we see a major change in the concept of the heroic Adventurer lighting out on his mythic quest. As part of the 1990s new principle of display, heroism no longer resides solely in the solitary figure of the male hero. The noble attribute can now, and in fact more often does, reside in the female or in a collective group, often led by a heroic female. While in the past we were mostly encouraged to integrate epic narrative according to principles of an Aristotelian or Cartesian schema, the new structuring principles of the late 1980s (self-consciousness, irony, and parody) push through such pragmatic limitations. A distinctive new subversiveness and intertextuality is set in motion.

In *Reflexivity in Film and Literature: From Don Quixote to Jean-Luc Godard*, Robert Stam posits that such intertextuality can be divided into five distinct categories:

1. "Celebrity Intertextuality," by which a famous star or celebrity is used to evoke a certain cultural milieu.
2. "Genetic Intertextuality," in which someone or something closely connected to a famous star or character is used.
3. "Intratextuality," in which a text refers back to itself in an overtly self-referential way.
4. "Auto-citation," when the creator, or creators, of a text use it to refer back to their own previous texts.
5. "Mendacious Intertextuality," by which a text creates a pseudo-intertextual reference or references all its own.[1]

Along with considering the ways in which these five categories of intertextuality operate, this chapter will also focus on the surprisingly subversive ways the heroic female — whom we classify as the fifth mythic archetype of the Epic Miniseries: The Avenging Angel/Great Goddess— will often mold, take charge of, and lead a group of individuals on the mythic quest of the 1990s and well into the next century.

Before we explore the use made of the Avenging Angel, we will next summarize the ways the televisual artists of the 1990s positioned themselves in favor of stretching the genre of the epic miniseries by working in five specific areas, any one or two of which suggest their new aesthetic stance: (1) areas of subject matter — this includes a greater emphasis placed on such topics as ambiguous sexuality, drug use, the surreal, the supernatural, and the fantastic; (2) areas of style — the continuance of certain Brechtian techniques, Minimalism, withdrawal from traditional epic narrative and character development, and the use of more abstracted forms; (3) areas of the self-conscious, ironic, and parodic — an obvious separating point from the majority of epic miniseries of the past; (4) areas of the use of intertextuality, which threads its way through several epic narrative strategies; (5) areas concerning the use of the archetype of the Avenging Angel, whose transcendent presence will have a most pervasive and persuasive influence all throughout the 1990s.

The Birth of the Avenging Angel

Like Botticelli's Venus rising up from the watery depths, skimming to the shore on a glittery golden half-shell, the Avenging Angel, who will dominate the 1990s, appears in several incarnations during the decade. What several of these incarnations amount to are variations of the archetype of the Great Goddess. Adele Getty says of the great mythic archetype:

> She is the Great Mother of the World, Giver of Life, The great nurturer, sustainer and healer. Yet she is also The Bringer of Death, the one who can grant immortality and liberation. The Goddess giveth and the Goddess taketh away. She is capable of infinite compassion in one form and of total annihilation in another. In short, she is the embodiment of all we know as life itself; her story is as old as life itself, for she is life itself. She is all Time — past, present, future; she is form and formlessness.... Throughout the Art of the World we find her as the all-powerful creative energy of the Lifeforce. Without the Great Goddess we are nothing; with her, our capacity is filled with a vital energy that carries us forward into the future.[3]

In light of Getty's words, we would only add, for our purposes, that the type of the Avenging Angel of the Epic Miniseries (our version of Getty's Great Goddess) can be further divided into two main categories: (1) The Avenging Matriarch; (2) The Matriarchal Avenger. Although these categories can and most often do overlap, there still exist some important distinctions between them.

The Avenging Angel

The 1980s presented an extraordinary number of talented actresses starring in a wide range of epic miniseries: Ingrid Bergman, Julie Christie, Faye Dunaway, Farrah Fawcett, Sophia Loren, Lee Remick, Stefanie Powers, Jane Seymour, and Oprah Winfrey, to name only some of the most outstanding. For the most part these and other talented actresses, with some exceptions, were presented in melodramatic renditions of the mythic configuration of the Wife (Mother)/Whore dyad. If the idea of constructing a full-scale dramatic epic miniseries around a specific female star had occurred in the 1970s and continued throughout the 1980s, it was not until the 1990s that all those skittish network executives and producers realized a lavish televisual production built around a strong, dynamic female character could ensure them high returns. With the arrival of the 1990s, in conjunction with the ending of the golden age of the epic miniseries, the networks felt the need to please television's largely female audience, still faithful to watching epic miniseries, more pressingly than ever before.[4]

CBS, traditionally a stronghold of mostly male-starring epic miniseries, decided to meet the need of pleasing this female televisual audience head-on. The network mounted an impressive succession of productions featuring a wide array of incarnations of the Avenging Angel. In this way, CBS provided female fans with the satisfying emotional catharsis that was sought. This was achieved by the presentation of a selection of stunning actresses like Shelley Long, Valerie

Bertinelli, Halle Berry, Ruby Dee, Molly Ringwald, Anne Bancroft, Diane Lane, Dana Delaney, and Angelina Jolie, playing regal, energetic, and hearty mythic women in ten solid CBS epic miniseries. Of the other networks, ABC contributed three entries; NBC, two; while A&E, FOX, PBS, and TNT offered one superior depiction each of the Avenging Angel.

Perhaps the thing that links all of these depictions is the emphasis on the quality of female charisma, that unique electromagnetism that is a "scintillating fusion of the masculine and the feminine."[5] Max Weber defines charisma as "an extraordinary, supernatural, divine power,"[6] which is above all deeply mysterious. In classical antiquity, we see the goddess Athena gives some of her own celestial charisma that creates "a golden mist around her head" and causes her whole being to emit "a blaze of blindingly pure light" to Odysseus in *The Iliad*. Camille Paglia believes charisma can possess a strong component of androgyny that can give the charismatic woman a powerful "masculine force and severity."[7] Indeed, we see what Paglia is getting at in several of the remarkable performances in the following gallery of Avenging Angels.

The Avenging Matriarch

The first depiction of the Avenging Matriarch we get comes in *The Kennedys of Massachusetts* (ABC, 1990), with the great matriarchal figure of the iconic Rose Kennedy (Annette O'Toole). As the much-adored, convent-bred daughter of the Mayor of Boston, John "Honey Fitz" Fitzgerald (Charles Durning), Rose signifies the grand prize that Joseph "Joe" Kennedy (William Petersen) must wrest away to provide him with the class and clout he so desperately needs to conquer the frigid Protestant climate with the burgeoning force of his Boston Irish Catholicism.

As Joe busies himself building up his massive fortune, and not always by the most ethical of means, he finds plenty of time to bed reigning Hollywood sex-goddess Gloria Swanson (Madolyn Smith Osborne, who is, without a doubt, one of the most spectacular representations of the mythic type of the Whore in the whole Epic Miniseries Pantheon). Rose comes to understand the exorbitantly high price she and her children will have to pay for her husband's many excesses and indiscretions. To escape Joe's inordinate avariciousness and chronic womanizing, Rose retreats, with her heart charred and rosary beads clenched tightly in her closed fists, into the lofty mysticism of her Roman Catholicism. As Joe's assaults against her intensify, Rose learns to brandish her faith and piety as a lethal weapon to beat him off.

So fierce does her resolve against her husband grow, eventually she is ready for anything he might throw her way. Thus, when she learns he has had her beloved emotionally disturbed daughter Rosemary (Deirdre Lovejoy), tragically lobotomized, Rose closes him out of her heart forever. Ultimately her intense faith gives her the perfect revenge she needs against her perfidious husband. When he's felled by a stroke, paralyzed, Rose hovers around his bed much like an ecumenical vulture, chiding him and endlessly reciting her Rosary — something she knew didn't comfort Old Joe much but infuriated and exasperated him in his physical and mental torture and helplessness. Whoever said revenge is a dish best served cold must have had Rose Kennedy in mind. Still, being the favorite daughter of a master Boston politico, Rose understands the importance of keeping up appearances at all costs, and rallies behind son John F. Kennedy (Steven Weber) in his mythic quest to capture the White House. The epic action, fittingly, concludes with the charismatic JFK triumphantly conquering the American body politic, and Rose smiling her own private triumphant smile, the charred heart of her maternal body shining ever brightly.

The next Avenging Matriarch arrives in the form of Valerie Bertinelli's feisty Italian-American, working-class heroine Angela Cimarelli, avenging a beloved sister's murder in *In a Child's Name* (CBS 1991). Like Rose Kennedy, Bertinelli's Angela also finds herself having to do battle against a ruthless man. Only this time the man makes Joe Kennedy look like a household saint. Angela's nemesis is her narcissistic, weight-lifting, wife-beating, coke-snorting, arrogant WASP brother-in-law, Ken Taylor (played by Michael Ontkean as a Nazi-like sociopath). Not only does this deranged sadist bludgeon Angela's beloved elder sister Teresa (Karla Tamburrelli) to death with a barbell, he also has the audacity to grant full custody of the murdered Teresa's baby, and Angela's nephew, Andrew (Andy Hirsch), to his exceedingly creepy, incredibly mean-spirited mother and father (Louise Fletcher, David Huddleston), while committing grand perjury and calumny by saying his late wife, Angela's sister, had sexually abused their infant son. He also has his parents portray Angela's family as low-life Italian Mafia types, something such bigoted WASPs are all too ready to believe and testify in court. The mother even goes so far as saying that the late Teresa had made lesbian overtures to her. There is no bottom to the evil the man and his parents spout against the late Teresa and her close-knit family.

Just as we saw the beleaguered Rose Kennedy rise up and call upon every saint in Heaven to join her in a Holy Crusade against husband Joe, Angela does likewise with her supportive husband, Jerry (the excellent Christopher Meloni), as well as all the rest of her close-knit, working-class, New Jersey family, friends, and neighbors, to form "The Save Baby Andrew Campaign." All those effete Midwestern WASPs are not quite prepared for the collective wild surge of Mediterranean Matriarchal Power headed their way.

While the iconic mother of a family of famous American politicians is celebrated in *The Kennedys of Massachusetts*, the no less iconic grandmother of a famous American writer is rightfully recognized in the epic miniseries *Queen* (CBS, 1993), based on the tumultuous life of Alex Haley's white-appearing paternal grandmother Queen (Halle Berry in an impassioned performance).

Similar to *Roots*, *Queen* has been designed in an attempt to repeat the ratings and critical success of its illustrious predecessor and to appeal to both Black and White audiences alike. The epic action encompasses such historical topics as slavery, the Civil War, the emancipation of the slaves, and the troubled postwar Reconstruction Period. Queen, the daughter of slave girl Easter (Jasmine Guy) and James Jackson (Tim Daly), the arrogant son of the plantation owner, lives her life as both White and Black. But much like the conflicted heroine of *Pinky* (Elia Kazan, 1949), Queen is a tormented figure, fitting into neither of her dualistic roles. Her interracial mix literally and figuratively makes her the embodiment of the conflicts and internal pressures of both the racially torn nation and the epic narrative of *Queen*.

After the Civil War and the death of her mother, Queen lights out on a picaresque journey worthy of Defoe or Fielding. Yet what her journey is really about is the mythic epic quest for self-identity that has thus far so eluded her. The masterful photography of Tony Imi provides the richly detailed mise-en-scène that visualizes Queen's eternal struggle: privileged vistas of opulent, colonnaded plantations, endless miles of lucrative cotton and tobacco fields (seemingly worked by an army of slaves), and elegant balls and parties are juxtaposed against scenes of unending physical, emotional, and spiritual injustices committed against downtrodden Black men and women.

If *Queen* does not resonate with the same all-consuming mythic grandeur of *Roots* or even its beautifully rendered sequel *Roots: The Next Generations*, it is nonetheless splendidly conceived and executed. Its evocation of the expansive American landscape is as beautifully realized as it was in *Roots*. And in the character of Queen Haley, we are presented with a haunting image of the Matriarch struggling through all of the tensions and stresses of life, until she finally learns to take pride in her race and herself. By then, of course, after much torment, Queen has also married Alec Haley (Danny Glover) and given birth to son Simon (Patrick Malone), who grows up to become the father of Alex. With this Queen can take her rightful place alongside the five remarkable women of Roots— Nyo Boto, Binta, Bell, Kizzy, and Matilda — as a signifier of African American grace, comfort, and indomitable woman's power.

In addition to *Queen*, 1993 witnessed two other epic miniseries with appealing depictions of Avenging Matriarchs, *Family Pictures* (ABC, 1993) and *A Matter of Justice* (NBC, 1993), which make it something of a banner year. Anjelica Huston as Lainey Eberlain in *Family Pictures* and Patty Duke as Mary Browne in *A Matter of Justice* offer dual portraits of the Avenging Matriarch in her most Mother Courage–like mode. In each text, the heroine is fully prepared to move Heaven and Earth for the sake of her children. As it happens, both mothers are particularly devoted to sons. This gives each epic miniseries an Oedipal characteristic and each heroine the primal force of an unfathomable Mother Nature wrought with a chthonian savagery more than capable of demolishing anyone or anything that gets in her way.

For Huston's Lainey what mostly gets in her way is husband David (Sam Neill), who blames her for the autism of son Randall (Jamie Harold). For Duke's Mary, it is her salacious, White-trailer-trash daughter-in-law, Dusty (Alexandra Power), who makes the fatal mistake of murdering Mary's beloved soldier son Chris (Jason London) and, adding further insult to injury, dares to stand in the way of the grieving Mary gaining custody of her toddler granddaughter. But in the end, neither Neil's accusing husband nor Power's sluttish daughter-in-law stands a chance when confronted with the grinding force of an Avenging Matriarch revved up to full throttle.

As in 1993, the year 1994 also witnessed three depictions of the mythic type of the Avenging Angel in the form of the Avenging Matriarch: *Tales of the City* (PBS, 1994), *The Stand* (CBS, 1994), and *Oldest Living Confederate Widow Tells All* (CBS, 1994). Since the first two texts are discussed in further detail below, we will next turn to *Oldest Confederate Widow Tells All*, with its epic narrative that unfolds in two different ways: first, through the garrulous reminiscences of 100-year-old heroine Lucy Marsden (Anne Bancroft), the Oldest Confederate Widow; and second, through the story of Lucy as a young woman (Diane Lane), the child-wife of Captain "Cap" William Marsden (Donald Sutherland). Only 14 years old when she marries Cap (he is over 50), the naïve, virginal Lucy is understandably in total awe of her larger-than-life, heroic husband, who is considerably older than even her own father. This theme of a young woman's fulfillment only being made possible through her relationship with the father, or a father-like surrogate, is carried over into many of the heroines we classify as Matriarchal Avengers. Still, the father-daughter relationship is one that can be wrought with dangerous tension. In *Confederate Widow*, this occurs when Lucy realizes her husband's Civil War obsession threatens the well-being of her children. Like Rose Kennedy, Lucy must wage a private war against her husband. Instead of Catholicism, she turns to her feisty, voodoo practicing housekeeper, Castalia (Cicely Tyson), for her spiritual guidance. Under her mystical tutelage, Lucy blossoms from naïve child-wife to fierce Steel Magnolia.

The tension that develops between the newly empowered Lucy and her increasingly obstinate husband brings into play several codified epic miniseries oppositions like passivity and activity, male and female, darkness and light. But the more Cap persists in moving toward the darkness, all the more determined Lucy becomes to keep herself and her children in the light. In this regard, the final showdown between husband and wife has an inevitability about it: Lucy's empowered femininity allows her to win out over the tendency of the more traditional positioning of woman within the epic narrative. Thus, the beautiful expression on Bancroft's face when she speaks of her love for all her deceased children at the end creates a special space for the Oldest Confederate Widow, and one which both affirms yet slyly subverts tradition: Lucy both embodies and transcends her own stereotype.

Much like Bancroft, the heroines of the next two epic miniseries, *Buffalo Girls* (CBS, 1995) and *True Women* (CBS, 1997), also succeed at embodying and transcending their own stereotypes. In *Buffalo Girls*, Calamity Jane (Anjelica Huston) composes a series of letters to the daughter she conceived of after a wild Dionysian fling with Wild Bill Hickok (Sam Elliot) but gave up at birth. As she writes, Calamity falls into a deeply self-reflective mood. Her mood affects the construction of the rest of the epic narrative. Because she writes at a time when the fabled Old West is passing away from historical actuality, Calamity

Avenging Angel I (Transcending Stereotype): Rough-and-ready Calamity Jane (Anjelica Huston) on a mythic quest to find the beloved daughter she gave up at birth. *Buffalo Girls* (CBS, 1995).

decides to light out on a mythic journey to England with Buffalo Bill Cody's (Peter Coyote) nostalgic pageant of the Wild Old West of legend and lore. She seeks something rooted in temporal England that she cannot find in spatial America: her lost daughter. And in finding her girl she will erase her sense of displacement and loss of identity and replace them with Mother Love. Although Huston's Calamity is indeed something of a misfit, the actress plays her like a cross-dressing butch lesbian who manages to defy all categories of gender definition. But make no mistake about it: on the outside Calamity Jane may look like a man, but on the inside she is all woman. After her long mythic journey, when she is reunited with her daughter, she is a Woman with the heart of an Avenging Matriarch.

The epic narrative of *True Women*, based on the 1994 best-selling book by Janice Woods Windle and directed by Karen Arthur, focuses on three women of the same family: Sarah Ashby McClure (Dana Delaney), Euphemia Ashby King (Annabeth Gish), and Georgia Lawshe Woods (Angelina Jolie). An unlikely mix of romanticism and realism, *True Women* unabashedly wallows in its own melodrama, underscored by the codified tropes of mise-en-scène and music. At the same time, it can be surprisingly tough-minded: The women must battle the harsh natural elements of the Old West like attacking Indians, raiding Klu Klux Klansmen, and the proverbial dominating husband.

Because she is the most complex and conflicted of the women, Jolie's Georgia is the most fascinating. The spoiled, pampered, overly-privileged daughter of a wealthy plantation owner, she eventually marries the handsome and ambitious Dr. Peter Woods (Jeffrey Nordling) and moves to Texas to establish a thriving plantation of her own. All of that changes for her, however, when she discovers she is part Indian.

After that life-changing discovery, Georgia's story treads much of the same thematic territory as Halle Berry's in *Queen*. When this happens, the epic narrative of *True Women* unfolds through two separate and different ways of relating character to mise-en-scène. While one of these ways is concerned with lies and deception, the other is concerned with truth and enlightenment. Through the presentation of the first way, Georgia is depicted as a glossy, hard-edged Scarlett O'Hara–like Southern belle (in what seems an homage to Vivien Leigh's most famous role [see *Darlings of the Gods* below]). She is seen forever tossing her curls, pouting prettily, flirting outrageously, slave owning, and land fetishizing, often against sumptuous, way-too-garish, brightly-lit panoramas of grandiose Southern aristocracy. But when she finally faces up to her divided heritage, she undergoes some major life-altering changes, in scenes of somber décor and a more muted color scheme. This causes lies and deception to give way to truth and enlightenment, as excessive romanticism gives way to a deeper realism, and Georgia is transformed from a flighty Southern belle into a mature, warm-hearted, slave-emancipating mother — in a word, a "True" Woman. Only then is she ready to take her place alongside of Delaney's Sarah and Gish's

Euphemia as a signifier of the Avenging Matriarch in this world as well as the next.

The Matriarchal Avenger

If the main focus of heroines depicted as Avenging Matriarchs is first and foremost on their identities as mothers on a mythic quest to right some profound wrong, the Matriarchal Avengers are Avengers first, although many of them are also mothers. The emphasis here is on the need to do battle against some injustice in a patriarchal world. Although the heroines in this second category are iconic, legendary, mostly real-life women — only Shelley Long as Truddi Chase (not famous) and the women of *Bella Mafia* (not real) do not qualify as such — the need for achieving satisfaction and exacting a justifiable revenge is palpable.

As a little girl, Truddi Chase — Shelley Long in *Voices Within: The Lives of Truddi Chase* (ABC, 1990) — is unrelentingly pursued by her sexually abusive, sadistic stepfather (Ernie Lively), as are her younger brother and sister. When not sexually violating his children, this evil monster is torturing and starving dogs to death beneath Truddi's bedroom window and cutting her pet rabbit's throat in front of her. To battle such trauma, the heroine escapes into a multiplicity of protective personalities (whom Truddi takes to calling her "Troops"). The epic action begins with Truddi and her collective Troops beginning a mythic quest to hunt down and put an end to the evil stepfather who has so unspeakably betrayed her and her siblings.

Playing Truddi, Long gives off a spooky, otherworldly aura that puts her in touch with a secret woman's place none of the men in her life will ever even begin to fathom or understand. This includes her advertising guru husband (John Rubinstein) and her compassionate therapist, Dr. Phillips (Tom Conti). But if none of the men in her life can understand her, Truddi finally comes to appreciate the fact that her Troops (which she admits can sometimes become a most troubling system to contend with) give her the jazzy rhythms and complex disjunctures of a painting by Picasso or Braque.

From the jazzy, visual tension of a Cubist painting to the monumentalized icons of Imperial Russia, we next turn to Catherine the Great in *Young Catherine* (TNT, 1991). Similar to Truddi Chase, the young Catherine (aka Princess Sophie of Germany, played by Julia Ormond) must rely upon internal and otherworldly forces of womanly intuition to deal with all the emotional upheavals thrust upon her. First she is shipped off to the Russia of 1744 as the betrothed to the Grand Duke Peter (Reece Dinsdale). Then, under the dominance of the Empress Elizabeth (Vanessa Redgrave), she is made to change her name from Sophie to Catherine, forced to convert to the Orthodox Church, and to accept the miserable fact that her husband is a sadistic madman who shuns his young wife but takes mistresses and likes to smash toy soldiers and shriek a good deal.

But if all the oppressive Russian characters do their utmost to crush young Catherine's spirit, she mysteriously only grows stronger. Try as her enemies might to get the better of her, the source of her young woman's secret power forever eludes them. Before they get a chance to discover the origins of that power, Catherine, like Truddi, rallies troops of her own, including British Ambassador Sir Charles (Christopher Plummer), cunning court priest Archimandrite Todorsky (John Shrapnel), and her tall, dark, handsome soldier lover Count Gregory Orlov (Mark Frankel). While the mise-en-scène of *Young Catherine* presents Imperial Russia with a hard, ravishing beauty, we gradually see the demure young Catherine metamorphose into something just as hard and ravishingly beautiful. No longer the passive young female of masculinist desire, Catherine stands resplendent as a Russian icon, having avenged herself on all her enemies. She has achieved the goal of her epic quest and been crowned the supreme Empress of all the Russians, a divine epiphany of Woman triumphant, immutable, and eternal.

In 1936, producer David O. Selznick began an epic quest to find the perfect actress to play the once-in-a-lifetime role of Scarlett O'Hara in his epic cinematic production of *Gone with the Wind* (Victor Fleming, 1939). Of course, his quest would end with his discovery of the exquisitely beautiful English actress Vivien Leigh. Paradoxically, the two-time Oscar winner (she won Oscars for both *Gone with the Wind* and *A Streetcar Named Desire* [Elia Kazan, 1951]), despite her fragile Dresden doll-like appearance, became famous for playing bitchy, unscrupulous, destructive heroines who use their smoldering eroticism to get what they want out of men and life. Mel Martin, who plays Leigh in the epic miniseries *Darlings of the Gods* (A&E, 1991), embodies this aspect of the actress's persona, along with the growing streak of mental instability that leads to her increasing disillusionment and ultimate unraveling.

The epic action focuses on the 1948 Australian tour of the Old Vic Theatre. In agreeing to the tour, Laurence Olivier (Anthony Higgins) has the ulterior motive of taking his wife Leigh along to play the classics opposite him and, hopefully, provide her with a much-needed psychological uplift. High-strung, imperious, and on constant edge, Leigh is the Matriarchal Avenger as Unstable Femme Fatale, and she is the bejeweled centerpiece of the epic narrative.

Often oddly emotionally disconnected, Leigh floats across the Australian Outback on a mythic quest of her own to find the perfect male lover to lift her flagging spirits and alleviate her chic ennui. She eventually finds him in the appealing person of handsome, young Australian actor Peter Finch (Jerome Ehlers). Sadly, like so much else in her life, Leigh's relief proves intense but all too brief. When in the end, Leigh is metaphorically left standing alone onstage, having lost her young lover as well as her husband's trust and good will, she recalls Anna Magnani at the end of the classic *The Golden Coach* (Jean Renoir,

1953), and "the depth of her own loneliness seems to be the real truth and pity of all the roles she ever played."[8]

We next move from one immortal Englishwoman to another with the presentation of *Diana: Her True Story* (NBC, 1993), a frank portrait of the trials and tribulations of Diana, Princess of Wales (Serena Scott Thomas). After Queen Elizabeth (Anne Stallybrass) pressures the rapidly aging Prince Charles (David Threlfall) into getting married, his manipulative, married mistress, Camilla Parker-Bowles (Elizabeth Garvie) coaxes him into taking blushing, virginal noblewoman-schoolgirl Diana Spencer for his child-bride. Through Camilla's manipulations, the triangular relationship of the epic narrative falls into place: King, Queen, Royal Mistress. But after giving birth to her two sons, Diana is promptly thrust back into the dark shadows from whence she came while Charles resumes his adulterous affair with manipulative Camilla. (Diana later said of this period in her life: "There were three of us in this marriage, so it was a bit crowded.")

When Diana learns the full extent of the deliberate evil perpetrated against her, the man of her dreams goes from being Prince Charming to The Evil Prince of Darkness in league with Madame Satan to destroy the beautiful Princess. Internalizing her despair and disappointment, Diana exhibits an unexpected masochistic flair for the sort of melodramatic excess that has fueled many an epic miniseries. She takes to starving her body. She slashes it with razors and broken glass, stabs it with knives and scissors, and even hurls herself down the famous staircase at Kensington Palace. Fortunately, before she can totally annihilate herself, Diana experiences a personal epiphany of sorts. Instead of destroying herself, she will use her secret woman's powers far more constructively.

Towards this end, a cadre of courtiers is summoned. Their assignment: to transform the ugly little duckling Charles and Camilla believe Diana to be into the enormously glamorous and fabulous Princess Di — The People's Princess. From then on, Diana's sense of fashion and how to look magnificent in front of the camera rivals Marilyn Monroe's, and she transforms herself into an extraordinarily luminous being. Like Catherine the Great, she also rallies troops of her own, as well as a phalanx of handsome young lovers, to do battle against the dark forces of the Evil Prince and his ogre-like Royal Mistress Camilla.

From the fabled splendors of Buckingham Palace, our mythic journey next takes us to the sophisticated chicness of New York City, by way of Hollywood royalty, with the depiction of the life and times of actress Mia Farrow (Patsy Kensit) in *Love and Betrayal: The Mia Farrow Story* (FOX, 1995). The daughter of director John Farrow and Tarzan's most memorable movie Jane, Maureen O'Sullivan, the unbelievably fragile and insecure, waif-like Farrow leads an easy life filled with easy opportunity. She gains wealth and fame while still a teenager starring in the TV soap opera *Peyton Place* (ABC, 1964–69), and becomes a movie star with her sensational performance as the tormented young woman chosen to bear Satan's baby in *Rosemary's Baby* (Roman Polanski, 1968). No less sensational are the unconventional circumstances of her private life, starting with her marriages to the considerably older Frank Sinatra (Richard Mueñz) and composer André Previn (Robert LuPone). But Farrow's marriage to these two legendary men is not the main thrust of the epic narrative. That arrives with the introduction of Farrow's longtime companion, Woody Allen (Dennis Boutsikaris in an inspired performance).

Initially, Allen is depicted as the emotionally hung-up, intensely neurotic but fairly lovable Jewish New Yorker we know from all of his classic films. However, when he sets his directorial (dictatorial?) sights on Farrow's nubile young daughter, the dreamy, Lolita-like Soon-Yi (Grace Una), the epic narrative focus shifts dramatically (melodramatically?). Consequently, Allen goes from being an endearing Charlie Chaplin–type to a Fagin-like predator, the very personification of the "Evil One" that Farrow's mother deems him to be. In one arrestingly surreal and slyly ironic scene, Farrow imagines herself as Polanski's Rosemary again having sex with Allen, who is suddenly transformed into the Devil, complete with scaly reptilian skin and piercing red eyes. After this scene, the configuration of a perverse triangular structure (consisting of Allen, Mother [Farrow], and Daughter [Soon-Ye]) is forced onto the proceedings, throwing the epic narrative into chaotic upheaval.

It is through the use of this triangular arrangement that the multiple dimensions of Allen's unexpected brand of patriarchal evil is manifested. In response, Farrow prepares for the epic battle with the "Evil One" to come. She has her home blessed by a priest, baptizes all her children and, clutching her rosary beads tighter than did even Rose Kennedy, she calls upon the forces of her ex-husbands, Sinatra and Previn (her aging Knights-in-shining-armor), and instructs her irate mother to unleash a continuous torrent of "Junoesque thunderbolts at Allen from her stronghold on the West Coast."[9] But Farrow's real "secret weapon" consists of her own secret troops (her multiracial household of fiercely loyal children), who together with Farrow drive the "Evil One" and his teenaged concubine out of their lives forever. By exhibiting such a flair for revenge and melodrama, Farrow aligns herself with many other great heroines of the epic miniseries. From fragile, insecure Hollywood waif, Farrow becomes as volatile and formidable as Shakespeare's Cleopatra, only with a better fate in store for her at the end. Having retreated triumphantly to her matriarchal fortress high above the glittery Manhattan skyline, Farrow signifies the Great Mother transforming chaos back into order with her mysterious female principle. As she gives and sustains life, it is to her that all must finally return, or else.

Yet another depiction of the Great Goddess at her most sensational comes in the form of *Liz: The Elizabeth Taylor Story* (NBC, 1995), starring Sherilyn Fenn as the ultimate Hollywood superstar. Perhaps it was inevitable that the life story of the ravishingly beautiful Taylor—with all of her scandalous love affairs, multiple marriages and multiple divorces, chronic health problems, various addictions, and conspicuous consumptions—would be transformed into an epic miniseries. After all, she is "probably the only Hollywood star whose entire life both on and off the silver screen has become the stuff of pure legend."[10]

Incredibly enough, all of the memorable highlights of her life are fitted into place. There are enactments from Taylor's most famous movies,[11] including, the most controversial one of all, *Cleopatra* (Joseph L. Mankiewicz, 1963), for which she became the very first star ever to command a million-dollar paycheck, and scandalized all of Christendom when she set her still-married-to-Eddie-Fisher sights on her married leading man, Richard Burton (Angus Macfadyen), whom Taylor married and divorced twice (the 1950s headlines of the triangular construct of "Debbie, Eddie, Liz" became, in the 1960s, "Sybil, Dick, Liz"). There are also all of her other husbands: Conrad "Nicky" Hilton (Eric Gustavson), Michael Wilding (Nigel Havers), Mike Todd (Ray Wise), Eddie Fisher (Corey Parker), John Warner (Charles Frank), and Larry Fortensky (Michael McGrady).

Avenging Angel II (Transcending Mortality): The Eternal Elizabeth Taylor (Sherilyn Fenn, pictured) as *Cleopatra* prepares to lay siege on the love of her life—Richard Burton (Angus Macfadyen). *Liz: The Elizabeth Taylor Story* (ABC, 1995).

What emerges out of all this often comes across as an amphetimine-laced crash course through the assorted ups and downs of Taylor's monumental life. Fortunately, there is the dazzling presence of Sherilyn Fenn to anchor these various elements in place. The actress gives us a varied portrait of the immortal Liz in all her enigmatic glory and oceanic contradictions. There is the fragile, impossibly beautiful, violet-eyed MGM child star pushed by a ruthless stage mother to succeed; the tough and spoiled to the core Hollywood superstar of legend; and the aging Immortal Diva devoting her final years to helping others. Still, much of the time Fenn's Taylor comes off mostly as a Sacred Hollywood Monster eating up men, money, and movies, even faster than Lucy and Ethel gobbled up all those chocolates from the swift-moving conveyer belt in *I Love Lucy* (CBS, 1951–57). At the same time, Fenn also nicely registers the tenderly lyrical and deeply poetic sides of Taylor's personality, when she is transformed into her final incarnation as the Avenging Angel heading into epic battle for all the sufferers of AIDS.

A battle of another sort is waged by the four women of *Bella Mafia* (CBS, 1997). Vanessa Redgrave delivers another of her customary televisual star turns as stately Maifiosa matriarch Graziella Luciano. When her husband Don Roberto (Dennis Farina) and three sons are murdered by a rival Mob family, Redgrave's Graziella has no other choice but to avenge their deaths. Like Mia Farrow, she retreats to her matriarchal stronghold and rallies her troops, consisting of her three equally fierce daughters-in-law, Sophia (Nastassja Kinski), Moyra (Jennifer Tilly), and Teresa (Ileana Douglas). The four Luciano women begin their epic quest of methodically and systematically avenging the murder of each of their men. In many ways, they are the ultimate expression of those fierce heroines we met in 1988's *The Singing Detective*. Through seduction, guile, pluck, ruthless courage and iron determination, they triumph over their enemies and avenge all their murdered sons and husbands.

Lastly, the mythic quest for a form of revenge gets carried over into the final two epic miniseries considered: *Cleopatra* (ABC, 1999) and *Joan of Arc* (CBS, 1999). We are presented with two of the most legendary women of history depicted as Avenging Angels on personal quests to conquer various aspects of the patriarchal power structure. For Cleopatra, this is signified by the oppressive Roman Empire; for Joan, it is the superpowerful England and the Roman Catholic Church. With each woman's act of defiant transgression, she hopes to fuse epic thrust and monumental scope into a unified whole. Yet in assuming the role of Avenging Angel, each also brings the collective wrath of the patriarchy down on her defiant head.

On the surface, these two heroines could not be more unalike if they tried. Cleopatra (Leonor Varela), the infamous pagan seductress with the mysterious power to dissolve even the most active of males into a state of quivering female passivity, coyly toys with the affections of the two noblest Romans of all — Marc Anthony (Billy Zane) and Julius Caesar (Timothy Dalton). Joan of Arc (Leelee Sobieski), the chaste, virginal saint is guided by her celestial voices and Heavenly visions to drive out the Imperialistic English from her beloved France. But whether the heroine is sinner or saint, virgin or whore, schoolgirl or queen, is of no real consequence to the powerful men in control. What is of the utmost consequence is that the offending female be cut back down to size. This inherent antagonism between female transgression and male aggression leads to an often-unsettling ambivalence. Such ambivalence can lead to either the emancipation of the female or her annihilation. For Cleopatra and St. Joan, it is the latter that occurs. And so as each heroine is cut down to size, the Avenging Angel appears to be in retreat, at least for the time being.

Tales of the City

The ambivalence directed toward the mythic type of the Avenging Angel present in the two late 1990s texts—*Cleopatra* and *Joan of Arc*—is nowhere to be found in the use made of the figure in the character of Mrs. Anna Madrigal in *Tales of the City* (PBS, 1994) and Mother Abigail in *The Stand* (ABC, 1994). In *Tales*, based on a series of articles written by San Francisco journalist Armistead Maupin, the mysterious Anna Madrigal (Olympia Dukakis) is the owner of the otherworldly apartment complex at 28 Barbary Lane in San Francisco, which turns out to be just as mysterious as its owner. Mary Ann Singleton (Laura Linney), a naïve young woman from Cleveland, Ohio, becomes one of Anna's tenants. At Barbary Lane, Mary Ann meets spirited bisexual Mona Ramsey (Chloe Webb), smooth-talking gigolo waiter Brian Hawkins (Paul Gross), and sinister rooftop tenant Norman Williams (Stanley DeSantis). After yet another of his failed love affairs, Michael "Mouse" Tolliver (Marcus D'Amico), Mona's sweet-tempered gay friend, moves in with her. Each one of them, like Anna Madrigal, possesses secrets of his or her own.

Mary Ann gets a job as a secretary at the high-profile advertising firm of fatally ill Edgar Halcyon (Donald Moffat), and becomes briefly involved with devious bisexual Beauchamp Day (Thomas Gibson), who is married to Edgar's neurotic, promiscuous socialite daughter DeDe (Barbara Garrick). Edgar takes up with Anna, DeDe finds herself pregnant but is not certain of the father, and Michael gets involved with social-climbing gynecologist Dr. Jon Fielden (Bill Campbell). The relationship between Michael and Jon ends when the uptight Jon discovers Michael dancing in his underwear in a club contest. But Mona's love life takes an unexpected upturn when her successful, ultra-glamorous, neurotic African American ex-lover D'orothea Williams (Cynda Williams) returns from modeling in New York and invites Mona to move into her luxurious new home with her.

Down but not out, Michael continues with his endless quest to find the ever more elusive Mr. Right. As D'orothea's neurotic behavior worsens, her relationship with Mona grows rocky; meanwhile Jon (who is DeDe's gynecologist) has a sexual fling with her husband Beauchamp, which Jon soon ends. After discovering that Anna Madrigal is a transsexual, Norman, who is also an exploitive child pornographer and pedarast, blackmails Edgar with his discovery. But when Mary Ann finds out what Norman is up to, she confronts him, and he falls off a cliff, plunging to his death. The epic action concludes on the night of Christmas Eve. While Edgar succumbs to his fatal illness, Mary Ann, Michael, and Brian join Anna for her annual Christmas party. After she learns that D'orothea is really White (she's been secretly injecting herself with medications to make her appear Black), Mona returns home to 28 Barbary Lane to be united with her beloved "alternative" family for Christmas.

In one sense, *Tales of the City* is part of the televisual world of post-modern TV gamesmanship, what we associate with such 1980s texts as *Ellis Island*, *Alice in Wonderland*, *Sins*, and *Fresno*: the epic miniseries as a great televisual game that becomes a drama of audacity, experimentation, irony, and parody. In this mode, large parts of the epic narrative are opened up to pastiche, playfulness, fantasy, mystery, camp, melodramatic excess, and generous amounts of self-consciousness. With *Tales*, these aspects of the epic narrative are given full expression.

In another sense, we can view the epic miniseries as a kind of post-modern burlesque of the entire genre, beginning with its genesis in the classic British novels of the 19th century. A brief consideration of the many coincidental and often outlandish mechanisms of its interlocking plotlines demonstrates this point. For example, unbeknownst to Mary Ann, Anna just happens to get involved in an extramarital affair with her boss Edgar Halcyon; Jon becomes Michael's lover, DeDe's gynecologist, and her degenerate husband Beauchamp's bathhouse sex mate; Brian meets and attempts to pick up D'orothea, who has returned to San Francisco for the purpose of resuming her love affair with Mona; and Jon just so happens to enter the same bar at the exact moment that Michael is dancing in his underwear onstage.

There is even a burlesque-like, pastiche quality to such standard codified tropes of the epic miniseries as the use of music, mise-en-scène, and characterization. And the use of a series of famous guest stars is most amusing and inspired: stars such as Rod Steiger and Karen Black, and celebrated icons of the gay community — Ian McKellan, Paul Bartel, Bob Mackie, Lance Loud — are utilized to create instances of witty celebrity intertextuality. Steiger amusingly parodies his own "Method-style," overly-intense acting as a bookstore owner fond of uttering cryptic expressions; Black spoofs her own tendency to put on weight in her later years, playing herself as a fellow patient DeDe meets at a "Fat Farm"; McKellan, Bartel, Mackie, and Loud all send themselves up, playing a pack of rich and pampered "old queens" with nothing better to do with their time than attend posh dinner parties and bitch about everyone like the females in the classic film *The Women* (George Cukor, 1939). But not only are all of these stars generating a parodic comment on their own celebrity status, they are also sending up the whole codified trope of the use of famous guest stars in the epic miniseries.

In *Tales*, anarchy, chaos, racial denial, extensive drug use, and plenty of recreational sex are the norms. Such a dependence on controversy, outrageousness, and exaggeration turns epic narrative into a ribald, racy, three-ring-circus. Characters are brought on with all their deep, dark secrets in tow — including the three main protagonists, Mary Ann, Mona, and Michael — for their sheer entertainment value. Moreover, each is endearing in his or her own quirky way. But each also seems somehow incomplete and insufficient. No matter how hard she tries to fit in, Mary Ann always feels a bit vaguely out of place.

Avenging Angel III (Transcending Gender): Mrs. Anna Madrigal (Olympia Dukakis) tends to her Magical Garden of Earthly Delights at 28 Barbary Lane. *Tales of the City* (PBS, 1994).

Michael's endless, anxious quest to find the right man grows increasingly absurd. Mona searches for a center she can never seem to locate for herself. But actually, a center is something all the characters in *Tales* are in need of finding. Enter fairy godmother–like Mrs. Anna Madrigal.

Nothing if not deeply, deeply mysterious, Anna Madrigal is a flamboyant, hallucinogenic Earth Mother riding sky-high in the Epic Miniseries Universe. Like the legendary Sphinx, she is as old as Time itself, yet she is also strangely timeless. She is the Avenging Angel as Avenging Matriarch as Vaudevillian Superstar. While waving her magic wand of incense and a marijuana joint, Anna is fond of reciting Romantic poetry (which she usually does while exhaling sinuous plumes of that marijuana smoke). She also speaks openly of her apocalyptic premonitions, believes in the fantastical Atlantis, and tells her tenants at Barbary Lane they were all fated to be together with her. Like Clara in *Lonesome Dove*, Anna is a powerful maternal force connecting one character to another and providing safe harbor for all. The structure of Anna's central role, and her connection to the other characters, is visualized in Diagram 6.1:

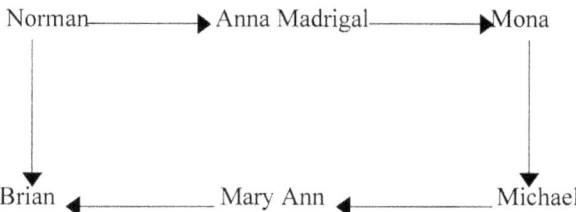

Diagram 6.1— The relationships of the characters of *Tales of the City*.

Not only does Anna possess an uncanny sex-surpassing power like Clara, she also possesses a gender-surpassing power. For Anna Madrigal has a "secret" of her own: she was actually born as Andrew, not Anna. Her "secret" then problematizes the traditional binary established between the customary boundary of "male" and "female" in the epic miniseries of the past. Further, as a positive representation of a male-to-female transgendered character, Anna in her own uniquely eccentric way provides a much-needed televisual anodyne to the inherent unpleasantness and homophobia typically associated with transgendered characters in the media. One example of this is the "pre-op transsexual" murderer (murderess?) Bobbi (Michael Caine) in the stylishly directed but morally problematic *Dressed to Kill* (Brian De Palma, 1980).

Most mercifully the loving, supremely maternal Anna is far removed from the troublesome gender dysphoria and psychotic anxiety depicted in *Dressed to Kill* and several other films.[12] Rather than raping, pillaging, maiming, and murdering, Anna is more likely to be tending to her homegrown marijuana crop, cooking up a gastronomic feast for her tenants, or generously dispensing her Wise Woman's advice. According to her, the center that all her tenants seek must be reached not only erotically, but intuitively, artistically, and finally magically. However, this is not meant to imply that Anna is in any way adverse to the Dionysian side of life. Her poetic mentions of internal fires, pulsing, secret Lifeforces, and her assorted love scenes with Edgar Halcyon link her to the same iconic-erotic territory the heroines in the novels of D.H. Lawrence occupy and celebrate. But first and foremost, Anna Madrigal is a mythical being, speaking the secret language of the cosmos. Anna believes love, like the truth, will set them all free. No longer confined by the burden of history, Anna is able to transcend the confines of all previous teleological limitations. As a representative of the Avenging Angel, Anna has also transgressed the rigid confines of traditional gender roles. This gives her an irrepressible element of mythic energy felt most especially by her tenants at Barbary Lane and Edgar (her High Priest of Love).

If Anna is the fairy godmother of *Tales*, Mary Ann is just as surely its fairy-tale princess. With her long, golden-blonde hair, big, sapphire-blue eyes, and lovely, warm smile, Mary Ann is like a modern-day incarnation of Lewis Carroll's Alice, incredulously making her way through the often-irrational exotic-erotic Wonderland of San Francisco. As with Alice in her Wonderland, Mary Ann always seems serenely self-composed. She's a cool, blonde beauty as sweet and wholesome as homemade bread and as guileless and American as Mom, God, and apple pie. She even attains the perfect aesthetic balance of a classical work of art. Forever smiling her Mona Lisa–like smile at everyone she encounters, she takes in stride the recreational drugs, the decadent discos, the seedy gay bathhouses, and all those endless one-night stands. Amazingly, through all that freedom and damnation, Mary Ann even eventually comes to love all of the multi-layered complexity of her life at 28 Barbary Lane, where so very many secrets are revealed and the consequences of those revelations can be freeing or damning. Much like Nurse Mills in *The Singing Detective*, Mary Ann spreads comfort and joy wherever she goes. She offers solace to Michael whenever another of his many love affairs fails him. To Mona she gives steadfast support through all her personal calamities. She even reaches out to the increasingly bizarre-acting Norman.

In fact, it is Mary Ann's connection to Norman that leads to her display of Nancy Drew–like sleuthing abilities. When she wants to learn what he is really up to, with a Goldilocksian surreptitiousness she sneaks inside his shabby rooftop apartment to get a peek inside his highly suspect, secret black briefcase. Still, Mary Ann does not achieve her most spectacular incarnation until she becomes a replica of Kim Novak's Madeleine from Hitchcock's sublime classic *Vertigo*. Likewise, when they recreate their self-conscious televisual homage to Hitchcock's cinematic masterpiece, the ironic-parodic power of director Alastair Reid and photographer Walt Lloyd reaches its creative peak. The bravura sequence begins with the opening chords of composer Bernard Hermann's famous theme from *Vertigo*. With this, Mary Ann emerges as a signifier for the Eternal Feminine. She has slipped off into a decadent, artificial televisual dream world, which seems unrelated in any way to the "real" world (and since that "real" world is, after all, San Francisco, that is saying a good deal). Further contributing to this effect, Mary Ann, while photographed through diffusion filters in soft, dreamy light, is dressed in luminous white, signifying the glamour, mystique, and the uncanny ghostliness she is now meant to represent.

In the scene of Mary Ann at the museum admiring the portrait of the exotic Carlotta Valdez (the 19th-century suicidal ancestor that Hitchcock's Madeleine believes is possessing her), she sits as if lost in a deep, hypnotic trance. Lloyd's camera moves in for a Hitchcockian close-up of Mary Ann's perfectly coifed blonde hair, then slowly tilts up while tracking forward into a close-up of the bouquet of flowers Carlotta holds in her hands. A similar camera movement begins with a close-up of Mary Ann's blonde hair, then slowly tracks back to another Hitchcockian close-up of Carlotta's equally blonde hair. These constant, lyrical, forward-and-backward tracking shots practically put us into the same sort of hypnotic trance that Mary Ann has slipped off into, even while there is a storm mounting and so much madness now swirling all around her.

If in one sense Mary Ann is like Madeleine in the way she is depicted to signify a reactive, passive, silent but exquisitely seductive feminine object of the controlling male gaze, in another sense she will soon become the antithesis of Hitchcock's doomed heroine. This happens when there is a sudden switch to the subjective female gaze of the camera (from Mary Ann's point-of-view), and she confronts Norman outside the museum. As she threatens to report him to the authorities for his pederastic and child-pornography activities and his blackmailing of Edgar Halcyon, she becomes more proactive, vocal, and defiantly forceful. Now she has been thrust into the role of active knowledge-seeker. Because the climactic scene takes place atop a steep cliff overlooking the pounding sea below, a surrealistic suspensefulness is created. Mary Ann is transformed from Kim Novak in *Vertigo* to Joan Fontaine in *Suspicion* (Hitchcock, 1941), and Norman, into a poor man's version of Gary Grant's scheming husband. But since she is depicted as being physically superior to him, not only in her physical movements but also in her dominance of the epic frame, she soon gains the upper hand. In true Hitchcockian style, the tables are quickly turned and Norman is the one sent plunging to his death below. *Deus ex machina*, Norman dies when Mary Ann confronts him with his own evil, which makes her the shining signifier for Woman Triumphant. Who would have ever imagined it possible that there inside the naively innocent Mary Ann Singleton of Cleveland, Ohio, beat the fierce heart of the Woman Warrior of the 1990s?

After her ordeal, Mary Ann returns to the maternalistic security of 28 Barbary Lane. As the "Black" D'orothea returns back home to her "White" mother and father for Christmas Eve, and DeDe holds her dying father's hand while telling him she is pregnant with his first grandchild, Mary Ann and the other "motherless" characters—Mona, Michael, and Brian—are able to return home and recover for themselves the Great Mother. In this they resemble the little lost boy in *Persona* (Ingmar Bergman, 1966), forever reaching out to touch the huge, superimposed female face of the Great Mother projected before him. The great difference between the characters in *Tales* and Bergman's little lost boy is they not only get to touch the Great Mother, she touches back.

The Stand

As difficult as the problems faced by Anna Madrigal and Mary Ann may seem, they pale in comparison to what the 106-year-old Mother Abigail (Ruby Dee) and the characters of *The Stand*, based on Stephen King's cult epic novel (1978, reissued 1990), face. Against the cataclysmic backdrop of an Imax-sized sense of the Apocalypse, a super-flu epidemic called "Captain Trips" is released by the American government when a biological warfare experiment goes disastrously wrong. Practically everyone in the country dies, except for various ordinary people who are mysteriously immune to the deadly disease. These survivors find themselves compelled to gather for unknown reasons, for unknown purposes. Essentially, they gather into two groups: the Good and the Evil. The Forces of Good are led by Mother Abigail of Nebraska. They include Stu Redman (Gary Sinise), a rough-and-ready Texan (and the closest individual *The Stand* has to the traditional, solitary hero); ambitious, womanizing rock star Larry Underwood (Adam Storke); deaf-mute Nick Andros (Rob Lowe) and his dim-witted friend, Tom Cullen (Bill Fagerbakke); the elderly Professor Glen Bateman (Ray Walston) and retired Judge Farris (Ossie Davis); and Frannie Goldsmith (Molly Ringwald), an unwed, pregnant young woman who becomes Stu's love interest.

In violent opposition to the Forces of Good are Randall Flagg (Jamey Sheridan) and his Forces of Evil. A vicious, cop-murdering, anti–Semitic racist, Flagg is a being of supernatural Evil, an Emissary of Satan who often takes the form of an ominous-looking black crow to torment his many victims. He rules with black magic and dark glamour, as Satan will. He sets his Evil Forces up in Las Vegas. They are made up of Lieutenant Lloyd Henreid (Miguel Ferrer), wild-eyed arsonist Trashcan Man (Matt Frewer), and devil-may-care bad girl Julie Lawry (Shawnee Smith). Two other characters, the confused Nadine Cross (Laura San Giacomo) and Frannie's geeky neighbor Harold Lauder (Corin Nemec), are manipulated by Flagg. They also act as a connection between the worlds of Flagg and Mother Abigail.

Under Mother Abigail's leadership, the Forces of Good relocate to Boulder, Colorado, to create a new utopian society. When Harold kills Nick, the new society's leader, with a bomb, the community readies itself for the great epic battle that must be fought against the Forces of Evil. While Harold and Nadine join up with Flagg, which leads to Harold's murder and Nadine killing herself (rather than bear Flagg's unwanted child), Mother Abigail's health grows frail. But before dying she sends out Tom and Judge Farris to spy on Flagg to find out what he is planning. Then she sends four men (Stu, Larry, Professor Bateman, and Ralph Brentner) on a mythic quest to take a "stand" against Flagg.

Judge Farris is killed by Flagg's men, as is Professor Bateman. Stu is badly injured and cannot go on, but Tom escapes. Larry and Ralph are taken before an unruly mob to be crucified and their bodies torn apart. But before this can happen Trashcan Man, now totally deranged from excessive exposure to radiation, arrives on the scene with an atomic bomb to present to Flagg. Although neither Larry nor Ralph are able to "stand" against Flagg, they, he, and all the rest of his evil Las Vegas troops are consumed by the atomic blast. Stu, aided by Tom, eventually makes it back to Boulder to learn Frannie has given birth to a healthy baby girl, and he prepares for a new life with her.

Much like the characters in the classic science-fiction film *Close Encoun-*

ters of The Third Kind (Steven Spielberg, 1977), those of *The Stand* become obsessed with a visionary dream they cannot immediately comprehend. They are instructed to travel to an unknown place for an unclear purpose. If we originally think them peculiar, we soon think differently of them. They are the "Chosen Ones." Each has been chosen to serve an essential purpose. Together, they are the collective force needed to fight the Great Conflict. According to Edwin F. Casebeer, each of them is signifier for a specific mythic type. Stu Redman signifies "the Hero, the New Adam, the Survivor," while his love interest, heroine Frannie Goldsmith, is "the New Eve, the First Mother, Stu's cofounder of the New Eden." Harold Lauder is a signifier for "both Cain and Judas, the first murderer and traitor," Professor Glen Bateman is "the Great Teacher," the deaf-mute Nick Andros is "the God-appointed King," and Larry Underwood is a symbol of "the archetypal Everyman, upon whom act the history of the Earth and the will of God."[13]

The manifestation of God's will on Earth resides in the super-signifying figure of Mother Abigail. Mother Abigail lives alone on her Nebraska farm surrounded by giant cornfields. She sits on her front porch, strumming on her guitar, singing iconic spirituals, awaiting the arrival of the Chosen Ones, in whose visionary dreams she always appears. She is linked to love for nature, for space, for the Greater Purpose of all Life. Although this connection to the

Avenging Angel IV (Transcending Time & Space): Confused deaf-mute Nick Andros (Rob Lowe) seeks out the wise counsel of the 106-year-old Mother Abigail (Ruby Dee). *The Stand* (ABC, 1994).

land and nature link her to the pastoral and Dionysian, her spiritual fortitude and powerful sense of moral purpose give her a clear-eyed Apollonian balance, which is fitting since she is the leader of the Forces of Good, the female Savior of the World, and remains a profound inspiration to the others even after her death. If Anna Madrigal defies the confines of gender, Mother Abigail defies those of Time and Space. To put it simply, she transcends all such human limitations.

Much of Mother Abigail's uncanniness stems from her miraculous ability to know the future. Her miraculousness gives her a dialectic power and a duality manifested in the way she is able to combine the Dionysian and Apollonian forces. Although she may initially appear as an elderly Black woman of little means, in actuality she is the only real hope civilization has left to be redeemed. Undeniably, Mother Abigail exists in mythic archetype, but she also has a strong reference to the science-fictional. This referent is an apocalyptic vision of the world. Mother Abigail clearly understands that her ultimate heroic purpose is not to lead the others into the Great Battle to come. Instead, she is the symbol of connection, whose heroic purpose it is to unite the heroic forces that will fight against Flagg. This concept of the heroic experience existing as a communal effort, rather than solely in one heroic individual, is present in many epic miniseries of the 1990s. If the 1980s recognize and celebrate the heroic effort, those of the 1990s communize it.

The modulating factor in *The Stand* is the character of Stu Redman. At first he does not strike us as an impressive man. After all, he is an unemployed factory worker scraping by in an economically depressed small town in Texas. Obviously, he is a far cry from the matinee idol-like Adventurers of the 1980s. Then again, Stu is not meant to be a throwback to a past time. He is a signifier for a new version of the heroic Adventurer for a new time and place. Actually, his heroic attributes are indeed on a par with the heroes of the 1980s. He is the one who shuts down the gas pumps when a man, dying of Captain Trips, crashes into them with his car. Stu's ability to troubleshoot and think on his feet proves advantageous when he has to escape from the prison in which the U.S. government confines him for being one of those immune to Captain Trips. These heroic attributes, along with several other reasons, result in Mother Abigail choosing him as one of the four men to "stand" against Flagg in Las Vegas.

In many ways, the relationship that evolves between Stu and Frannie makes perfect sense. Not only is she the "New Eve" to his "New Adam," the two of them are also kindred spirits whose lives feed into the same great mythic stream. Like Stu, Frannie is much more than she initially appears to be. While a part of Frannie signifies the mythic type of the Wife/Mother, a larger part of her runs counter to such stereotypical categorization. Her natural spiritedness (resulting in her decision to carry her baby to term even after she is cruelly abandoned by her erstwhile boyfriend) sets her apart. If such an action would have relegated her to the type of the Whore in the past, in the end, Frannie resists any such reductive typecasting. Therefore, it is the character of the uncannily beautiful Nadine Cross who must bear the onus of the Whore in *The Stand*. But even in her case we see a noticeable running against the grain of the usual stereotypical aspects of the mythic type.

For example, when Nadine first meets Randall Flagg in the flesh in the desert at night, she finds herself, against her better judgment, attracted by his charisma and dark good looks, and he makes violent love to her. When he transforms himself into his real demonic visage, Nadine calls him her God. By doing so, she shuts herself off from God or any rescue by God in her horrific situation. Her long, beautiful hair turns a pure, ghostly white in Las Vegas and she shrieks out to Flagg's followers, "We are all dead and this is Hell!"

Later, as Flagg continues to reveal his true demonic form to her and continues to control and manipulate her sexual desires, Nadine fights back against him. And when towards the end Flagg violently rapes her, Nadine responds to the gross violation by committing suicide, killing Flagg's demonic baby as well as herself. Her final act of defiance against him is one of several indications that Flagg's Evil Empire is crumbling at an alarming rate.

Even though Flagg is ultimately destroyed, he manages to unleash a considerable amount of evil into the epic narrative. And although he often appears in the natural world, Flagg is really most at home amidst the gaudy technological spectacle of the modern-day Sodom and Gomorrah he makes of Las Vegas (more will be said on this matter below.) As a signifier of extreme evil, Flagg is the sum of countless other evil villains of the epic miniseries. Like the White slave-catchers of *Roots*, the Nazis of *Holocaust* and *War and Remembrance*, and the savage Blue Duck of *Lonesome Dove*, Flagg links a fascistic authoritarianism to the most primitive of instincts. Images of Flagg as an atavistic, sado-masochistic master, taking great pleasure in torturing men and dragging half-naked, screaming women to their doom, are the codified tropes of the eroticized fascism of *The Stand*. And just as the bodies of the victims of the Nazis bore a form of silent witness in *Holocaust* and *War and Remembrance*, the mise-en-scène of *The Stand* is no less drenched in totalitarian images of human pain, misery, and death. Conversely, Mother Abigail's mission to put an end to Flagg and everything he represents grows more and more urgent as the death rate of his victims escalates.

To conclude, we will analyze the way *The Stand* uses intertextuality, mise-en-scène, and music in some interesting and ironic ways. Director Mick Garris incorporates several instances of self-conscious intertextuality into the epic narrative. An example of celebrity intertextuality and auto-citation comes in the casting of the great actress Ruby Dee as Mother Abigail. With a career spanning several decades, Dee is famous for her deft performances as strong Black women on stage, screen, and television.[14] Although she was cast in the canonical *Roots*, scheduling problems would force her to drop out. As compensation, Dee would later play Alex Haley's paternal grandmother, Queen Haley, in *Roots: The Next Generations* (the same woman Halle Berry plays in the 1993 epic miniseries *Queen*). In essence, Dee's dignified presence in *The Stand* both evokes a certain cultural-historical milieu, and also serves as a referent linking her to the five mythic women of *Roots*—Binta, Nyo Boto, Bell, Kizzy, and Matilda, as well as Queen Haley. Viewed sitting on her front porch in Nebraska, singing iconic spirituals, Dee's Mother Abigail is the Avenging Angel as Divine and Nurturing Avenging Matriarch.

Examples of auto-citation and mendacious intertextuality are present in the way various celebrities appear in *The Stand*, often in ironic, cameo-like roles. These include several of Stephen King's close cult-director buddies: Tom Holland (Carl Hough), Sam Raimi (Bobby Terry), John Landis (Carl Dorr); basketball player Kareem Abdul-Jabbar (The Monster Shooter), and even King himself (as the eccentric Teddy Meizak). In more prominent guest starring roles are Ed Harris as the suicidal General Starkey, who blames himself for the outbreak of Captain Trips, and the superb actress Kathy Bates as defiant talk-show host Rae Flowers, whose penchant for speaking her mind comes at great cost to herself. Each of these personalities, all of whom are closely connected to King and his work,[15] is used to evoke and remind the audience of these close connections. Their presences also serve as a kind of doubling-back reference point to the many examples of famous film and television productions made from King's copious literary *oeuvre*.

The visual schematics of *The Stand* combine the classically composed scenes of the exalted American landscape of *Roots* with the more sparse, austere monumentality of *Holocaust*, as well as traces of the heightened visual excess associated with the epic miniseries of the late 1980s. Photographed under the supervision of Edward Pei, the mise-en-scène offers consistently rewarding images of natural, pastoral beauty in the wide-open spatial vistas of Nebraska and Colorado. But in three cases the beauty of the natural gives way to imagery infused with the power of myth to create a different sort of epic meaning altogether. The first consists of the visionary dream sequences in which the characters first experience Mother Abigail. In terms of iconography, the authenticity of pastoral-naturalistic evocation (the simplicity of Mother Abigail's farm house, the wind rippling through the expanse of corn fields, and the winding lane leading to her farm house off in the distance suggest the paintings of Grant Woods) gives way to the more conspicuous anti-realism of the Hollywood Studio of the classic period. Thus, the epic narrative is exposed and allowed to revel in its own self-conscious constructedness and blatant artificiality.

Similarly, color will frequently be used with the same sort of Expressionist daring that the camera of Dietrich Lohmann displayed in *War and Remembrance*. While Mother Abigail is typically bathed in a defused, celestial golden light, the mise-en-scène surrounding her is presented in palettical paroxysms of bold, hallucinogenic colors—blood-reds, acid yellows, electrical blues—which often verge on the overblown.

Color is also used in this same heightened, mythic way in the surrealistic scene when Flagg sends Nadine to seduce Harold. Here the mise-en-scène takes on the elemental imagery of blood-red raw meat, as if the garishness of the scene is emanating from the seductive blood-redness of the skintight, sequined gown Nadine wears. The entire epic frame is eventually drenched in the color red (which is traditionally symbolic of the desire of the flesh) as Nadine goes about what she has been sent to accomplish.

The climactic showdown between the Forces of Good and Evil, which takes place in Las Vegas, features the most assertive and elaborate use of heightened mise-en-scène, complete with flashing neon lights, eye-popping contrasts of garish color, phantasmagoria, exaggeration of visual style, irony, and extreme self-consciousness. Exaggerated and almost mechanistic in their movements and appearance, the weapon-toting Forces of Evil are a regimented public display of fascistic soldiers amidst the glittery luridness of an apocalyptical rock concert. Larry and Ralph are positioned on each side of the gigantic stage in illuminated horseshoe-like structures. Each man is crucified on a giant neon cross. Here is fascistic decadence on an epic scale. Looking like a strung-out rock star, a false evangelical prophet, a demagogic dynamo, Flagg emerges from a psychedelic burst of multi-colored flares and incandescent floodlights. As manipulative and exploitive as a decadent emperor of pagan Rome, Flagg prepares to pass sentence on the two innocent, crucified men. After reading a series of trumped-up charges, Flagg decrees that Larry and Ralph will be slowly torn apart, limb from limb. Of course before that happens, Trashcan Man unexpectedly appears to present Flagg with his gift of an atomic bomb.

At the time he was writing *The Stand*, King believed the coming of the future apocalypse was inevitable: "There was a feeling — I must admit — that I was doing a fast, happy tap-dance on the grave of the whole world. Its writing came during a troubled period for the world in general and America in particular."[16] The reality of biochemical warfare was then not simply a literary metaphor for King in his writing of *The Stand*: it was an all too harsh reality. But in the epic televisual adaptation of the novel, it becomes a harsh reality that has been set to the infectious melodic beat of the electric and acoustic guitar. King suggested to composer W.G. Snuffy Walden that he devise a mostly acoustic soundtrack. Walden's inspired approach to the trope of music resulted in a soundtrack in which solo acoustic guitar dominates much of the epic action. The composer does use fuller orchestral arrangements, but in only a few select places. In fact, it is only in the climactic last two hours, involving the final battle between the Forces of Good and Evil in Las Vegas, that the total spectrum of the rich orchestral palette is heard in full force. But at the end, when Stu and Frannie prepare to assume their roles as the new Adam and Eve, Walden's music shifts into a transcendently uplifting mode as the spirit of Mother Abigail continues to lead them into the future. How this provocation is negotiated in relation to the epic miniseries of the 21st century — how this concept will develop and evolve — will be of central concern in the next chapter.

Chapter 7

Outer and *Outré* Spaces

In the previous chapter, we considered how the epic miniseries of the 1990s were altered in various ways as a means of appealing to a dwindling televisual audience in a period of much change and uncertainty. This was evident in the genre's obvious shift away from some of the bold virtuosity of style and flamboyance of design exhibited in the epic miniseries of the latter part of the 1980s. With the arrival of the 1990s, texts tended to be organized more compactly and to be more self-consciously ironic, or even parodic. Both epic narrative and mythic characterization were affected by this altered sense of display. With the new decade, heroism no longer resided solely in the male alone; it could just as easily, and much more likely, reside in the female, most especially in the form of the fifth mythic type of the Avenging Angel. In addition, heroism could now also reside in the communal dynamic of a group of characters who were usually inspired by a powerful female figure.

Moreover, in the 1990s we also saw how the influence of a more experimental and playful approach to epic narrative structure, which had distinguished such foreign epic miniseries as *Scenes from a Marriage*, *Berlin Alexanderplatz*, and *The Singing Detective*, exerted itself on epic miniseries being made for American television. Further, faith and a belief in matters of a spiritual nature accounted for the transcendental dimensions of the characters of Anna Madrigal in *Tales of the City* and the moral authority of Mother Abigail of *The Stand*. In other words, by the end of the 1990s the heroic formula became more inclusive, and the idea of epic narrative became considerably more experimental and flexible.

At the same time, in the waning decade of the 20th century and the advent of the 21st, there came the birth of what we shall refer to as a more radical world terrorism, culminating in the devastating attacks of September 11, 2001. In the aftermath of this cataclysmic event, a greater, more ruthless sense of American Empire was ultimately triggered, which soon led to an infinitely greater spread of a militaristic overstretch. Suddenly, new flames were being fanned from old, dying embers, for new purposes. Within this historical-cultural context disturbing revelations of the torture of prisoners in Iraq and Guantanamo were made public. Gruesome imagery of torture from Abu Ghraib Prison (of naked humans being sexually degraded, tortured, and beaten) recalled some of the more grisly Nazi imagery of *Holocaust* and *War and Remembrance*, combined with aspects of the edgier fascistic-sadomasochistic-influenced imagery of *Berlin Alexanderplatz* and *The Stand*. Such imagery rather ostentatiously begins to usher in a certain grandiose totalitarianism, which at times can even be a surprisingly ascetic vision, of what the future of the epic miniseries might be like in the 21st century. What is most distinctive for our purposes about this New Millennial vision is how much it resembles Susan Sontag's influential essay "Fascinating Fascism":

> Fascistic aesthetics ... flow from (and justly) a preoccupation with situations of control, submissive behavior, extravagant effort, and the endurance of pain; they endorse two seemingly opposite states, egomania and servitude. The relations of domination and enslavement take the form of a characteristic pageantry: the massing of groups of people; the turning of people into things, the multiplication or replication of things; and the grouping of people/things around an all-powerful, hypnotic leader-figure or force. The fascist dramaturgy centers on the orgiastic transactions between mighty forces and their puppets, uniformly garbed and shown in ever swelling numbers. Its choreography alternates between ceaseless motion and a congealed, static, "virile" posing. Fascist art glorifies surrender, it exalts mindlessness; it glamorizes death.[1]

Some examples of this more aggressive New Millennial development include the following epic miniseries: *Perfect Murder, Perfect Town* (CBS, 2000), a tabloid re-telling of the brutal sexual violation and murder of hyper-fetishized Baby Beauty Queen, JonBenét Ramsey; *American Tragedy* (CBS, 2000), a detailed examination of the behind-the-scenes wheeling-and-dealing of O.J. Simpson's famous "Dream Team" of powerful lawyers who succeeded in their quest to get him off an infamous double-murder charge; *Frank Herbert's "Dune"* (SciFi, 2000), a visionary epic tale of messianic hero Paul Atreides (Alec Newman) and his fight for power, aided by his Avenging Angel mother, Lady Jessica (Saskia Reeves), on the planet Dune; *Attila* (USA, 2001), the mythic quest for dominance over imperialistic Rome by Attila, King of the Huns (Gerard Butler); and *Hitler: The Rise of Evil* (CBS, 2003), which explores the bloodthirsty rise to power of the young Adolf Hitler in his power-hungry years before World War II. Each of these New Millennial texts employs elements of fascistic imagery for a variety of purposes, and in each we witness the same sort of things occurring. What this amounts to is the reiteration of some essential aspect of the fascistic aesthetic: the ruthless subordination of the powerless individual to the harsh grueling dictates of a cruel symbolic order of power, control, and authority, to project the expression of some cruel, inherently malevolent vision.

Still, as a means of combating and repudiating some of the more negative claims put forth by this New Millennial agenda, there is a continual reliance upon the mythic figure of the Avenging Angel. That said, it should next be pointed out that with the arrival of the 21st century we also begin to witness the nature of the mythic figure growing more complex and ambiguous. As a result, the Avenging Angel will sometimes appear indifferent, baffled, and even accusatory. The three epic miniseries analyzed in this chapter—*From the Earth to the Moon* (HBO, 1998), *The 10th Kingdom* (NBC, 2000), and *Angels in Amer-*

ica (HBO, 2003) — provide examples of all three viewpoints. Yet whatever the specifics or the ambivalence expressed, the Avenging Angel cannot be completely denied. True, there might be those occasions when the mythic type appears to be down for the count, but in the final analysis, pain, terror, misery, and dominance are no real match for the timeless vision of grace, beauty, rationality, and the eternal order that is the type of the Avenging Angel of the Epic Miniseries Pantheon.

From the Earth to the Moon

HBO's initial foray into the realm of the epic miniseries came in 1984 with the broadcasts of the eight-hour saga set in turn-of-the-century Australia, *All the Rivers Run*, and the six-hour adaptation of *The Far Pavilions*, set within the imperialism of British colonial India in the 19th century. However, the mighty cable giant would not score its mightiest epic miniseries success until the 1998 broadcast of *From the Earth to the Moon*.

From the Earth to the Moon begins in 1961 with Soviet Russia becoming the first of the world superpowers to launch a man into space. Riding high on a jingoistic wave of the anti–Communist sentiment of the times, President John F. Kennedy pledges that America will better Russia, landing a man on the Moon by the end of the 1960s. The Mercury Program is launched with Freedom 7 taking Astronaut Alan Shepard (Ted Levine) into outer space. Bolstered by this success, NASA readies to make good on Kennedy's bold promise to the nation. But in 1967, during a routine test for the flight of Apollo 1, tragedy strikes. A small electrical fire quickly explodes into a raging inferno, killing all three of the astronauts — Gus Grissom (Mark Rolston), Ed White (Chris Isaak), and Roger Chaffee (Ben Marley) — inside the space capsule. In the aftermath of the tragedy, America mourns for the dead astronauts' three young widows — Betty Grissom (Ruth Reid), Pat White (Jo Anderson), and Martha Chaffee (Rhoda Griffis) — and their fatherless children.

A year later, the outpouring of grief subsides. Three new astronauts — Wally Shirra (Mark Harmon), Don Eisele (John Mese), and Walt Cunningham (Fredric Lehne) — are successfully launched into space in Apollo 7. In 1968, the Russians announce plans to send a man to the Moon. Not to be out-done, America hurriedly readies the launch of Apollo 8 for lunar orbit. But this frantic activity takes a tremendous toll on astronauts Frank Borman (David Andrews), Jim Lovell (Tim Daly), and Bill Anders (Robert John Burke), as well as Borman's loyal wife, Susan (Rita Wilson). Fortunately, Apollo 8 succeeds.

Then, the culmination of the Space Program occurs on July 20, 1969, when the crew of Apollo 11 — Neil Armstrong (Tony Goldwyn), Edward "Buzz" Aldrin (Bryan Cranston), and Michael Collins (Cary Elwes) — fulfill President Kennedy's great dream of reaching the Moon. As Armstrong takes his legendary

"One small step for man ... one giant leap for mankind," billions watch on the Earth below.

In comparison to Apollo 11, most of the other missions to the Moon seem anti-climactic. These include the comedic mishaps of Astronauts Al Bean (David Foley), Peter Conrad (Paul McCrane), and Dick Gordon (Tom Verica) of Apollo 12; the ill-fated Apollo 13; the more successful Apollo 14, with astronauts Alan Shepard (Ted Levine), Edgar Mitchell (Gary Cole), and Gene Cernan (David Hugh Kelly); the equally successful Apollo 15, which results in the most thorough geological study of the Moon's surface; and in 1972, the last voyage to the Moon by Astronauts Cernan and Harrison "Jack" Schmitt (Tom Amandes) is juxtaposed against filmmaker Georges Méliès (Tchéky Karyo) and his loyal assistant Jean-Luc Despont (Tom Hanks) making the phantasmagorical film classic *Le voyage dans la lune* in the Paris of 1902 about a mythic trip to the Moon.

The vision of America in *From the Earth to the Moon* is of a clean-living, flag-waving, Bible-touting, hermetically sealed-off, picture-postcard earthly paradise. America is ruled over by strong, heroic White men. Accordingly, it is a space of hyper-masculine phallocentricity. This is signified by the large white classic columns holding up the White House — one of the premier symbols of American might. It is also signified by all the upward-thrusting of the phallic-shaped rocket ships that transport the virile American astronauts into the farthest reaches of outer space. These Apollonian alpha males are a privileged lot indicative of a particular, clean-cut, all–American, heterosexual, WASP archetype. And yes, they also have their fair share of what Tom Wolfe famously refers to as "The Right Stuff." They use their considerable manly courageousness to express their version of the American Will in the New Age of Aquarius. Their unique mythic quest is directed toward the great scientific unknown. In this, there is a strong transcendent quality to the achieving of their final goal. The pastoral nature of Emerson, Thoreau, Melville, and Whitman is projected onto an even greater cosmic scale. In their mythic quest to reach the Moon, perhaps these men believe they are bringing themselves closer to God, or maybe even becoming a bit God-like themselves.

In opposition to this, Norman Mailer describes these astronauts differently. He critically describes them as WASPs, but with Nazi-like brains, who like Dorf in *Holocaust* invent a euphemistic language all their own:

> The use of "we" was discouraged. "A joint exercise has demonstrated" became the substitution. "Other choices" become "peripheral secondary objectives." "Doing our best" was "obtaining maximum advantage possible." "Confidence" became "very high confidence level." "Ability to move" was a "mobility study." "Turn off" was "disable"; "turn on" became "enable."[2]

Still, with all their hyper-masculine-muscularity, their firm-fitting, futuristic-looking silvery space suits, their private, manly language, their sheer American stick-to-it-iveness, they are one impressive-looking lot who inspire total awe in all varieties of the Other (i.e., Blacks, Jews, gays, ethnics, women). Then again, these astronauts are meant to be the late 1990s and early 2000s version of the mythic type of the Adventurer. After all, they all firmly believe in the impossible, the exploration of the unknown, and the idea of the heroic romantic quest as great American Archetype on a cosmogonic scale.

Fittingly, the object toward which all this testosterone-fueled, alpha-male energy is directed is that most mysterious of femininely celestial bodies—the Dionysian Moon. As depicted in *From the Earth to the Moon*, the Man in the Moon is, just as in Jerry Herman's great Broadway musical hit *Mame* (1966), most decidedly a Lady. Like Anna Madrigal and Mother Abigail, the Moon is also very much an enigmatic feminine presence in possession of all sorts of otherworldly powers. This is precisely why all of the highly mentally and physically fit, scientifically adroit alpha males are united in their virile quest to conquer, calm, and claim the Moon for their own: she is the Eternal Female to their collective male frenzy and desire.

Sometimes the Moon's otherworldliness is depicted as enticingly dreamy. At those times she seems to exist in an alluring outer-spatial realm of delicious solitude that is all her own. She is, first and foremost, a symbol of the feminine (as opposed to the masculine symbols of the Sun and Earth). Further, the Moon controls the tide with her cyclical time of repetition and return. Her very iconographic roundness is full and complete, like the perfect circle of the feminine. This naturally puts the Moon in eternal conflict with the mathematical exactitude of the male-dominated Earth, with its linear sense of time and space and history and its utopian aspirations towards progress. On Earth, we see that all is sharp right angles and hierarchical permanence: the geometrical precision of the phallic-shaped NASA rocket ships, the clarity, order, and proportion of scientific equations, the Absolutist linearity of the formalistic projections of the labyrinths of the patriarchal passageways of power, shooting forever forward into the far distance. In dialectical opposition (which we have by now come to expect from the epic miniseries) to the Apollonian rigidity and geometrical precision and perfection of the Earth, there is the unruly Dionysian glory of the Moon. The Earth's "inner" spaces give way to the Moon's "outer" spaces, in which all is the chthonian obfuscation of non-geometrical chaos and disorder. To the ancient Babylonians, the moon was "The Queen of the Night," with all her secret powers that far exceeded those of the Sun, and reduced the Earth to a mere enfeebled stepchild.

In this same context, the Moon is then both cold and vengeful but also a fruitful goddess. She is Ishtar and Isis, healing yet demanding sacrifices to bestow her bounty. Like a large, milky-white pearl, she sails through inky black skies in all her awesome majesty, looking for hot male lovers to join her in blood, lust, and death. Like Cybele and Artemis, the Moon demands that her holy priests castrate themselves and offer up their lopped-off genitalia to prove their love of her. Further, the Moon is an enchantress like Circe, and all those alpha males who seek her often-fickle favor are so many spellbound sailors lusting after her to their inevitable doom upon the gnashing shoals of actual experience.

While the ancient Babylonians viewed the Moon as a symbol for the Great Mother, her Garboesque self-consciousness reduces all male Earthlings to so many blabbering fools. The first Earth male in *From the Earth to the Moon* reduced to such a state is President Kennedy (and considering his reputation as a Devil-may-care ladies' man, there is a certain logic to this). Unfortunately, he is shot down by a lunatic (a word, incidentally, derived from the Latin *luna*, "moon") in Dallas in 1963 and never gets to see America successfully land the first man on the Moon. But even the death of the President cannot deter all the alpha males of NASA from making his promise to the American people a shining reality, no matter the cost. Our first real indication of just how high that cost will be comes when astronauts Gus Grissom, Ed White, and Roger Chaffee are all burned to death when a routine test leads to a fatal disaster. And even though an entire nation mourns, the young widows grieve, and the children weep for their dead fathers, the Moon shows no emotion. As in Oscar Wilde's *outré* play *Salomé*, the Oscar Wildean Moon simply looks down upon it all from a far-off distance in cool detachment, "looking only for dead things."

There are times when the mise-en-scène of *From the Earth to the Moon* depicts the Moon as a silvery, luminous orb glowing in a limitless star-filled nighttime sky, like a perfect mythic circle, birth-life-death, the cycle-upon-cycle-upon-cycle of the infinitesimal External Return, without beginning or end. What care the Moon for all those foolish alpha males of Earth desperately seeking her fickle favor? And what should she make of their ludicrous attempts to get beyond themselves, always attempting to project themselves beyond the here and now into the vast spatiality, infinity, and immortality of the cosmic realm that is her domain? Yet even though she may care nothing for them, that is all the more the alpha males of Earth try to conquer and possess her. She is the elusive goddess of the eternal hunt they are forever attempting to capture.

Following the deaths of Grisson, White, and Chaffee, precautions are taken still to make good on President Kennedy's promise. Astronauts Frank Borman, Jim Lovell, and William Anders safely reach the Moon and make history when they actually remain in orbit and become the first three Earth men to look upon her elusive face close-up. But somewhat ungallantly, they describe the Moon as a "vast, lonely, forbidding-looking place ... a gaping expanse of total nothingness." In comparison, they view the Earth as a Rousseauvian paradisiacal oasis of bounty that its habitants must view with pride. This dialectic between Earth and Moon is visually depicted in the standard trope of the epic miniseries: as a system of binary opposites. Thus, the Earth is a presence; the Moon is an absence. As the Apollo 8 spacecraft orbits the Moon, the high-contrast, black-and-white imagery reveals an austere space set against a grim nighttime sky. And there, off in the far distance, is the luminous brilliance of the Earth, giving off a spectacular golden glow. Amazingly, the imperious Moon does not strike down these audacious astronauts for their impertinence to her. Could her reticence toward them be based on some commendable sense of solidarity for their wives, her Earthly sisters?

Like so many anxious Penelopes, the wives of the astronauts are forced to wait in unendurable patience as their Adventurer astronaut husbands go off satisfying their collective wanderlust. Of course sometimes a wife's wait ends badly. Betty Grissom, Pat White, and Martha Chaffee wait only to learn they have become young widows. So affected is Susan Borman by this ordeal, she actually prepares her own husband's eulogy when she learns there is a possibility the Apollo 8 might never make it back to Earth. The astronaut wives recall Julie in *Rich Man, Poor Man*, in the mode of prized trophy wife of the superrich Rudi Jordache. As with Julie, these wives are also always expected to project a perfect image of impeccably groomed feminine grace whatever pressures they are under. The moment a woman becomes an astronaut wife, she forfeits all claims to her privacy. She becomes a perfect, high-fashion mannequin to be paraded before the nation. In his 1979 book *The Right Stuff*, Tom Wolfe says of Betty Grissom that she was forced to learn to make heavy sacrifices "more frequently and live in depressing exhausted houses ... and always live with the very real fact that at any given moment there was an astonishingly good chance that her husband might be killed, *just like that*."[3] What Wolfe says of Betty Grissom's experience holds equally true of all the other waiting astronaut wives. The whole time, deep in her heart of hearts, an astronaut wife knows that if presented with a choice her foolish astronaut husband would throw her off for the Moon in a heartbeat. Although the Astronaut wives are, like their husbands, an aggregate of collective will — they signify a total female will as opposed to the collective male will of NASA. There's even a curious scene when a golden wedding ring is taken off an astronaut husband's finger and left to float off into deep space, far away from the vow of Holy Matrimony he once gave to his wife.

From the Earth to the Moon uses all five categories of intertextuality to an exceptional degree. An example of celebrity intertextuality is introduced in the person of superstar Tom Hanks, along with Ron Howard and Brian Grazer, all of whom were responsible for *Apollo 13* (Ron Howard, 1995), acting as executive producers for the epic miniseries. In addition, Hanks acts as the host, introduces each episode, directs the opening episode, takes an active hand in the writing of several episodes, and assumes the role of the assistant to director Méliès in the final fantastical episode. Genetic intertextuality is seen with the casting of Hanks's wife Rita Wilson in the stand-out role of Susan Borman, and with Sally Field, his close friend and leading lady in several films, who directs the eleventh episode and appears in the role of astronaut wife Trudy Cooper.

Intertextuality is most evident in the episode dramatizing the ill-fated mission of Apollo 13, in which Hanks played astronaut Jim Lovell and uttered the now famous line, "Houston, we have a problem...." On another level, this self-conscious reference back to the success of Apollo 13 also serves as an autocitation in the way it refers back to the earlier famed space movie of Hanks, Howard, and Grazer.

The trope of pseudo-intertextuality occurs throughout the epic narrative with the extensive use made of Lane Smith as television newscaster Emmett Seaborn, who with his continuous reporting on the events of the Apollo mission often acts as a one-man Greek chorus. Smith's character is presented in pseudo-television broadcasts, which create a constant flow of doubling-back references to the events that are depicted on screen. Another example of this same sort of pseudo-intertextuality is seen in the marvelously inspired and painstakingly detailed re-creation of *Le voyage dans la lune* in the concluding episode.

While the astronauts of the Apollo Moon Mission depicted certainly do possess their fair share of "The Right Stuff," as did those of the Mercury Project, there is something different between the two crews. Those of the Apollo mission lack the sort of subversive, individualistic spiritedness that informed those earlier astronauts. Instead, we notice more of a uniformity at play. For Mailer, this uniforming development came with some negative connotations. He believed it transformed the Apollo Moon Mission astronauts into interchangeable parts in a great authoritarian machine and stripped them of personality, autonomy, and individuality. But to temper the potential danger of this effect, although the television-makers do indeed move the emphasis away from the concept of the romantic solitary heroic figure (exemplified in the type of the Adventurer), they tactfully shift it toward the paradigm of the achievement of the heroic collective. Therefore, the combined excellence of the team, the crew, the group, and the mission itself matters infinitely more than that of any one individual.[4]

The emphasis on the idea of the group working toward the common good leads to other significant changes. There is an idea at play of epic narrative starting to grow out of itself. In other words, epic narrative is beginning to generate more epic narrative. The key to this process lies in the concept of a post-modern sense of epic narrative responding to a broader social-political-cultural sense of purpose (the process reaches its apotheosis in *Angels in America*). There is additionally a movement away from a more tightly structural narrative fixedness toward relativity, a rejection of a traditionally stable form leading to a much looser, more stream-of-consciousness fluidity and indeterminacy (as was superbly achieved in *Berlin Alexanderplatz* and *The Singing Detective*), a moving away from straightforwardness toward a genre better able to reflect the regions of the unconscious and unknown of a new century. Perhaps a traditional, fixed sense of epic narrative is no longer appropriate for the epic tales that need to be told at the end of one century and the start of another.

A striking effect of this process is the way a character previously kept in the background in one part of the epic narrative suddenly moves into the foreground, only to return later to the background again, or else to be brought forward again as needed. Two examples of this occur with the characters of Alan Shepard and Susan Borman. We are first introduced to Shepard at the start of the epic narrative when he is chosen as the first astronaut to venture into outer space. But because of a chronic inner-ear disorder, he is grounded for a ten-year period and virtually dropped from the epic narrative. Then, after undergoing an experimental ear operation and grueling physical therapy, he returns to the foreground again in time to live out his life-long dream of traveling to the Moon. The real beauty of this epic narrative fluidity is the way it allows various elements of the complex epic storyline to jump back and forth in time and place as a means of providing essential information needed for audiences to appreciate the full breadth of Shepard's final accomplishment.[5]

In like fashion, Susan Borman plays a major role in the fourth episode, only to disappear from view, and then reappear as part of the female ensemble of the eleventh episode, which examines the difficult role the astronaut wives have to play. The narrative complexities of this episode make it the most ingeniously conceived and strikingly designed of the entire epic miniseries. Beginning with a posh NASA fashion show, each of the wives, radiating a luminous high glamorousness, models the very latest of 1960s haute couture. As each wife makes her way down the fashion runway, the epic narrative shifts fluidly back and forth in time and space, unveiling the details of each woman's personal experience. We learn, for instance, the devastating toll the untimely death of Ed White had on his wife, Pat, and their children. Believing with some justification that the NASA community is no longer interested in her without her husband, Pat cuts all ties. Growing increasingly depressed, she turns to pills and alcohol for comfort, and eventually commits suicide. The pressure of being the "perfect" astronaut wife also takes quite a toll on Susan Borman. Like Pat, she also turns to alcohol. However, unlike Pat, she seeks help and is eventually cured of her addiction. In a final ironic note, we learn that Susan's marriage to Frank is one of the very few NASA marriages that does not end in personal disillusionment and bitter divorce.

But even with the emphasis on the heroic-group dynamic and a more fluid style of epic narrative, there is no denying the fact that there are still those privileged moments when it is necessary for the epic narrative to highlight the singular power of one heroic individual acting in the historical Now. We saw examples of this with Susan Borman's story, and also with Alan Shepard's taking command of Apollo 14. Then, of course, there is the defining moment of July 29, 1969, when Neil Armstrong becomes the first man ever to walk on the Moon. Because of the historic monumentality of the event and its canonical place in the history of epic narrative, we shall conclude our discussion with a reading of the way the canonical tropes of mise-en-scène and music are employed to make the "Moonwalk" sequence the indisputable high point of the entire epic narrative.

The tour-de-force sequence begins with Armstrong and Aldrin inside the space capsule thanking God for their safe arrival to the Moon. The shiny surfaces of the interior of the space capsule surrounding the Astronauts give the mise-en-scène a lustrous metallic sheen. As the men pray, the music takes on the quality of a celestial liturgy. A choir of hushed voices is heard, signifying the awesome religious, transcendent nature of what is taking place on screen. Then, when Armstrong begins his descent from the space module, his movements are slow and sluggish. It is as if he is entering an imaginary dream space. There is a cut to NASA headquarters, where all of the other alpha males of Earth gaze up in utter amazement at a giant television screen. In the grainy black-and-white imagery of the television, Armstrong's descent is seen in colossal dimensions. The hushed solemnity of the choir singing gradually subsides, and the music shifts into an exuberant, fully orchestral sound, similar to the theme music at the beginning of each episode. The force of the music continues to swell until it becomes a triumphant symphonic fanfare, aurally reflecting every aspect of the epic action on screen. Upon reaching the Moon's surface, Armstrong describes it as being fine and powdery, which corrects what the crew of the Apollo 8 had said earlier. With Armstrong standing on the Moon's surface, the camera expands out from a close-up to a stunning long shot. A solitary expanse of lunar landscape, devoid of any signs of life, yet still eerily beautiful, stretches out, far off into the distance.[6] The camera slowly pans upward offering a majestic vista of the star-filled, pitch-dark sky. Armstrong gazes up into the sky at the transfixing sight of the Earth in the distance.

At this point, Aldrin joins Armstrong. Together they praise the stark, minimalistic beauty of the Moon. With the raising of the American flag, the Moon is declared a place of magnificent desolation, but also of terrifying glory and ambivalent beauty. Finally, the alpha males of the planet Earth get it. In rendering unto the Moon what is only her proper due — honor, respect, fear, awe — they will not have to discover if the power of her avenging wrath is as imposing as her magnificent desolation.

The 10th Kingdom

The wrath of the Moon in *From the Earth to the Moon* is relatively tame in comparison to that of the Evil Queen (Diane Wiest) in *The 10th Kingdom*. Understandably, Prince Wendell (Daniel Lapaine) makes a special point of going to the prison, where she has been confined for the rest of her unnatural life, to deny her request for parole. At the same time, Relish the Troll King (Ed O'Neill) is at the prison to free his three obnoxious Troll children: Burly (Hugh O'Gorman), Blabberwort (Dawnn Lewis), and Bluebell (Jeremiah Birkett). In the process, Relish also frees the Evil Queen. After the Trolls attack Prince Wendell, the Evil Queen casts a spell on him: he and a dog named Prince switch bodies. After escaping, Prince jumps through the Magic Mirror, winding up in the cosmopolitan "10th Kingdom" (aka New York City). The Evil Queen sends the three troll children and Wolf (Scott Cohen), a half-man half-wolf, to recapture Prince. But Virginia Lewis (Kimberly Williams), a confused young woman, and her unhappy father Tony (John Larroquette), follow Prince back to his world through the Magic Mirror.

Virginia, Tony, Wolf (who has fallen in love with Virginia), and Prince set out on a mythic quest to find the Magic Mirror to return them home. At the same time, the Evil Queen hatches an evil plot to use the dog she has transformed into Prince Wendell to destroy the House of White and gain total control the Nine Kingdoms. As Virginia and her friends continue on their quest, they face many trials and tribulations based on several famous fairy-tales: Virginia's hair grows to Rapunzel-length; she enters a shepherding contest against the saucy Sally Peep, a direct descendent of Little Bo Peep; Tony acquires the Golden Touch and turns Prince into solid gold; and when the Magic Mirror accidentally shatters, Snow White (Camryn Manheim) gifts Virginia with a new Magic Mirror, informing her that her fate and that of the Nine Kingdoms are interwoven together.

With the Magic Mirror of Snow White, Virginia discovers that the Evil Queen is the mother who had abandoned her in childhood. After much effort, Virginia and her friends arrive at the castle where the Evil Queen plans to have the fake Prince Wendell crowned King. Among the illustrious guests attending the lavish coronation celebration are Queen Red Riding Hood III (Kim Thomson), the King of the Elves (Chris Cooks), and the incredibly well-preserved, 200-year-old Cinderella (Ann-Margret). When Virginia and Tony find out the Evil Queen plans to poison all the guests, they vow to stop her. A confrontation between the Evil Queen and Virginia ends with the daughter having to kill the mother in self-defense with the Poison Comb. Prince Wendell is reunited with his body and crowned King. While Tony decides to stay on in the Nine Kingdoms, Virginia (who is pregnant with a "wolf-cub") and her beloved Wolf return home to New York City.

The 10th Kingdom offers an example of the epic miniseries in the form of a fairy-tale fantasy mythic quest that ends in transcendence. However, when it was first broadcast, critics and audiences responded none too favorably. What they failed to realize at the time is that *The 10th Kingdom* required one to make an adjustment away from the classic epic miniseries of the Golden Age, toward something new and different. The best way to appreciate the text is to focus on the way its many, often ironic and parodic references to famous fairy-tales operate.

Several of these references are cleverly interwoven into the 10-hour-long epic structure. We are presented with such well-known fairy-tale immortals as

Snow White, Cinderella, King Midas, and the descendants of Little Bo Peep and Little Red Riding Hood. There are also multiple references and allusions made to several other famous fairy tales, like *Rapunzel, Sleeping Beauty, Goldilocks and the Three Bears,* and *The Emperor's New Clothes*. And like any good fairy-tale, there is a dark element of savage realism and naked horror to the text. When taken together, all these references, allusions, and darker elements appear in one form or another, serving as so many adjuncts to the central mythic quest of the principals—Virginia, Tony, Wolf, and Prince. While all this is happening on one level, there is a whole other level of story and meaning gradually being added to the epic narrative. The full impact of this process only becomes fully apparent in the final two hours of *The 10th Kingdom*. This is precipitated by Virginia's understanding that the true nature of her mythic quest is quite different from what she had at first believed it to be.

Out of all these developments, an intricately plotted epic miniseries for the New Millennium results. It is humorous and playful, satirical and farcical, campy and deadly serious, fantastical and even complex when it needs to be. In particular, many scenes utilize several of these elements at the same time. When the lascivious Wolf is first shown a picture of Virginia he is totally baffled: He can't figure out whether he wants to make love to her or eat her. (Although he does get to try to cook her campy New York high-society grandmother.) While the three grotesque troll children hunt down Tony and Virginia to kill them, they do so to the infectious beat of the Bee Gees musical soundtrack from *Saturday Night Fever* (John Badham, 1977), which constantly plays from the CD player they steal from Virginia and believe to be a potent magic box. Since it is so multi-faceted, deepens in its final hours, and has been assembled with a smooth-as-silk-mechanical expertise (and even ends with a 21st century version of "They-all-lived-happily-ever-after" Hollywood-like finish), *The 10th Kingdom* concludes on a satisfying, affirmative note.

It was Freud who put forward the idea of interpreting the deeper, darker aspects of fairy tales psychologically, and Bruno Bethleheim who provided one of the most authoritative texts on the subject with *The Uses of Enchantment: The Meaning and Importance of Fairytales*.[7] However, for the most part, the psychological implications in *The 10th Kingdom* are implicit rather than explicit (with the exception of Virginia's relationship to the Evil Queen). Therefore, they never really get in the way or complicate the swift-moving epic narrative all that much. Since the main emphasis is on the tropes of style and fantastical mise-en-scène, it is essential that such psychological implications be handled lightly, and only grow and deepen in a gradual way.

A good example of how this technique works comes in the way the relationship between Virginia and Wolf is developed. Initially, Wolf is presented as a comical figure (his satyrical behavior around beautiful women makes it easy to understand how he got his name). Yet Wolf is also capable of surprising paradoxes. Take the scene when he attempts to smooth-talk the reluctant, virginal Virginia (hence her name) into stroking his big, thick, bushy tail, which Virginia does with a neat Freudian touch.[8]

In a sublimely ribald scene such as the one of his getting Virginia to engage in a little tail-stroking foreplay, Wolf signifies a phallic form of existence, pure and simple. But since Wolf is not a static figure (as the Evil Queen appears to be), he gradually begins to display "an ambivalence about whether to live by the pleasure principle or the reality principle."[9] His ambivalence ultimately leads to his acquiring a greater understanding between the two. By choosing the former, Wolf will doubtlessly receive instant gratification. But choosing the latter leads to his moral growth, deeper happiness, and final transcendence, not only for himself, but for Virginia as well. This point is restated when Wolf declares his deep love for Virginia, and moves from a phallic to a more intimate form of relating to her.

When Wolf asks Virginia for her hand in marriage, he goes out of his way to create the ultimate romantic evening. This involves his purchase of the valuable Magical Singing Ring as an engagement present for her. It consists of a lively pearl that spins joyously through the air while singing of Wolf's love. But the Ring is only one of the many magical motifs incorporated into the fantasy structure of the epic narrative. Other magical motifs include the Magical Mirror, the Magical Golden Key that frees Tony from prison, the Magical Golden Touch that turns Prince into gold, the Poison Apple the Evil Queen uses to kill her enemies, the Magical Bird that guides Virginia and friends out of the Enchanted Forest, and the Poison Comb the Evil Queen uses to kill Virginia, to name a few.

Along with drawing upon the magical motifs of so many famous fairy tales, *The 10th Kingdom* utilizes the tropes of music, mise-en-scène, lavish spectacle, various forms of intertextuality, and the dialectical opposition of good/evil, light/dark, and passive/active. Since the central focus of the epic narrative ultimately revolves around the primal conflict between Virginia and the Evil Queen, we will next consider the way these tropes are used to delineate each of their characters. Like Natalie in *The Winds of War* and *War and Remembrance*, Virginia is a version of the Contemporary Untyped Woman. Except in her case, there is a certain level of psychological unfullfilment in evidence. While she is engaged in the mythic quest for the Magical Mirror, Virginia learns that the nature of her real quest is the Eternal Return, what Nietzsche referred to as the circularity of all ethical experience. However, in the case of *The 10th Kingdom*, the object of the Eternal Return is the Great Mother.

Virginia does not fully understand what she is searching for until she encounters Snow White. Music, mise-en-scène, epic televisual spectacle, and intertextuality are employed to reinforce the scene's dramatic import. Astonished by her discovery, Virginia happens upon a big white space that looks like something out of an Andersen fairy tale. Constructed out of ice and snow, the white-on-white space is illuminated in brilliant high-key lighting, which creates a soft glossy sheen. It is here Virginia comes upon the lifeless body of Snow White encased in a coffin of solid ice. As Virginia approaches the coffin, Snow White, dressed in a luminous white gown and black corset, magically rises from the dead. Her cherry-red lips provide the only touch of real color to the mise-en-scène.[10]

With the casting of the opulently zaftig Camryn Manheim as the traditionally svelte Snow White, a humorous note of celebrity intertextuality is added to the scene. Similarly humorous is the casting of the eternally youthful-looking Ann-Margret as the eternally youthful-looking 200-year-old Cinderella, and that of Diane Wiest—who became famous for playing intensely neurotic modern-day New Yorkers in the films of Woody Allen—as Virginia's intensely neurotic New York Mother, who later becomes the intensely psychotic Evil Queen. A complex instance of self-referential intertextuality involves Snow White telling Virginia her life story, concluding with her being poisoned by her evil stepmother, which closely parallels the circumstances of Virginia's own life.

Virginia's encounter with Snow White also serves to put into sharper focus that of all the fairy tales utilized, it is the story of Snow White that mainly influences the epic narrative. Principally, this is signified in the depiction of the narcissistic Evil Queen of *Snow White*. Consumed with jealousy over her younger, more beautiful stepdaughter, she commands that the hunter murder the girl. But in *The 10th Kingdom*, the old tale is given a modern twist: The Evil Queen is the heroine's mother and intends to kill her own daughter herself.

Hence, all of the darker elements running through the epic narrative coalesce around the problematic figure of the Evil Queen. She is Darkness seeking Darkness. She can love only herself. She can only plot, dominate, destroy, poison and bend all those around her to her own dark will. This makes her an Avenging Angel on a twisted, nihilistic course of total dominance and annihilation. Like Mary Carey in *The Thorn Birds*, the Evil Queen is also the possessor of real phallic power. This phallic scenario is signified by the hard-edged allure of the powerful Magical Mirror, inherited from Snow White's evil stepmother, which the Queen is forever gazing into. Whenever she does this, the Evil Queen is "fixated to a primitive narcissism ... and makes clear her identity as a woman who cannot positively relate, nor can anybody positively identify with her."[11]

For Freud, the intense pleasure derived from looking (scopophilia) is ultimately connected to sexual desire, which he believed to be just as powerful in the female as the male. But since looking is traditionally equated with active maleness, the passive female is forced to repress scopophilic desire through marriage and learn to look away. As a corollary to this, Laura Mulvey argues it is the male hero who is the active controller of fantasy, and so controls the power of the look. Active scopophilia and even sadism become aligned with the male who traditionally controls the course of both the gaze and epic narrative. As a result, the female comes to be "coded for strong visual and erotic impact so that she connotes to-be-looked-at-ness."[12]

But of course in *The 10th Kingdom*, it is the Evil Queen who controls the gaze. Through the power of her Magical Mirror, she controls not only the look, but also the drive that is the active source of its energy — the libido. Since there is no other character in *The 10th Kingdom* anywhere near as powerful, active, and controlling as the Evil Queen, the continuance of the Nine Kingdoms depends solely upon her destruction. It falls upon Virginia, in the guise of the Avenging Angel, to put an end to the Evil Queen's reign, assuring the safety of the Nine Kingdoms and the royal House of White.

Virginia's first indication of the importance of the role she will ultimately play occurs when Snow White tells her that her fate and that of the Nine Kingdoms are inextricably interconnected. But when Virginia first learns the true identity of the evil Queen, she cannot accept it. Is this vicious woman the same unnatural mother who tried to drown her in the bathtub as a seven-year-old child? When she does accept the awful truth, Virginia firmly believes she can perhaps reason with this mad woman, her own mother. If she herself has been transformed in this Magical Land, from ugly duckling to a beautiful Princess, perhaps it is possible for her mother to change as well. However, as Virginia's status rises, it is matched by the decline of the Evil Queen. With this Virginia eventually comes to displace the Evil Queen as the controller of the gaze. While Virginia does learn of the Evil Queen's "true" identity, the Queen does not learn that Virginia is her daughter. Further, it is only after she totally displaces the Evil Queen (the phallic mother) that both Virginia and the Nine Kingdoms are truly free.

With the killing of the Evil Queen, the male discourse that typically dominates epic narrative is displaced and superseded by one controlled by a young woman. In destroying the phallic mother, the conditions are put into place for Virginia herself to become the phallic mother. (Virginia is "phallic" for the epic narrative in that she is signified within pre–Oedipal relations.) However, when the pregnant Virginia decides to leave her father behind in the Nine Kingdoms and return back home to The 10th Kingdom of New York City with Wolf by her side, two things happen in congruence. First, she proves that her true personality has indeed been formed and her inner conflicts resolved. She is no longer the frightened little girl she once was whose mother tried to kill her. Now she has become her higher transcendent self. Fearless, brave, and dauntless, she has allowed love to blossom in her heart at last. She is finally ready to separate from the father and begin a new life. Second, she also proves she is the diametrical opposite of her mother. Whereas the mother is evil, the daughter is good; the mother is static, the daughter, dynamic; the mother cold, cruel, and unloving; the daughter warm, kind, and loving. Put simply, Virginia becomes the loving mother of every child's fairy-tale fantasy. And the epic tale ends happily ever after, after all.

In the end, *The 10th Kingdom* is a work whose meaning and method cohabit in a visionary epic space that reaches for the new heights of fantasy, mythic characterization, and otherworldly visual beauty started in the 1990s with such televisual texts as *Gulliver's Travels* (1996), *The Odyssey* (1997), and *Merlin* (1998). All of these qualities are carried over into the next and final text detailed in this study, the sublime *Angels in America* (HBO, 2003), one of the greatest visionary epic miniseries ever to have been financed for and broadcast on American television.

Angels in America

Playwright Tony Kushner's two-part epic play *Angels in America* is considered by many to be the greatest work of drama written by an American in the past thirty years. David Savaran says, "Not within memory has a new American play been canonized by the press as rapidly as *Angels in America*."[13] The tricky task of transforming Kushner's visionary theatrical masterpiece into an epic miniseries for television was eventually taken on by master filmmaker Mike Nichols. He assembled one of the most spectacular casts of actors ever to have appeared in an epic miniseries. Under his masterful direction, established superstars Al Pacino, Meryl Streep, Emma Thompson, and several younger, highly acclaimed New York stage actors—Mary-Louise Parker, Jeffrey Wright, Patrick Wilson, Ben Shenkman, Justin Kirk—formed a television dream cast in cable giant HBO's 2003 visionary epic miniseries.

The epic action begins in New York City in the 1980s. Louis (Ben Shenkman), an intensely neurotic, gay Jewish man, panics when he discovers his long-time lover, Prior Walter (Justin Kirk), has AIDS. As Prior's condition worsens, Louis withdraws even further from him. He also betrays Prior when he gets involved with reactionary, bi-sexual, Mormon law clerk Joe Pitt (Patrick Wilson). With this odd union, ultra-liberal gay New Yorker melds with arch–Conservative Mormon pseudo-straight who is married to the delusional, pill-popping Harper (Mary-Louise Parker) and works for proto-fascistic, closeted homosexual Roy Cohn (Al Pacino). When Louis can no longer deal with Prior's illness, he leaves him. After Joe leaves Harper, he and Louis move in together.

Virtually alone, except for visits from his kind-hearted, flamboyant, dragqueen caretaker, Belize (Jeffrey Wright), Prior is first visited by the ghosts of his ancestors—Prior Walter #1 (Michael Gambon) and Prior Walter #2 (Simon Callow)—who announce to him the coming of the magnificent Angel of America (Emma Thompson), who will inform Prior he has been chosen to become a Great Prophet. While also alone, Harper experiences ever more elaborate drug-induced hallucinations, in which she and her imaginary deceitful companion, Mr. Lies (Jeffrey Wright), travel to fantasy worlds together. In an attempt to save her son's shattered marriage, Joe's formidable, no-nonsense mother, Hannah (Meryl Streep), moves to New York from Salt Lake City and eventually befriends Prior. Meanwhile Cohn, who has also been diagnosed with AIDS, is hospitalized. His only companions are Belize and the ghost of Ethel Rosenberg (Meryl Streep), whom he had executed in the 1950s, along with her husband Julius, for high treason.

When Belize tells Louis that Joe works for Cohn, he confronts Joe. After a violent fight breaks out between them, Louis leaves Joe and attempts to reconcile with Prior. As the end of Cohn's life nears, Ethel informs him he has been disbarred and is no longer a lawyer. But after he dies, she, along with Louis, recites the Kaddish (the Jewish prayer for the dead) for him. Prior's situation turns out more positively. After having wild sex with and wrestling the Angel of America, he is allowed to enter Heaven. There, he convinces the Angels to bless him and grant him more life. Back on Earth, Prior forgives Louis, but tells him they can never be a couple again. A vibrant Hannah remains in New York. Harper leaves Joe and lights out for a mythic quest of her own across the spatial frontiers of America. But before she leaves, Harper hands Joe her pills and tells him to go off exploring somewhere or other. Although the AIDS epidemic continues, Prior vows to live on and do all he can to fight the devastating effects of AIDS.

Since limitations of time and space preclude the sort of real in-depth study an epic miniseries of the quality of *Angels in America* fully warrants, our focus will be primarily on the use of mise-en-scène, music, and a revolving series of famous guest stars in Nichols's adaptation. Attention will also be paid to the way the epic narrative uses the Avenging Angel (in the four characters of Streep's Hannah and Ethel Rosenberg, Kirk's Prior, and Thompson's Angel of America), various forms of intertextuality, and the way Pacino's proto-fascistic portrayal of Roy Cohn presents us with one of the all-time great larger-than-life evil villains of the Epic Miniseries Pantheon.

Nothing if not a study in sharp contrasts, Cohn first made his name in the early 1950s as the right-hand man of the infamous anti–Communist Joseph McCarthy, during the Senate investigations into the supposed Communist influence in America. Cohn was also highly instrumental in the trial and execution of Julius and Ethel Rosenberg for high treason. Although the broken and alcoholic McCarthy died ignobly in 1957, Cohn would go on to achieve considerable wealth and fame. But if his seemed a fairy-tale existence, there was a darker side as well. Cohn was a secret homosexual in private, even though he was vehemently anti-gay in public, and he was diagnosed with AIDS in the 1980s. (Cohn even pressured his physician into publicly stating that he had liver cancer, not AIDS.) Although he spent much of his life moving among the rich and powerful, in the last months of his life that he was disbarred and left to die alone. It is precisely at this point in his life that Ethel Rosenberg, in the form of the Avenging Angel, appears in the epic narrative. On their first encounter, Cohn says to Ethel, "I have forced my way into history. I ain't never gonna die." Then, when she triumphantly responds, "History is about to break wide open. Millennium approaches,"[14] the dialogical schematic of the epic narrative is firmly established.

Not surprisingly Kushner's depiction of Cohn is highly controversial. He is presented as a comic, larger-than-life figure, as vain and vindictive as Master Moore in *Roots* and Erik Dorf in *Holocaust*. But at the same time, Cohn is an actor, a poseur. He is a closeted homosexual. Thus he evidences the same sort of sexual degeneracy the figure of the Jew as Other is made to signify in the historical-sexual memory espoused by the Nazis in *Holocaust*. And even if Cohn is depicted as "almost Jacobean in his snarling and vigorous excesses,"[15] in spite of ourselves we find something oddly, subversively attractive, due to the sheer force of Pacino's electrifying and complex performance, about a character who is such an odd amalgamation of power, greed, and denial.

Whenever Ethel Rosenberg appears to Cohn, director of photography Stephen Goldblatt uses heightened color to achieve a stylized dialectic effect. For example, Ethel is usually bathed in an otherworldly, soft blue light, which connotes a higher mystical, spiritual realm. But for Cohn, the lighting and colors are broodingly dark, even when he and Ethel appear in the same epic frame. At times, this technique creates the sense that we are looking at solid blocks of pure color. Another example of this comes when the Angel of America first appears to Prior. While everything associated with Prior in the scene is dark and shadowy, the Angel towers above him in a radiant burst of golden intensity.

The same sense of epic sweep used to depict Ethel and the Angel of America gets carried over into the depiction of Hannah. When she leaves her pastoral Mormon home in Utah for the strange and forbidden environs of New York City, Hannah is a determined woman with an epic mission to perform. One way or another, she has set her steely resolve toward putting the broken pieces of her sexually confused son's failing marriage back together by any means possible. (At one point, she tells Harper that although life is terribly disappointing, through faith and hard work it can probably be made more bearable.) Visually, Goldblatt conveys this harder aspect of Hannah's character in the scene when she forces her way into Joe and Harper's dank, dark, unkempt apartment, jolting the epic frame with the illuminating white-heat of her eerie brand of commonsensical clarity. But of course, like Virginia in *The 10th Kingdom*, Hannah will undergo a great personal illumination and transcendence of her own, when she gets transformed, glorified, and magnified forever by the Angel of America.

With the mention of the transformational scenes, we must next speak of the overall technical expertise of the epic miniseries. Mike Nichols is a master of lyrical camera placement and movement within the epic frame. Consider, for instance, the scene in Prior's bedroom when the Angel of America hovers over him in long shot, while proclaiming her many commands to him. As she speaks, shots of her face in Olympian-sized close-ups looking down at Prior are contrasted with shots of him fearfully looking up at her in long shot, looking even smaller and all the more puny for it. But when she and the sexually aroused Prior come together in mid-air to "consummate" their spiritual connection (Prior gets aroused whenever the Angel comes near), the act is viewed in long shot again:

Avenging Angel V: The Ascension of the Angel of America (Emma Thompson). *Angels in America* (HBO, 2003).

Their clothing is burnt away in heavenly golden flames, which engulf both their nude bodies, as they wildly copulate in mid-air, making this, hands-down, the most memorable sex scene in the whole Epic Miniseries Pantheon.

All throughout the course of the epic narrative, the camera fluidly catches the most significant action and details we should see and know about. In another scene, Joe and Cohn are seated at the bar of a posh New York restaurant. While Joe goes on about his marital problems with Harper, the two men in medium shot are juxtaposed with lingering close-ups of Roy's hand seductively and aggressively massaging Joe's shoulder as he attempts to convince him to leave the increasingly unstable Harper. Then, with one breathtaking movement, the camera pulls back out of the posh interior and travels across the street past waiting horses and carriages as it plunges deeper and deeper into the shadowy underworld of Central Park at night. The colors grow dark and ominous, as the camera comes to a stop on the scene of Louis, having abandoned Prior for having AIDS, soliciting sex from a leather-clad, macho stranger.

Equally expert is the brilliant photography of Stephen Goldblatt. In the dazzlingly stylized dream/fantasy sequence in which Prior unexpectedly encounters the hallucinatory Harper, Goldblatt pays a special televisual homage to cinematographer Henri Alekan's Gustave Doré–like imagery from *Beauty and the Beast* (Jean Cocteau, 1946).[16] After falling asleep while reading a book about Cocteau's life, Prior finds himself dressed in full drag, plunged into a surrealistic black-and-white fantasy space, which has the curtained lighting of a Surrealist painting by Dali. Muscular arms holding candelabras jut out of the walls providing light, and marble statues with moving eyes follow whomever enters the magical space. When Harper announces to Prior that both she and her husband Joe are Mormons, he retorts that both he and her husband are homosexuals. Perhaps because she is in such an out-of-body, other-worldly dreamscape, Harper finds it easier to accept what she has realized intuitively all along. Fittingly, the remarkable sequence concludes with both Prior and Harper staring up intently at the monumental simplicity of the hemispheric dome as a white feather drifts gracefully down from the ceiling's round opening, announcing the coming of the Angel of America.

Afterward, whenever life becomes too much for Harper to bear, she usually escapes to a fantasy Antarctica of her own mind. Goldblatt's camera shows us a dazzling study of several shades of white-on-white, in which the white-clad bodies of Harper and her traveling companion, the deceitful Mr. Lies, cut a starkly imposing figure against a pale-blue ocean in the distance, thrillingly evoking both the art of the Impressionists and the Abstract Formalism of Russian Constructivists like Kandinsky and Malevich.

Even the musical score of composer Thomas Newman backs up and elaborates upon many of these same points. There is the scene when Prior fantasizes Louis has returned to him and the epic frame is transformed into a glowing Busby Berkeley–like movie musical set, complete with the two men dancing to the romantic theme song of *Breakfast at Tiffany's*, "Moon River" (Blake Edwards, 1961). Later, a spirited Black drag queen sings a lively spiritual with a Lena Horne–esque force at the Jean Genet–like funeral service for a famous New York drag queen who has died of AIDS. And Newman's main theme, with its haunting mix of loss and triumph, alternates masterfully between being almost too painfully brooding one moment, and impossibly, voluptuously beautiful the next.

In fact, Newman's music helps to reinforce the rhythmic resourceful-ness by which the various complex connections between all the characters are represented. In this music-like arrangement, we see an intricate Star of David–shaped dance configuration being created. As the various characters come together, separate, and go on to form new relationships, a fluid, waltz-like arrangement is established. It is the ambiguity of these different relational arrangements that provides *Angels* with its rich texture and music-like construction. This structure can be visualized as the positions and movements of the ten central characters on a dance floor; we see them as arranged in two concentric circles. In this arrangement, the "mortal" characters are on the outside, the four "immortals" or iconic figures on the inside. Fittingly, because of the dynamic, swirling properties of the waltz's unitary, one-to-a-bar meter, it has a long association with the idea of all life forming an uncontrolled Dionysian dance, which can further be depicted as a Dance in the arms of Death. This uncontrolled Dionysian Dance of Life and Death is visualized in 7.1:

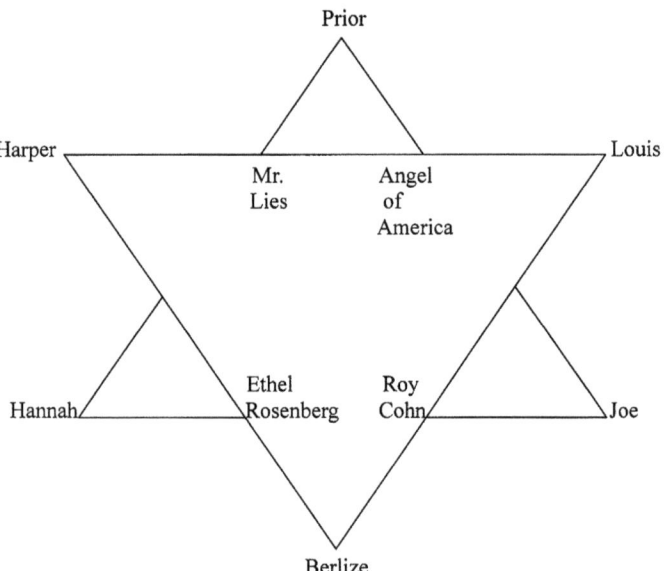

Diagram 7.1 — The Dionysian Dance of Life and Death of *Angels in America*.

Clearly then, there is so much taking place in *Angels*, it is impossible to grasp all of it in only one viewing. There are elements of symbolic visual and psychological geometry. For example, Prior unleashing the full wrath of his anger at Louis for abandoning him for having AIDS occurs simultaneously with the scene of Harper exploding at Joe for his callous neglect and betrayal of her. Both scenes combine to comment upon one another and form a psychological as well as a televisual triumph. Or there are other things like the way the codified trope of using a revolving set of guest stars is combined with the 1990s trope of intertextuality for an ironic and parodic effect (much as we saw happen in the likewise gay-themed *Tales of the City*).

Angels provides several examples of celebrity intertextuality with such iconic superstars as Streep, Pacino, and Thompson being used to evoke their personal connections to a certain cinematic milieu of the highest artistic caliber. Instances of auto-citation are present in the way Nichols casts Streep and Thompson in leading roles. Both actresses are closely connected to his acclaimed cinematic oeuvre. Streep was his leading lady in the films *Silkwood* (1983), *Heartburn* (1986), and *Postcards from the Edge* (1990). Thompson starred in his *Primary Colors* (1998) and the superb *Wit* (HBO, 2001), about a brilliant English literary professor dying of ovarian cancer.

But the best and most complex form of intertextuality grows out of the way an actor is made panoptic and invisible at the same time — both all-seeing and barely seen — as he or she is linked up to the intricate workings of the epic narrative. A certain kind of measured, musical-like arrangement (and therefore a symbolic visual geometry) is behind such ubiquity. Moreover, the arrangement of a ubiquitous epic narrative has a strong connection to the stylistic daring behind the actor playing multiple roles. When taken together, ubiquitous epic narrative and the playing of multiple roles become a form of common linkage, replacement, and a sense of continuous rebirth.

We see this in the way Jeffrey Wright is made to appear in various different parts of the epic narrative as different people: He is the flamboyant, campy drag-queen, Belize; he is the smooth-talking, macho Mr. Lies, who acts as Harper's personal guide through her druggy hallucinations; and he is also the incredibly patient caretaker who prepares Cohn for death. (Cohn even asks him if he is Death.) Thus, Wright's multiple roles make him seem impossibly everywhere at once. But really, is such ubiquity any more difficult for us to accept than the hallucinatory spaces of Harper's fantasies or Prior's dreams, or the very presence in the text of the Angel of America? We think not.

Another form of bold narrative space opened up in *Angels* is a consequence of its three-part structure and its many repeated references to, and appearances of, the Angel of America. Along with Prior and Hannah, the Angel forms the third point of the triangular power center of *Angels*. This three-part structure and the full implications of the triangular relationship it represents comes together in the multiplicity of characters played by Streep, Thompson, and

Kirk. As previously mentioned, Streep plays the ancient Rabbi Isidor Chemelwitz, who delivers the eulogy for Louis's deceased grandmother, and Streep is also two of the Avenging Angels of the epic narrative: the stoic Mormon matriarch Hannah Pitt, and the spirit of Ethel Rosenberg. Thompson is the straight-talking Nurse Emily, who cares for Prior; the demented bag lady, who predicts that everyone will be mad in the New Millennium, and who, in a comical scene, somehow manages to pull it together long enough to give the angry Hannah directions to get to New York City; and she is the resplendent Angel of America. Kirk is the hero, Prior, stricken with AIDS, seemingly left to extinguish on his deathbed; he is also the macho leather-clad stranger Louis has anonymous sex with in Central Park; and the newly empowered Prior as Avenging Angel is chosen to live on and become the voice for all the voiceless sufferers of AIDS. In the end, we may be left to wonder which of all these multiple roles is real, or they all are, or if perhaps none of them are?

The closing tableau gives us Prior, who has AIDS; Louis, his repentant Jewish ex-lover; Belize, a Black man with a penchant for drag; and Hannah, a totally transformed Mormon woman with a sexually confused son, reuniting at the majestic Bethesda Fountain with its legendary healing waters in Central Park on a bright, cold autumn day.[17] Like the characters of 28 Barbary Lane in *Tales of the City*, they form the model of the new alternative family of the late 20th and early 21st centuries. While they speak together of the fall of the Berlin Wall, the end of the Cold War, the democratization of Russia, the changing of the world, and the celebration of life itself, the Bethesda Angel hovers high above them, dominating all, moving both them and us into yet another different sort of new epic space. If we may not totally believe in Prior's vision of the future, nor completely understand the full meaning and implications of the new epic space, we are prepared to live with this ambiguity. After all, there is much in this life we cannot understand that we have learned to live with. Also, in *Angels*, so much does seem to be put right in the end: Kaposi's Sarcoma becomes Divine Stigmata; Slavery becomes Freedom; Pain becomes Joy; Suffering becomes Divinity. Just as we have learned to accept the tropes of panopticity and invisibility of the multiple lives of the mythic characters, we know the ubiquitousness of the characters and the epic narrative of *Angels in America* has taken us much further afield than most of the epic miniseries made for American television ever have before. Like a giant Möbius strip, the text has a surprising way of turning back in on itself, returning everyone to the mythic epic space where it all began. Only now, like Prior, we too realize the privileged "fabulousness" of just being allowed to return, of being alive, of simply being permitted to go on....

Afterword: Where We Are and Where Are We Going

The progression from *QB VII* to *Rich Man, Poor Man/Roots/Holocaust* to *Shogun*, from *Brideshead Revisited* to *The Winds of War* and *War and Remembrance* and *The Singing Detective*, from *Lonesome Dove* and *From the Earth to the Moon* to *Angels in America* and beyond has been a long one. It reveals that the tactical preparations for an epic miniseries capable of transporting us into pastoral and Edenic fantasies of many varieties—enticing with the attractions of limitless space and spatiality, promising the transformation of self and ego—enriches the meaning of these and so many other televisual texts discussed and not discussed in this book. In retrospect, we see that the early epic miniseries of the 1970s stressed the clash between the individual, the source of freedom or anarchy, with society and community, the source of order or oppression. Those of the 1980s focused on the individual and the promise of the real possibility of revelation, the redoing of one's life, and the search for transformation. And those of the 1990s and into the New Millennium close with the unit of the heroic group attaining that sense of rebirth—the power of transcendence.

Accordingly, much like Prior, Louis, Hannah, Harper, and Belize, all gathered together at the Bethesda Fountain in Central Park at the conclusion of *Angels in America*, we are made aware that, much like the development and trajectory of the epic miniseries, our beginning might very well be there at the moment of our ending, just as the ending is implicit at the start. Hence, birth-death-rebirth are all one, as are epic narrative, mythic characterization, and the eternal dream of transcendence. Although it may be true that the golden age of the epic miniseries has come and gone, nonetheless, we firmly believe that there will always be those privileged spaces where that "fabulous invalid"—the epic miniseries—will remain a viable televisual presence. True, methods and meanings change; history and epic narrative become romances and fables, which become allegories, labyrinths, and legends. And yet, one thing always remains a constant: the story of the epic miniseries of American television is America's story, and so it is our own continuing story as well.

Epic Miniseries Credits

Scenes from a Marriage (PBS, 1974)

Length: 6 hours
Number of Episodes: 6
Cinematograph
Producer: Lars-Owe Carlberg
Director & Teleplaywriter: Ingmar Bergman
Production Designer: Björn Thulin
Costume Designer: Inger Pehrsson
Editor: Siv Lundgren
Photographer: Sven Nykvist
Cast: Liv Ullmann (Marianne), Erland Josephson (Johan), Bibi Andersson (Katarina), Jan Malmsjö (Peter), Gunnel Lindblom (Eva), Anita Wall (Interviewer for Woman's Magazine), Barbro Hiort af Ornäs (Mrs. Jacobi), Bertil Norström (Arne), Wenche Foss (Marianne's Mother).

QB VII (ABC, 1974)

Length: 6½ hours
Number of Episodes: 2
Douglas S. Cramer Productions, Screen Gem, Columbia Pictures Television
Producer: Douglas S. Cramer
Director: Tom Gries
Teleplaywriter: Edward Anhalt (from the novel by Leon Uris)
Composer: Jerry Goldsmith
Production Designers: Maurice Fowler, Ross Bellah
Costume Designer: Judy Moorcroft
Editors: Byron "Buzz" Brandt, Irving C. Rosenbaum
Photographers: Paul Beeson, Robert L. Morrison
Cast: Ben Gazzara (Abe Cady), Anthony Hopkins (Dr. Adam Kelno), Leslie Caron (Angela Kelno), Lee Remick (Lady Margaret Alexander Weidman), Juliet Mills (Samantha Cady), Dan O'Herlihy (David Shawcross), Robert Stephens (Robert Highsmith), Anthony Quayle (Tom Bannister), Milo O'Shea (Dr. Stanislaus Lotaki), John Gielgud (Clinton-Meek), Edith Evans (Dr. Parmentier), Jack Hawkins (Justice Gilloy), Judy Carne (Natalie), Kristoffer Tabori (Ben Cady), Joseph Wiseman (Morris Cady), Anthony Andrews (Stephen Kelno), Signe Hasso (Lena Kronska), Sam Jaffe (Dr. Mark Tessler), Alan Napier (Semple), Grégoire Aslan (Sheik Hassan), Lana Wood (Sue Scanlon), Julian Glover (Igor Zaminski), Robert Hutton (Ambassador Richards), Michael Gough (Dr. Fletcher).

Rich Man, Poor Man (ABC, 1976)

Length: 12 hours
Number of Episodes: 8
Universal Television
Executive Producer: Harve Bennett
Producer: Jon Epstein
Directors: David Greene, Boris Sagal
Teleplaywriter: Dean Riesner (from the novel by Irwin Shaw)
Composer: Alex North
Production Designer: John E. Chilberg II
Costume Designer: Charles Waldo
Editors: Douglas Stewart, Richard Bracken
Photographers: Howard R. Schwartz, Russell L. Metty
Cast: Peter Strauss (Rudy Jordache), Nick Nolte (Tom Jordache), Susan Blakely (Julie Prescott), Edward Asner (Axel Jordache), Dorothy McGuire (Mary Jor-

dache), Dick Butkus (Al Fanducci), Michael Evans (Arnold Simms), Gloria Grahame (Sue Prescott), Robert Reed (Teddy Boylan), Steve Allen (Bayard Nicholas), Bill Bixby (Willie Abbott), Kim Darby (Virginia Calderwood), Fionnula Flanagan (Clothilde), Ray Milland (Duncan Calderwood), Talia Shire (Teresa Santoro), William Smith (Falconetti), Van Johnson (Marsh Goodwin), Dorothy Malone (Irene Goodwin), Andrew Duggan (Colonel Deiner), Kay Lenz (Kate), Leigh J. McCloskey (Billy), Michael Morgan (Wesley).

Captains and the Kings (NBC, 1976)

Length: 9 hours
Number of Episodes: 6
Roy Huggins Productions
Executive Producer: Roy Huggins
Producer: Jo Swerling Jr.
Directors: Allen Reisner, Doug Heyes
Teleplaywriters: Doug Heyes, Elinor Karpf, Steven Karpf (from the novel by Taylor Caldwell)
Composer: Elmer Bernstein
Production Designers: John Corso, Joseph R. Jennings
Costume Designer: Roberta Weiner
Editors: Christopher Nelson, Edwin F. England, Larry D. Lester, Lawrence J. Vallario
Photographers: Isidore Mankofsky, Ric Waite, Vilis Lapenieks
Cast: Richard Jordan (Joseph Armagh), Perry King (Rory Armagh), Patty Duke (Bernadette Hennessey Armagh), Ray Bolger (R.J. Squibbs), Blair Brown (Elizabeth Healey Hennessey), John Carradine (Father Hale), Katherine Crawford (Moira Armagh), Charles Durning (Ed Healey), Henry Fonda (Senator Enfield Bassett), Celeste Holm (Sister Angela), John Houseman (Judge Newell Chisolm), David Huffman (Sean Armagh), Burl Ives (Old Syrup), Harvey Jason (Haroun "Harry" Zieff), Vic Morrow (Tom Hennessey), Barbara Parkins (Martinique), Joanna Pettet (Katherine Hennessey), Jane Seymour (Marjorie Chisholm Armagh), Ann Sothern (Mrs. Finch), Robert Vaughn (Charles Desmond), Beverly D'Angelo (Missy Emmy), Cliff De Young (Brian Armagh).

Roots (ABC, 1977)

Length: 12 hours
Number of Episodes: 8
David L. Wolper Productions, Warner Brothers Television
Executive Producer: David L. Wolper
Producer: Stan Margulies
Directors: David Greene, John Erman, Gilbert Moses, Marvin J. Chomsky
Teleplaywriters: Ernest Kinoy, James Lee, M. Charles Cohen, William Blinn (from the novel by Alex Haley)
Composers: Quincy Jones, Gerald Fried
Production Designers: Jan Scott, Joseph R. Jenning
Costume Designer: Jack Martell
Editors: Neil Travis, James T. Heckert, Peter Kirby
Photographers: Stevan Larner, Joseph M. Wilcots
Cast: LeVar Burton/John Amos (Kunta Kinte), Ben Vereen (Chicken George), Louis Gossett Jr. (Fiddler), Cicely Tyson (Binta), Leslie Uggams (Kizzy), Edward Asner (Captain Davies), Lorne Greene (John Reynolds), Chuck Connors (Master Tom Moore), Lloyd Bridges (Evan Brent), Richard Roundtree (Sam Bennett), Madge Sinclair (Bell), Gary Collins (Grill), Raymond St. Jacques (The Drummer), Sandy Duncan (Missy Anne Richards), Scatman Crothers (Mingo), Olivia Cole (Mathilda), George Hamilton (Stephen Bennett), Georg Stanford Brown (Tom Harvey), Lynne Moody (Irene Harvey), Vic Morrow (Ames), Robert Reed (Dr. William Reynolds), Lynda Day George (Mrs. Reynolds), Doug McClure (Jimmy Brent), Brad Davis (Ol' George Johnson), Thalmus Rasulala (Omoro), O.J. Simpson (Kadi Touray), Maya Angelou

(Nyo Boto), Ian McShane (Sir Ian Russell).

King (NBC, 1978)

Length: 6 hours
Number of Episodes: 3
Abby Mann Productions, Filmways
Executive Producer: Edward S. Feldman
Producer: Paul Maslansky
Director & Teleplaywriter: Abby Mann
Composer: Billy Goldenberg
Production Designer: James Spencer
Costume Designer: Nancy Stewart
Editors: Byron "Buzz" Brandt, David R. Berlatsky, Richard C. Meyer
Photographer: Michael Chapman
Cast: Paul Winfield (Martin Luther King Jr.), Cicely Tyson (Coretta King), Tony Bennett (Himself), Roscoe Lee Brown (Philip Harrison), Lonny Chapman (Chief Frank Holloman), Ossie Davis (Martin Luther King Sr.), Cliff De Young (Robert F. Kennedy), Al Freeman Jr. (Damon Lockwood), Clu Gulager (William Sullivan), Steven Hill (Stanley Levinson), William Jordan (President John F. Kennedy), Warren Kemmerling (Lyndon Baines Johnson), Lincoln Kilpatrick (Jerry Waring), Kenneth McMillan (Bull Connor), Howard Rollins Jr. (Andrew Young), David Spielberg (David Beamer), Dolph Sweet (J. Edgar Hoover), Dick Anthony Williams (Malcolm X), Julian Bond (Himself), Ramsey Clark (Himself), Roger Robinson (Reverend Fred Shuttlesworth), Frances Foster (Alberta King), Ernie Banks (Ralph Abernathy), Art Evans (A. D. King), Yolanda King (Rosa Parks).

Holocaust (NBC, 1978)

Length: 7½ hours
Number of Episodes: 4
Titus Productions
Executive Producer: Herbert Brodkin
Producer: Robert "Buzz" Berger
Director: Marvin J. Chomsky
Teleplaywriter: Gerald Green
Composer: Morton Gould
Production Designer: Wilfred J. Shingleton
Costume Designers: Edith Almoslino, Peggy Farrell
Editors: Craig McKay, Robert Reitano, Stephen A. Rotter
Photographer: Brian West
Cast: Fritz Weaver (Dr. Josef Weiss), Rosemary Harris (Berta Weiss), James Woods (Karl Weiss), Meryl Streep (Inga Helms Weiss), Joseph Bottoms (Rudi Weiss), Blanche Baker (Anna Weiss), Sam Wanamaker (Moses Weiss), Michael Moriarty (Erik Dorf), Deborah Norton (Marta Dorf), Robert Stephens (Kurt Dorf), David Warner (Reinhard Heydrich), Ian Holm (Heinrich Himmler), Tom Bell (Adolf Eichmann), Tovah Feldshuh (Helena Slomova), George Rose (Lowy), Nigel Hawthorne (Oldendorf), Michael Beck (Hans Helms).

Shogun (NBC, 1980)

Length: 12 hours
Number of Episodes: 5
Paramount Network Television, NBC Productions
Executive Producer: James Clavell
Producer: Eric Bercovici
Director: Jerry London
Teleplaywriter: Eric Bercovici (from the novel by James Clavell)
Composer: Maurice Jarre
Production Designer: Joseph R. Jennings
Costume Designer: Shin Nishida
Editors: Benjamin A. Weissman, Bill Luciano, Donald R. Rode, James T. Heckert, Jerry Young
Photographer: Andrew Laszlo
Cast: Richard Chamberlain (John Blackthorne), Toshirô Mifune (Toranga), Yôko Shimada (Lady Mariko), Frankie Sakai (Yab), Alan Badel (Father dell'Aqua), Michael Hordern (Friar Domingo), Damien Thomas (Father Alvito), John Rhys-Davies (Vasco Rodriguez), Vladek Sheybal (Captain Ferriera), George Innes (Johann daVinck), Leon Lissek (Father Sebastio), Yuki Meguro (Omi), Nobuo Kaneko (Ishido),

Hideo Takamatsu (Buntaro), Edward Peel (Pieterzoon), Eric Richard (Maetsukker), Stewart MacKenzie (Croocq). Narrated by Orson Welles.

Brideshead Revisited (PBS, 1981)

Length: 14 hours
Number of Episodes: 11
Granada International
Producer: Derek Granger
Directors: Charles Sturridge, Michael Lindsay-Hogg
Teleplaywriter: John Mortimer (from the novel by Evelyn Waugh)
Composer: Geoffrey Burgon
Production Designers: Peter Phillips, Terry Pritchard, Chris Truelove
Costume Designer: Jane Robinson
Editor: Anthony Ham
Photographer: Ray Goode
Cast: Jeremy Irons (Charles Ryder), Diana Quick (Julia Flyte), Simon Jones (Lord Brideshead "Bridey"), Roger Milner (Wilcox), Phoebe Nicholls (Cordelia Flyte), Charles Keating (Rex Mottram), Claire Bloom (Lady Marchmain), John Gielgud (Edward Ryder), Jeremy Sinden (Boy Mulcaster), Mona Washbourne (Nanny Hawkins), John Grillo (Mr. Samgrass), Nicholas Grace (Anthony Blanche), Jane Asher (Celia Ryder), Laurence Olivier (Lord Marchmain), Stéphane Audran (Cara), Richard Hope (Lieutenant Hooper), Colin Higgins (Patridge).

Berlin Alexanderplatz (PBS, 1982)

Length: 15 hours
Number of Episodes: 14
Bavaria/RAI Television
Producer: Peter Märthesheimer
Director & Teleplaywriter: Rainer Werner Fassbinder (from the novel by Alfred Döblin)
Production Designer: Helmut Gassner, Werner Achmans, Jurgën Henze
Costume Designer: Barbara Baum
Editors: Juliane Lorenz, Franz Walsch
Photographer: Xaver Schwarzenberger
Cast: Günter Lamprecht (Franz Biberkopf), Hanna Schygulla (Eva), Barbara Sukowa (Mieze), Gottfried John (Reinhold), Franz Buchrieser (Meck), Claus Holm (Wirt), Brigitte Mira (Frau Bast), Ivan Desny (Pums), Roger Fritz (Herbert), Werner Asam (Fritz), Karin Baal (Mina), Harry Baer (Richard), Wolfgang Bathke (Redner), Axel Bauer (Dreske), Hark Bohm (Lüders), Liselotte Eder (Mrs. Pums), Irm Hermann (Trude), Günther Kaufmann (Theo), Vitus Zeplichal (Rudi), Margit Carstensen (Terah), Elisabeth Trissenaar (Lina), Barbara Valentin (Ida).

Marco Polo (NBC, 1982)

Length: 10 hours
Number of Episodes: 4
RAI Uno, Cristaldi-Labella Productions
Executive Producers: Franco Cristaldi, Giovanni Bertolucci
Producer: Vincenzo Labella
Director: Giuliano Montaldo
Teleplaywriters: David Butler, Giuliano Montaldo, Vincenzo Labella
Composer: Ennio Morricone
Production Designer: Luciano Riccieri
Costume Designer: Enrico Sabbatini
Editor: John A. Martinelli
Photographer: Pasqualino De Santis
Cast: Ken Marshall (Marco Polo), Denholm Elliott (Niccolo Polo), Anne Bancroft (Signora Polo), F. Murray Abraham (Jacopo), John Gielgud (The Doge), John Houseman (The Patriarch), Burt Lancaster (Pope Gregory X), Tony Lo Bianco (Brother Nicholas), Ian McShane (Ali Ben Yussouf), Leonard Nimoy (Achmet), Beulah Quo (Empress Chabi), Ying Ruocheng (Kublai Khan), Sada Thompson (Aunt Flora), David Warner (Rustichello), Mario Adorf (Giovanni), Georgia Slowe (Catherina), Kathryn Dowling (Monica), Soon-Teck Oh (Yang Zhu), Riccardo Cucciolla (Uncle Zane), Bruno Zanin (Giulio),

Hal Buckley (Brother William), Marilù Tolo (Fiammetta), Alexander Picolo (Marco Polo as a Boy), John Dicks (Brother Philip), Junichi Ishida (Prince Chinkin).

The Winds of War
(ABC, 1983)

Length: 16 hours
Number of Episodes: 7
Dan Curtis Productions, Paramount Network Television
Producer & Director: Dan Curtis
Teleplaywriter: Herman Wouk (from his own novel)
Composer: Bob Cobert
Production Designer: Jackson De Govia
Costume Designer: James P. Cullen
Editors: Bernard Gribble, Earl Herdan, Gary L. Smith, Jack Tucker, John F Burnett, Peter Zinner
Photographer: Charles Correll
Cast: Robert Mitchum (Victor "Pug" Henry), Ali MacGraw (Natalie Jastrow), Jan-Michael Vincent (Byron Henry), John Houseman (Aaron Jastrow), Polly Bergen (Rhoda Henry), Lisa Eilbacher (Madeline Henry), David Dukes (Leslie Slote), Topol (Berel Jastrow), Ben Murphy (Warren Henry), Peter Graves (Fred "Palmer" Kirby), Jeremy Kemp (Brigadier General Armin von Roon), Ralph Bellamy (Franklin D. Roosevelt), Victoria Tennant (Pamela Tudsbury), Elizabeth Hoffman (Eleanor Roosevelt), Günter Meisner (Adolf Hitler), Anton Diffring (Joachim von Ribbentrop), Rene Kolldehoff (Hermann Goering), Howard Lang (Winston Churchill), Anatoly Chaguinian (Josef Stalin), Enzo Castellari (Benito Mussolini), Sky Dumont (Count Galliano Ciano), Edmund Purdom (Luigi Gianelli), Roy Poole (Harry Hopkins), Michael Logan (Alistair "Talky" Tudsbury), Tom McFadden (Hugh Cleveland), John Carter (Colonel William Forrest), Ferdy Mayne (Ludwig Rosenthal). Narrated by William Woodson.

The Thorn Birds
(ABC, 1983)

Length: 10 hours
Number of Episodes: 4
David Wolper–Stan Margulies Productions, Edward Lewis Production, Warner Brothers Television
Executive Producers: David Wolper, Edward Lewis
Producer: Stan Margulies
Director: Daryl Duke
Teleplaywriter: Carmen Culver (from the novel by Colleen McMcCullough)
Composer: Henry Mancini
Production Designer: Robert MacKichan
Costume Designer: William Travilla
Editors: Robert F. Shugrue, David Saxon, C. Timothy O'Meara
Photographer: Bill Butler
Cast: Richard Chamberlain (Father Ralph de Bricassart), Rachel Ward (Meggie Cleary), Jean Simmons (Fiona "Fee" Cleary), Ken Howard (Rainer Hartheim), Mare Winningham (Justine O'Neill), Piper Laurie (Anne Mueller), Richard Kiley (Paddy Cleary), Earl Holliman (Luddie Mueller), Bryan Brown (Luke O'Neill), Philip Anglim (Dane O'Neill), Barbara Stanwyck (Mary Carson), Christopher Plummer (Vittorio Contini-Verchese), John Friedrich (Frank Cleary), Allyn Ann McLerie (Mrs. Smith), Sydney Penny (Young Meggie), Stephen Burns (Jack Cleary), Brett Cullen (Bob Cleary).

Lace (ABC, 1984)

Length: 5 hours
Number of Episodes: 2
Lorimar Productions
Executive Producers: Gary Adelson, David Jacobs
Producer: Preston Fischer
Director: Billy Hale
Teleplaywriter: Elliott Baker (from the novel by Shirley Conran)
Composer: Nick Bicât
Production Designer: Allan Cameron
Costume Designer: Barbara Lane

Editors: John F. Link, Derek Trigg, Peter Boita
Photographer: Phil Meheux
Cast: Bess Armstrong (Judy Hale), Brooke Adams (Pagan Tralone), Arielle Dombasle (Maxine Pascal), Angela Lansbury (Aunt Hortense Boutin), Phoebe Cates (Lili), Anthony Higgins (Abdullah), Herbert Lom (Monsieur Chardin), Anthony Quayle (Dr. Geneste), Honor Blackman (Selma), Nickolas Grace (Sir Christopher Swann), Leigh Lawson (Count Charles de Chazelle), Simon Chandler (Nick Cliffe), Trevor Eve (Tom Schwartz), Francois Guétary (Pierre).

Ellis Island (CBS, 1984)

Length: 7 hours
Number of Episodes: 3
Pantheon Productions, Telepictures Corporation
Executive Producers: Gabriel Katzka, Frank Konisberg
Producer: Nick Gillot
Director: Jerry London
Teleplaywriter: Fred Mustard Stewart, Christopher Newman (from the novel by Fred Mustard Stewart)
Composer: John Addison
Production Designer: Robert Laing
Costume Designer: Barbara Lane
Editors: John J. Dumas, Bernard Gribble, James Galloway
Photographers: Jack Hildyard, Dudley Lovell, Ennio Guarnieri
Cast: Peter Riegert (Jacob Rubinstein/Jake Rubin), Greg Martyn (Marco Santorelli), Claire Bloom (Rebecca Weiler), Judi Bowker (Georgiana O'Donnell), Kate Burton (Vanessa Ogden), Joan Greenwood (Madame Levitska), Ann Jillian (Nellie Byfield), Lila Kaye (Kathleen O'Donnell), Stubby Kaye (Abe Shulman), Alice Krige (Bridgett O'Donnell), Cherie Lunghi (Una Marbury), Melba Moore (Flora Mitchum), Milo O'Shea (Casey O'Donnell), Emma Samms (Violet Weiler), Ben Vereen (Roscoe Haines), Faye Dunaway (Maud Charteris), Richard Burton (Senator Phipps Ogden), Michael Byrne (Dr. Carl Travers), Liam Neeson (Kevin Murray), Natasha Richardson (Young Whore).

Hollywood Wives (ABC, 1985)

Length: 6 hours
Number of Episodes: 3
Aaron Spelling Productions
Executive Producers: Aaron Spelling, Douglas S. Cramer
Producer: Howard W. Koch
Director: Robert Day
Teleplaywriter: Robert L. McCullough (from the novel by Jackie Collins)
Composer: Lalo Schifrin
Production Designer: John E. Chilberg II
Costume Designer: Nolan Miller
Editors: John M. Woodcock, Fred A. Chulack, Ray Daniels
Photographer: William W. Spencer
Cast: Candice Bergen (Elaine Conti), Joanna Cassidy (Marilee Gray), Mary Crosby (Karen Lancaster), Angie Dickinson (Sadie La Salle), Steve Forrest (Ross Conti), Anthony Hopkins (Neil Gray), Roddy McDowall (Jason Swankle), Stefanie Powers (Montana Gray), Suzanne Somers (Gina Germaine), Robert Stack (George Lancaster), Rod Steiger (Oliver Easterne), Andrew Stevens (Buddy Hudson), Catherine Mary Stewart (Angel Hudson), Frances Bergen (Pamela Lancaster).

Christopher Columbus (CBS, 1985)

Length: 6 hours
Number of Episodes: 2
RAI, Antenne 2, Bavaria Atelier GmbH, Lorimar Productions
Executive Producers: Malcolm Stuart, Ervin Zavada
Producers: Silvio Clementelli, Anna Maria Clementelli
Director: Alberto Lattuada

Teleplaywriter: Laurence Heath (based on screenplay by Andriano Bolzoni, Alberto Lattuada, Tulio Pinelli)
Composer: Riz Ortolani
Production Designer: Mario Chiari
Costume Designer: Maria De Matteis
Editor: Russell Lloyd
Photography: Franco Di Giacomo
Cast: Gabriel Byrne (Christopher Columbus), Faye Dunaway (Queen Isabella), Oliver Reed (Martin Pinzon), Max Von Sydow (King John of Portugal), Eli Wallach (Hernando De Talavera), Massimo Girotti (Duke Medina Celi), Nicol Williamson (King Ferdinand), Raf Vallone (José Vizinko), Rossano Brazzi (Diego Ortiz De Vilhegas), Virna Lisi (Dona Moniz Perestrello), Audrey Matson (Dona Felipa Perestello), Mark Buffery (Bartholomew Columbus), Anne Canovas (Beatriz Enriquez), Hal Yamanouchi (Guacanabo), Michel Auclair (Luis De Santangel), Elpidia Carrillo (Coana), Larry Lamb (Don Castillo), Stefano Madia (Frederico), Murray Melvin (Father Linares), Jack Watson (Father Marchena).

Alice in Wonderland (CBS, 1985)

Length: 4 hours
Number of Episodes: 2
Irwin Allen Productions, Procter & Gamble Productions, Columbia Pictures Television
Producer: Irwin Allen
Director: Harry Harris
Teleplaywriter: Paul Zindel (from the novel by Lewis Carroll)
Composer: Morton Stevens
Production Designer: Phil Jefferies
Costume Designer: Paul Zastupnevich
Editors: Richard E. Rabjohn, James W. Miller
Photography: Fred J. Koenekamp
Cast: Natalie Gregory (Alice), Sheila Allen (Alice's Mother), Steve Allen (Man in Paper Suit), Scott Baio (Pig), Ernest Borgnine (Lion), Beau Bridges (Unicorn), Lloyd Bridges (White Knight), Red Buttons (White Rabbit), Sid Caesar (Gryphon), Carol Channing (White Queen), Imogene Coca (Cook), Sammy Davis Jr. (Caterpillar/Father William), Patrick Duffy (Goat), George Gobel (Gnat), Eydie Gormé and Steve Lawrence (Tweedledee and Tweedledum), Merv Griffin (Conductor), Sherman Hemsley (Mouse), Ann Jillian (Red Queen), Arte Johnson (Dormouse), Harvey Korman (White Knight), Karl Malden (Walrus), Roddy McDowall (March Hare), Jayne Meadows (Queen of Hearts), Donna Mills (Rose), Pat Morita (Horse), Robert Morley (King of Hearts), Anthony Newley (Mad Hatter), Louis Nye (Carpenter), Donald O'Connor (Lory Bird), Martha Raye (Duchess), Telly Savalas (Cheshire Cat), John Stamos (Messenger), Ringo Starr (Mock Turtle), Sally Struthers (Tiger Lily), Jack Warden (Owl), Jonathan Winters (Humpty Dumpty), Shelly Winters (Dodo Bird).

Peter the Great (NBC, 1986)

Length: 8 hours
Number of Episodes: 4
PTG Productions, NBC Productions
Producer: Marvin J. Chomsky
Directors: Marvin J. Chomsky, Lawrence Schiller
Teleplaywriter: Edward Anhalt (from the book by Robert K. Massie)
Composer: Laurence Rosenthal
Production Designers: Alexander Popov, John Blezard
Costume Designers: Ella Maklakova, Sibylle Ulsamer
Editors: James T. Heckert, Bill Parker
Photographer: Vittorio Storaro
Cast: Maximilian Schell (Peter the Great), Vanessa Redgrave (Sophia), Laurence Olivier (King William III), Omar Sharif (Prince Feodor Romodanovsky), Jan Niklas (Peter as a Young Man), Trevor Howard (Sir Isaac Newton), Lili Palmer (Natalya), Hanna Schygulla (Catherine Skevronskaya), Renée Soutendijk (Anna

Mons), Elke Sommer (Queen Charlotte), Ursula Andress (Athalie), Mel Ferrer (King Frederick), Helmut Griem (Alexander Menshikov), Jeremy Kemp (Colonel Patrick Gordon), Natalya Andreichenko (Eudoxia), Boris Plotnikov (Alexis), Jan Malmsjö (Patriarch), Geoffrey Whitehead (Prince Vasily Golitsyn), Mike Gwilym (Shafirov), Algis Arlauskas (Father Theodosius), Denis De Marne (the Adult Peter in selected scenes).

Sins (CBS, 1986)

Length: 7 hours
Number of Episodes: 3
Grief-Dore Company, Collins-Holm Productions, New World Television
Executive Producers: Joan Collins, Peter Holm
Producer: Steve Krantz
Director: Douglas Hickox
Teleplaywriter: Laurence Heath (from the novel by Judith Gould)
Composers: Francis Lai (Additional Music by Michel Legrand)
Production Designer: François De Lamothe
Costume Designers: Valentino, Michel Fresnay
Editor: Michael Brown
Photographer: Jean Tournier
Cast: Joan Collins (Helene Junot), Jean-Pierre Aumont (Count De Ville), Marisa Berenson (Luba Tcherina), Steven Berkoff (Karl Von Eiderfeld), Joseph Bologna (Steve Bryant), Elizabeth Bourgine (Jeanne), Judi Bowker (Natalie Junot), Capucine (Odile), Timothy Dalton (Edmund Junot), Arielle Dombasle (Jacqueline Gore), James Farentino (David Westfield), Paul Freeman (Mueller), Allen Garfield (Adam Gore), Giancarlo Giannini (Marcello D'Itri), Lauren Hutton (ZZ Bryant), Gene Kelly (Eric Hovland), Catherine Mary Stewart (Young Helene), William Allen Young (Jacques Danvers), Feodor Atkine (Chameleon), Faith Brook (Julia Westfield), John McEnery (Defense Lawyer), Regine (Madame Liu).

Fresno (CBS, 1986)

Length: 6 hours
Number of Episodes: 5
MTM Entertainment
Executive Producer: Barry Kemp
Producer: R.W. Goodwin
Director: Jeff Bleckner
Teleplaywriters: Barry Kemp, Mark Ganzel, Michael Petryni
Composer: John Morris
Production Designer: Tommy Goetz
Costume Designer: Bob Mackie
Editor: Andrew Chulack
Photographer: Robert Steadman
Cast: Carol Burnett (Charlotte Kensington), Dabney Coleman (Tyler Cane), Gregory Harrison (Torch), Teri Garr (Talon Kensington), Charles Grodin (Cane Kensington), Luis Avalos (Juan), Pat Corley (Earl Duke), Valerie Mahaffey (Tiffany Kensington), Anthony Heald (Kevin Kensington), Teresa Ganzel (Bobbi Jo Bobb), Bill Paxton (Billy Joe Bobb), Jerry Van Dyke (Tucker Agajanian), Charles Keating (Charles), Melanie Chartoff (Desiree De Mornay), Michael Richardson (2nd Henchman), J.E. Freeman (1st Henchman), Jeffrey Jones (Mr. Acme), Tom Poston (Doc Parseghian), Louise Latham (Ethel Duke), Henry Darrow (Commandante), Tammy Lauren (Candy Cane), Natalie Gregory (China Kensington), James Staley (Kyle Tensinger), José Quintero (Don Diego de la Peña).

Mario Puzo's *"The Fortunate Pilgrim"* (NBC, 1988)

Length: 5 hours
Number of Episodes: 2
A Carlo and Alex Ponti Production, Rete-Europa
Executive Producer: Carlo Ponti
Producer: Alex Ponti
Director: Stuart Cooper
Teleplaywriter: John McGreevey (from the novel by Mario Puzo)

Composers: Lucio Dalla, Mauro Malavasi
Production Designer: Wolf Kroeger
Costume Designer: Enrico Sabbatini
Editor: Michael S. Murphy
Photographer: Reginald Morris
Cast: Sophia Loren (Lucia Angeluzzi Corbo), Edward James Olmos (Frank Corbo), John Turturro (Larry Angeluzzi), Anna Strasberg (Cousin Filomena), Yorgo Voyagis (Tony Angeluzzi), Mirjana Karanovic (Clara Cinglata), Annabella Sciorra (Octavia Angeluzzi), Ron Marquette (Vinnie Angeluzzi), Harold P. Pruett (Gino Corbo), Hal Holbrook (Dr. Andrew McKaig), Roxann Biggs (Louisa Marconozzi), Edward Wiley (Lo Squalo), Helen Stirling (Zia Louche).

Onassis: The Richest Man in the World (ABC, 1988)

Length: 4 hours
Number of Episodes: 2
The Konigsberg-Sanitsky Company, Television Espanola SA
Executive Producers: Frank Konigsberg, Larry Sanitsky
Producer: Alfred R. Kelman
Director: Waris Hussein
Teleplaywriters: Jacqueline Feather, David Seidler (from the book *Ari: The Life & Times of Aristotle Onassis* by Peter Evans)
Composer: Billy Goldenberg
Production Designer: Gil Parrondo
Costume Designer: Yvonne Blake
Editor: David Saxon
Photographer: Alan Doberman
Cast: Raul Julia (Aristotle Onassis), Jane Seymour (Maria Callas), Francesca Annis (Jacqueline Kennedy Onassis), Elias Koteas (Young Aristotle), Beatie Edney (Tina Onassis), Anthony Zerbe (Stavros Livanos), John Kapelos (Constantine Gratsos), Anthony Quinn (Socrates Onassis), Robert Krantz (Young Gratsos), Lorenzo Quinn (Alexander Onassis), Geoffrey Hutchings (Peter Meneghini), Dimitra Arliss (Artemis), Shanit Keter (Young Artemis), Harriet Bagnall (Christina Onassis), James F. Kelly (Bobby Kennedy), Joris Stuyck (Teddy Kennedy), Giannis Voglis (Uncle Alexander), Thorley Walters (Winston Churchill), David Gilliam (John F. Kennedy), Garrick Hagon (Roy Cohn), Richard Svare (Billy Baldwin), Marella Oppenheim (Lee Radziwill), John Ticehurst (Cardinal Cushing).

The Singing Detective (PBS, 1988)

Length: 6 hours
Number of Episodes: 6
BBC, The Australian Broadcasting Corporation
Executive Producer: Rick McCallum
Producers: John Harris, Kenith Trodd
Director: John Amiel
Teleplaywriter: Dennis Potter
Composer: Stanley Myers
Production Designer: Jim Clay
Costume Designer: Hazel Pethig
Editors: Bill Wright, Sue Wyatt
Photographer: Ken Westbury
Cast: Michael Gambon (Philip Marlow), Patrick Malahide (Mark Binney/Finney/Raymond Binney), Joanne Whalley (Nurse Mills), Janet Suzman (Nicola), Alison Steadman (Mrs. Marlow), Imelda Staunton (Nurse White), Jim Carter (Mr. Marlow), Bill Paterson (Dr. Gibbon), David Ryall (Mr. Hall), Gerald Horan (Reginald), Leslie French (Mr. Tomkey), Ron Cook (1st Mysterious Man), George Rossi (2nd Mysterious Man), Sharon D. Clarke (Night Nurse), Lyndon Davies (Young Philip), Janet Henfrey (Schoolteacher), William Speakman (Young Mark Binney), Wally Thomas (Grandad Baxter), Charles Simon (George Adams), Kate McKenzie (Sonia), Simon Chandler (Dr. Finlay), Ken Stott (Uncle John), Jo Cameron Brown (Aunt Emily), Niven Boyd (1st Soldier), David Thewlis (2nd Soldier).

War and Remembrance (ABC, 1988–89)

Length: 30 hours
Number of Episodes: 12
Dan Curtis Productions, Jadran Films, ABC Circle Films
Executive Producer: Dan Curtis
Producer: Barbara Steele
Director: Dan Curtis
Teleplaywriters: Earl W. Wallace, Dan Curtis, Herman Wouk (from the novel by Herman Wouk)
Composer: Bob Cobert
Production Designer: Guy Comtois
Costume Designer: John S. Perry
Editors: Peter Zinner, John F. Burnett, Gary Smith
Photographer: Dietrich Lohmann
Cast: Robert Mitchum (Victor "Pug" Henry), Jane Seymour (Natalie Jastrow Henry), Hart Bochner (Byron Henry), Victoria Tennant (Pamela Tudsbury), Polly Bergen (Rhoda Henry), David Dukes (Leslie Slote), John Gielgud (Aaron Jastrow), Michael Woods (Warren Henry), Sharon Stone (Janice Henry), Robert Morley (Alistair "Talky" Tudsbury), Barry Bostwick (Commander Carter "Lady" Aster), Sami Frey (Avram Rabinovitz), Topol (Berel Jastrow), John Rhys-Davies (Sammy Mutterperl), Ian McShane (Phillip Rule), Bill Wallis (Werner Beck), Peter Graves (Palmer Kirby), Leslie Hope (Madeline Henry), Ralph Bellamy (Franklin D. Roosevelt), Richard Dysart (Harry Truman), E.G. Marshall (General Dwight Eisenhower), Jeremy Kemp (Brigadier General Armin von Roon), Nicholas Pryor (J. Robert Oppenheimer), Steven Berkoff (Adolph Hitler), Kristie Polley (Eva Braun), Robert Stephens (Major Karl Rahn), Robert Hardy (Winston Churchill), William R. Moses (Simon Anderson), Mike Connors (Colonel Harrison "Hack" Peters), Howard Duff (William Tuttle), Nina Foch (Comtesse de Chambrun), Pat Hingle (Admiral William "Bull" Halsey), G.D. Spradlin (Admiral Raymond A. Spruance), G.W. Bailey (Commander Jim Grigg), Barry Morse (Colonel General Franz Halder), Brian Blessed (General Yevlenko), Eddie Albert (Breckinridge Lang), Hardy Kruger (Field Marshall Erwin Rommel), Sky Dumont (Claus von Stauffenberg), Barbara Steele (Elsa McMahon), Michael Madsen (Lieutenant "Foof" Turkell), Milton Johns (Adolf Eichmann), Günther Maria Halmer (Rudolph Hoess).

Lonesome Dove (CBS, 1989)

Length: 8 hours
Number of Episodes: 4
Motown Productions, Panagaea, Quintex Entertainment
Executive Producers: Suzanne de Passe, Bill Wittliff
Producer: Dyson Lovell
Director: Simon Wincer
Teleplaywriter: Bill Witliff (from the novel by Larry McMurtry)
Composer: Basil Poledouris
Production Designer: Cary White
Costume Designer: Van Broughton Ramsey
Editor: Corky Ehlers
Photographer: Doug Milsome
Cast: Robert Duvall (Augustus "Gus" McCrae), Tommy Lee Jones (Woodrow F. Call), Danny Glover (Joshua Deets), Diane Lane, (Lorena Wood), Robert Urich (Jake Spoon), Frederic Forrest (Blue Duck), D.B. Sweeney (Dish Boggett), Ricky Schroder (Newt Dobbs), Anjelica Huston (Clara Allen), Chris Cooper (Sheriff July Johnson), Timothy Scott (Pea Eye Parker), Glenne Headly (Elmira Johnson), Barry Corbin (Deputy Roscoe Brown), William Sanderson (Lippy Jones), Barry Tubb (Jasper Fant), Gavan O'Herlihy (Dan Suggs), Steve Buscemi (Luke), Helena Humann (Peach Johnson), Adam Faraizl (Joe Boot), Nina Siemaszko (Janey).

Small Sacrifices (ABC, 1989)

Length: 4 hours
Number of Episodes: 2

Louis Rudolph Films, Motown Productions, Allacrom Ltd., Fries Entertainment
Executive Producers: Suzanne de Passe, Louis Randolph
Producer: S. Bryan Hickox
Director: David Greene
Teleplaywriter: Joyce Eliason (from the book by Ann Rule)
Composer: Peter Manning Robinson
Production Designer: Brent Thomas
Costume Designer: Larry Wells
Editor: Parkie Singh
Photographer: Ron Orieux
Cast: Farrah Fawcett (Diana Downs), Gordon Clapp (Doug Welch), Ryan O'Neal (Lew Lewiston), John Shea (Frank Joziak), Emily Perkins (Karen Downs), Garry Chalk (Boyd Paul Downs), Ken James (Daryl Chapman), Sean McCann (Russell Wade), Garwin Sanford (Matt Jensen), Tom Butler (Wally Beck), Elan Ross Gibson (Rosalind Dyring), Lynne Cormack (Lola Jaziak), Jayne Eastwood (Evelyn Slaven), Christopher Carvalho (Robbie Downs).

The Kennedys of Massachusetts (ABC, 1990)

Length: 6 hours
Number of Episodes: 3
Edgar J. Scherick Associates, Orion Television
Executive Producers: Edgar J. Scherick, Susan Pollock
Producer: Lynn Raynor
Director: Lamont Johnson
Teleplaywriter: William Hanley (from the book *The Fitzgeralds and the Kennedys: An American Saga* by Doris Kearns Goodwin)
Composer: David Shire
Production Designer: Jan Scott
Costume Designer: Shelley Komarov
Editor: Susan B. Browdy
Photographer: Laszlo George
Cast: William Petersen (Joseph P. Kennedy), Annette O'Toole (Rose Kennedy), Charles Durning ("Honey Fitz" Fitzgerald), Tracy Pollan (Kathleen Kennedy), Pat Hingle (P.J. Kennedy), Steven Weber (John F. Kennedy), Campbell Scott (Joseph P. Kennedy Jr.), Madolyn Smith Osborne (Gloria Swanson), Josef Sommer (Franklin D. Roosevelt), Tim Halligan (Eddie Moore), Jean De Baer (Josie Fitzgerald), William Duff-Griffin (Henry Fitzgerald), Eddie Jones (Jim Fitzgerald), Lily Knight (Pat Wilson), Olek Krupa (Erich von Stroheim), Sullivan Brown (King George), Richard Clarke (Neville Chamberlain), Brian Tierney (Jimmy Roosevelt).

Voices Within: The Lives of Truddi Chase (ABC, 1990)

Length: 4 hours
Number of Episodes: 2
Itzbinson Long Productions, P.A. Productions Inc., New World Television
Executive Producers: E. Jack Neuman, Helen Verno
Producer: Harry R. Sherman
Director: Lamont Johnson
Teleplaywriter: E. Jack Neuman (from the book *When Rabbit Howls* by Truddi Chase)
Composer: Charles Fox
Production Designer: Paul Peters
Costume Designer: Shelley Komarov
Editor: Susan B. Browdy
Photographer: William Wages
Cast: Shelley Long (Truddi Chase), Tom Conti (Dr. Phillips), John Rubinstein (Norman De Roin), Alan Fudge (Albert Johnson), Jamie Rose (Maureen), Christine Healy (Sharon Barnes), Ernie Lively (Paul), Frank Converse (Peter Morgan), Robert Costanzo (Eddie), Guido Koock (Charles), Tiffany Ballenger (Truddi at age 8), John Beshara (Police Officer), Val Bettin (Playwright), Irina Cashen (Truddi at age 6), Carl Ciarfalio (Colin Keefe).

Young Catherine (TNT, 1991)

Length: 4 hours
Number of Episodes: 2

Turner Pictures, Consolidated Entertainment, Lenfilm, RAI, Tele-Munchen Fernsen, CTV Television Network
Executive Producers: Michael Deeley, Stephen Smallwood
Producer: Neville C. Thompson
Director: Michael Anderson
Teleplaywriter: Chris Bryant
Composer: Isaak Shvarts
Production Designers: Natalia Vasilieva, Harold Thrasher
Costume Designer: Larissa Konnikova
Editor: Ron Wisman
Photographer: Ernest Day
Cast: Vanessa Redgrave (Empress Elizabeth), Julia Ormond (Catherine), Christopher Plummer (Sir Charles), Franco Nero (Count Voronstov), Marthe Keller (Johnanna), Maximilian Schell (Frederick the Great), Mark Frankel (Count Gregory Orlov), Reece Dinsdale (Grand Duke Peter), Anna Kanakis (Countess Voronstova), John Shrapnel (Archimandrite Todorsky), Hartmut Becker (Catherine's Father), Laurie Holden (Countess Dashkova), Katharine Schlesinger (Elizabeth Voronstova), Katya Galitzine (Maria Choglokov), Rory Edwards (Alexis Orlov), Chris Bryant (Doctor Lande).

Darlings of the Gods (A&E, 1991)

Length: 4 hours
Number of Episodes: 2
Thames Television
Executive Producers: Sandra Levy, John Hambly
Producers: Roger Simpson, Roger Le Mesurier
Director: Catherine Millar
Teleplaywriters: Roger Simpson, Graeme Farmer (from the book by Garry O'Connor)
Composer: Brian May
Production Designer: Colin Gersch
Costume Designer: Jim Murray
Editor: Edward McQueen Mason
Photographer: Ian Warburton
Cast: Anthony Higgins (Laurence Olivier), Mel Martin (Vivien Leigh), Jerome Ehlers (Peter Finch), Rhys McConnochie (Ralph Richardson), Anthony Hawkins (Cecil Tennant), Lindy Davies (Antonia Vaughan), Barry Quin (Dan Cunningham), Jackie Kelleher (Elsie Beyer), Nicki Paull (June Kelly), Shane Briant (Cecil Beaton), Kevin Miles (Lord Esker), Jon Finlayson (Tyrone Guthrie), Charles Dance (Michael St. Dennis), Frederick Court (Peter Cushing).

In a Child's Name (CBS, 1991)

Length: 4 hours
Number of Episodes: 2
New World Television
Executive Producers: Dan Wigutow, Helen Verno
Producers: Donald C. Klune, Christopher Canaan
Director: Tom McLoughlin
Teleplaywriters: Bill Phillips, Charles Walker (from the book by Peter Maas)
Composer: Richard Stone
Production Designer: Ward Preston
Costume Designer: Geoffrey S. Grimsman
Editors: Charles Bornstein, Michael Berman
Photographer: Daryn Okada
Cast: Valerie Bertinelli (Angela Cimarelli), Michael Ontkean (Kenneth Taylor), Timothy Carhart (Lieutenant Robert Fausak), David Huddleston (Zack Taylor), John Karlen (Joe Silvano), Caroline Kava (Janice Miller), Christopher Meloni (Jerry Cimarelli), Joanna Merlin (Frances Silvano), Mitchell Ryan (Peter Chappell), Karla Tamburrelli (Teresa Silvano Taylor), Andy Hirsch (Andrew Silvano), Vincent Guastaferro (Inspector Malinowski), Louise Fletcher (Jean Taylor), Nancy McLoughlin (Marilyn Taylor), Eric Tilley (Tom Taylor), James Cromwell (Thomas Hobbs), Lou Criscuolo (Peter Maas).

Queen (CBS, 1993)

Length: 6 hours
Number of Episodes: 3
The Wolper Organization, Warner Brothers Television
Executive Producers: David L. Wolper, Bernard Sofronski
Producer: Mark M. Wolper
Director: John Erman
Teleplaywriter: David Stevens (from the novel by Alex Haley)
Composer: Michael Small
Production Designer: Roger Maus
Costume Designer: Helen Butler Barbon
Editors: Paul LaMastra, James Galloway
Photographer: Tony Imi
Cast: Halle Berry (Queen Haley), Ann-Margret (Sally Jackson), Patricia Clarkson (Lizzie Perkins), Tim Daly (James Jackson Jr.), Ossie Davis (Parson Dick), Danny Glover (Alec Haley), Jasmine Guy (Easter), Raven Symone (The Young Queen), Martin Sheen (James Jackson Sr.), Madge Sinclair (Dora), Sada Thompson (Miss Mandy), Paul Winfield (Cap'n Jack), Dennis Haysbert (Davis), Victor Garber (Digby), Lonette McKee (Alice), Elizabeth Wilson (Miss Gippy), George Grizzard (Mr. Cherry), Frances Conroy (Mrs. Benson), Richard Jenkins (Mr. Benson), Linda Hart (Mrs. Henderson), Jane Krakowski (Jane Jackson), Lorraine Toussaint (Joyce).

Family Pictures (ABC, 1993)

Length: 4 hours
Number of Episodes: 2
Alexander-Enright & Associates, Hearst Entertainment
Executive Producers: Don Enright, Les Alexander
Producer: Joseph Broido
Director: Philip Saville
Teleplaywriter: Jennifer Miller (from the novel by Sue Miller)
Composer: Johnny Harris
Production Designer: Perri Gorrara
Costume Designers: Diana Irwin, Vickie Saito
Editor: Debra Karen
Photographer: Elemér Ragályi
Cast: Anjelica Huston (Lainey Eberlin), Sam Neill (Dr. David Eberlin), Kyra Sedgwick (Nina), Dermot Mulroney (Mack), Janet-Laine Green (Tony Baker), Jamie Harrold (Randall), Torri Higginson (Liddie), Kaya McGregor (Marie), Nahanni Johnstone (Jill), Barbara Barnes-Hopkins (Retta).

Diana: Her True Story (NBC, 1993)

Martin Poll Films
Executive Producer: Martin Poll
Producer: Hugh Benson
Director: Kevin Connor
Teleplaywriter: Stephen Zito (from the book by Andrew Morton)
Composer: Ken Thorne
Production Designer: Keith Wilson
Costume Designer: Graham Wilson
Editors: Barry Peters, Brian Smedley-Aston
Photographer: Doug Milsome
Cast: Serena Scott Thomas (Princess Diana), David Threlfall (Prince Charles), Elizabeth Garvie (Camilla Parker-Bowles), Anne Stallybrass (Queen Elizabeth), Donald Douglas (Prince Phillip), Jemma Redgrave (Carolyn), Jeremy Child (Alfred Drake-Kinney), William Franklyn (Lord Montbatten), Jean Anderson (Lady Fermoy), Aletta Lawson (Princess Anne), Helen Masters (Sarah Spencer), Camelia Hayes O'Herlihy (Jane Spencer), Gabrielle Blunt (Queen Mother), Christopher Bowen (James Gilbey), Nicholas Bastian (Prince William), Barclay Wright (Prince Harry), Anthony Calf (Captain James Hewitt).

A Matter of Justice (NBC, 1993)

Length: 4 hours
Number of Episodes: 2

Ron Gilbert Associates, Hill-Fields Entertainment
Executive Producers: Leonard Hill, Joel Fields, Ron Gilbert
Producers: Ardythe Goergens, Bernadette Caulfield
Director: Michael Switzer
Teleplaywriter: Dennis Turner
Composer: David Michael Frank
Production Designer: Elayne Barbara Cedar
Costume Designer: Rosalie Wallace
Editor: Mark Rosenbaum
Photographer: Robert Draper
Cast: Patty Duke (Mary Brown), Martin Sheen (Jack Brown), Alexandra Powers (Charlene "Dusty" Johnson), Jason London (Chris Brown), Jeff Kober (Talbot), Cole Hauser (Private Ralph "Rocky" Jackson), Danny Nucci (Vince Grella), T. Max Graham (Harry Amblin), Charles S. Dutton (Arlo McDaniel), Christopher John Fields (Agent Warren Matthews), Lynette Walden (Patty), Robin Burrows (Diane), Jodie Markell (Sandra).

Tales of the City (PBS, 1994)

Length: 6 hours
Number of Episodes: 6
Channel 4 Television
Executive Producers: Richard Kramer, Tim Bevan, Sigurjon Sighvatsson, Armistead Maupin
Producer: Alan Mark Poul
Director: Alastair Reid
Teleplaywriter: Richard Kramer (from the novel by Armistead Maupin)
Composer: John Keane
Production Designer: Victoria Paul
Costume Designer: Molly Maginnis
Editor: David Gamble
Photographer: Walt Lloyd
Cast: Olympia Dukakis (Mrs. Anna Madrigal), Donald Moffat (Edgar Warfield Halcyon), Chloe Webb (Mona Ramsey), Laura Linney (Mary Ann Singleton), Marcus D'Amico (Michael "Mouse" Tolliver), Bill Campbell (Dr. Jon Philip Fielding), Thomas Gibson (Beauchamp Day), Paul Gross (Brian Hawkins), Barbara Garrick (Deirdre "DeDe" Halcyon Day), Nina Foch (Frances "Frannie" Ligon Halcyon), Stanley De Santis (Norman Williams), Cynda Williams (D'orothea Wilson), Edie Adams (Ruby Miller), Meagen Fay (Binky Gruen), Mary Kay Place (Prue Giroux), Parker Posey (Connie Bradshaw), Michael Jeter (Carson Callas), Swoosie Kurtz (Betty Ramsey), Paul Dooley (Herbert L. Tolliver), Belita Morena (Alice Tolliver), Lance Loud (William Deveraux Hill), Bob Mackie (Richard Evan Hampton), Paul Bartel (Charles Hillary Lord), Karen Black (Herself), Rod Steiger (Bookstore Owner).

Oldest Living Confederate Widow Tells All (CBS, 1994)

Length: 4 hours
Number of Episodes: 2
Konigsberg-Sanitsky Productions, RHI Entertainment
Executive Producers: Frank Konigsberg, Larry Sanitsky
Producer: Jack Clements
Director: Ken Cameron
Teleplaywriter: Joyce Eliason (from the novel by Allan Gurganus)
Composer: Mark Snow
Production Designer: Charles C. Bennett
Costume Designer: Van Broughton Ramsey
Photographer: Edward Pei
Cast: Diane Lane (Lucy Honicut Marsden), Donald Sutherland (Captain William Marsden), Cicely Tyson (Castalia), Anne Bancroft (Lucy Marsden at 100), Blythe Danner (Bianca Honicut), E.G. Marshall (Professor Taw), Gwen Verdon (Etta Pell), Camille Cooper (Shirley Wilgus), Maureen Mueller (Lady Marsden), Kathryn Morris (Zondro), Wil Horneff (Willie Marsden), Jesse Zeigler (Ned Marsden), Ed Grady (General Robert E. Lee).

The Stand (ABC, 1994)

Length: 8 hours
Number of Episodes: 4
Laurel Productions, Greengrass Productions
Executive Producers: Richard R. Rubinstein, Stephen King
Producer: Mitchell Galin
Director: Mick Garris
Teleplaywriter: Stephen King (from his own novel)
Composer: W.G. Snuffy Walden
Production Designer: Nelson Coates
Costume Designer: Lina Matheson
Editor: Patrick McMahon
Photographer: Edward Pei
Cast: Gary Sinise (Stu Redman), Molly Ringwald (Fran Goldsmith), Jamey Sheridan (Randall Flagg), Ruby Dee (Mother Abigail), Laura San Giacomo (Nadine Cross), Ossie Davis (Judge Farris), Miguel Ferrer (Lieutenant Llyod Henreid), Corin Nemec (Harold Lauder), Matt Frewer (Trashcan Man), Adam Storke (Larry Underwood), Ray Walston (Glen Bateman), Bill Fagerbakke (Tom Cullen), Rob Lowe (Nick Andros), Ed Harris (General Starkey), Kathy Bates (Rae Flowers), Peter Van Norden (Ralph Brentner), Rick Aviles (Ratman), Max Wright (Herbert Denninger), Patrick Kilpatrick (Ray Booth), Ray McKinnon (Charles Campion), Shawnee Smith (Julie Lawry), Kareem Abdul-Jabbar (The Monster Shouter), Stephen King (Teddy Weizak), Tom Holland (Carl Hough), John Landis (Russ Dorr), Sam Raimi (Bobby Terry).

Love and Betrayal: The Mia Farrow Story (Fox, 1995)

Length: 4 hours
Number of Episodes: 2
Fox Circle Productions
Executive Producer: Tarquin Gotch
Producer: Terence A. Donnelly
Director: Karen Arthur
Teleplaywriter: Cynthia A. Cherbak (from the books *Mia & Woody: Love and Betrayal* by Kristi Groteke and Marjorie Rosen, and *Mia: The Life of Mia Farrow* by Edward Z. Epstein and Joe Morella)
Composer: David Michael Frank
Production Designer: David Davis
Costume Designer: Judy Truchan
Editor: Caroline Biggerstaff
Photographer: Thomas Neuwirth
Cast: Patsy Kensit (Mia Farrow), Dennis Boutsikaris (Woody Allen), Richard Mueñz (Frank Sinatra), Robert LuPone (André Previn), Frances Helm (Maureen O'Sullivan), Taryn Davis (Dylan), Heidi von Palleske (Young Maureen O'Sullivan), Stephen Pearlman (Elkan Abramowitz), Tovah Feldshuh (Eleanor Alter), Grace Una (Soon-Yi Previn), Nigel Bennett (John Farrow), Lynne Cormack (Dory Previn), Christine Andreas (Ava Gardner), Robin Dunne (Fletcher Previn), Natalie Miller (Young Mia), Bruce McCarty (Roman Polanski), Chandra West (Mariel Hemingway), Damon Redfern (Robert Redford), Julian Lennon (John Lennon), Mark Richardson (Paul McCartney).

Buffalo Girls (CBS, 1995)

Length: 4 hours
Number of Episodes: 2
Cabin Fever Entertainment, de Passe Entertainment, CBS Entertainment Productions
Executive Producer: Suzanne de Passe
Producers: Sandra Saxon Brice, Suzanne Coston
Director: Rod Hardy
Teleplaywriter: Cynthia Whitcomb (from the novel by Larry McMurtry)
Composer: Lee Holdridge
Production Designer: Cary White
Costume Designer: Van Broughton Ramsey
Editor: Richard Bracken
Photographer: David Connell
Cast: Anjelica Huston (Calamity Jane), Melanie Griffith (Dora Du Fran), Gabriel Byrne (Teddy Blue), Peter Coyote (Buffalo Bill Cody), Tracey Walter (Jim Ragg), Floyd Red Crow Westerman

(No Ears), Jack Palance (Bartle Bone), Reba McEntire (Annie Oakley), Sam Elliot (Wild Bill Hickok), Charlaine Woodward (Doosie), John Diehl (General Custer), Liev Schreiber (Ogden Verdeaux), Andrew Bicknell (Captain O'Neill), Paul Lazar (Doc Rames), Russell Means (Chief Sitting Bull), Geoffrey Bateman (Prince of Wales), Julie Bevan (Duchess of Warwick), Peter Birch (Lord Windhouvern), Hannah Taylor-Gordon (Janey).

Liz: The Elizabeth Taylor Story (NBC, 1995)

Length: 4 hours
Number of Episodes: 2
Lester Persky Productions
Executive Producer: Lester Persky
Producer: Hugh Benson
Director: Kevin Connor
Teleplaywriter: Burr Douglas (aka Gerald Ayres) (from the book *Liz* by C. David Heymann)
Composer: Ken Thorne
Production Designer: James J. Agazzi
Costume Designer: Jane Robinson
Editors: Barry Peters, Corky Ehlers
Photographer: Doug Milsome
Cast: Sherilyn Fenn (Elizabeth Taylor), Angus Macfadyen (Richard Burton), Eric Gustavson (Nicky Hilton), Nigel Havers (Michael Wilding), Ray Wise (Mike Todd), Corey Parker (Eddie Fisher), Charles Frank (John Warner), Michael McGrady (Larry Fortensky), Katherine Helmond (Hedda Hopper), Kevin McCarthy (Sol Siegel), William McNamara (Montgomery Clift), Christine Healy (Sara Taylor), Dan McVicker (Rock Hudson), John Saxon (Richard Brooks), Judith Jones (Debbie Reynolds), John Fink (Francis Taylor), Michael Cavanaugh (Walter Wagner), Jon Menick (Phillippe Halsam), Eugene Roche (George Stevens), Victor Raider-Wexler (Joseph L. Mankiewicz), Patricia North (Sybil Burton).

True Women (CBS, 1997)

Length: 4 hours
Number of Episodes: 2
Craig Anderson Production, Hallmark Entertainment
Executive Producer: Craig Anderson
Producer: Lynn Raynor
Director: Karen Arthur
Teleplaywriter: Christopher Lofton (from the book by Janice Woods Windle)
Composer: Bruce Broughton
Production Designer: Rodger Maus
Costume Designer: Vicki Sánchez
Editor: Corky Ehlers
Photographer: Tom Neuwirth
Cast: Dana Delaney (Sarah Ashby McClure), Annabeth Gish (Euphemia Ashby King), Angelina Jolie (Georgia Lawshe Woods), Tina Majorino (Young Euphemia), Rachel Leigh Cook (Young Georgia), Michael York (Captain Lawshe), Jeffrey Nordling (Dr. Peter Woods), Salli Richardson (Martha Benny), Tony Todd (Ed Tom), Terence Mann (Captain Haller), Julie Carmen (Cherokee Lawshe), Matthew Glave (William King), Anne Marie Tremko (Mattie Lockhart), Powers Boothe (Bartlett McClure), Charles S. Dutton (Josiah).

Bella Mafia (CBS, 1997)

Length: 4 hours
Number of Episodes: 2
The Konigsberg Company
Executive Producer: Frank Konigsberg
Producer: Jack Clements
Director: David Greene
Teleplaywriter: Lynda La Plante (from her own novel)
Composer: Joseph Vitarelli
Production Designer: Charles C. Bennett
Costume Designer: Enid Harris
Editor: Michael Brown
Photographer: Gordon Lonsdale
Cast: Vanessa Redgrave (Graziella Luciano), Dennis Farina (Don Roberto Luciano), Nastassja Kinski (Sophia), Jennifer Tilly (Moyra), Illeana Douglas (Teresa Scorpio), James Marsden (Luka

Luciano), Gina Philips (Rosa), Richard Portnow (Tony Moreno), Franco Nero (Mario Domino), Peter Bogdanovich (Vito Gianomo), Carmen Argenziano (Castellano), Michael Hayden (Michael Luciano), Michael Raynor (Nickie Diamond), Dimitra Arliss (Anna-Maria Scorpio), Tony Lo Bianco (Paul Carolla).

From the Earth to the Moon (HBO, 1998)

Length: 12 hours
Number of Episodes: 12
Imagine Entertainment, Clavius Base
Executive Producer: Tom Hanks
Producers: Ron Howard, Brian Grazer, Michael Bostick
Directors: David Carson, Sally Field, Gary Fleder, David Frankel, Tom Hanks, Frank Marshall, Jonathan Mostow, Jon Turteltaub, Graham Yost, Lili Fini Zanuck
Teleplaywriters: Remi Aubuchon, Amy Banker, Erik Bork, Jeff Fishkin, Tom Hanks, Karen Janszen, Steven Katz, Peter Osterland, Al Reinert, Andy Wolk, Graham Yost
Composers: Jeff Beal, Mason Daring, Brad Fiedel, James Newton Howard, Mark Isham, Michael Kamen, Mark Mancina, Marn Shaiman
Production Designer: Richard Toyon
Costume Designer: Chrisi Karvonides Dushenko
Editors: Eric Bork, Lisa Churgin, Laurie Grotstein, Richard Pearson, Christopher Rouse, Wendy Smith
Photographer: Gale Tattersall
Cast: Tom Amandes (Astronaut Harrison "Jack" Schmitt), David Andrews (Astronaut Frank Borman), Adam Baldwin (Astronaut Fred Haise), Robert John Burke (Astronaut William "Bill" Anders), Gary Cole (Astronaut Edgar Mitchell), Bryan Cranston (Astronaut Buzz Aldrin), Brett Cullen (Astronaut Dave Scott), Tim Daly (Astronaut James Lovell), J. Downing (Astronaut Charles Duke), Cary Elwes (Astronaut Michael Collins), Dave Foley (Astronaut Alan Bean), Tony Goldwyn (Astronaut Neil Armstrong), Mark Harmon (Astronaut Walter Schirra), Steve Hofvendahl (Astronaut Tom Stafford), Chris Isaak (Astronaut Edward White II), Zeljko Ivanek (Astronaut Ken Mattingly), Daniel Hugh Kelly (Astronaut Eugene Cernan), Fredric Lehne (Astronaut Walt Cunningham), Ted Levine (Astronaut Alan Shepard) Ben Marley (Astronaut Roger Chaffee), Paul McCrane (Astronaut Pete Conrad), John Mese (Astronaut Don Eisele), Kieran Mulroney (Astronaut Rusty Schweickart), George Newbern (Astronaut Stu Rooso), John Posey (Astronaut John Young), Michael Raynor (Astronaut Alan Worden), Mark Rolston (Astronaut Gus Grissom), Peter Scolari (Astronaut Pete Conrad), Nick Searcy (Astronaut Donald "Deke" Slayton), Robert C. Treveiler (Astronaut Gordon Cooper), Tom Verica (Astronaut Dick Gordon), Gareth Williams (Astronaut James Irwin), Steve Zahn (Astronaut Elliott See), Krista Adair (Jo Schirra), Jo Anderson (Pat White), Katie Austin (Susan Lovell), Wendy Crewson (Faye Stafford), Ann Cusack (Jan Armstong), Sally Field (Trudy Cooper), Joanna Garcia (Julie Shepard), Rhoda Griffis (Martha Chafee), Gwen Hollander (Laura Shepard), Kristie Horton (Barbara Lovell), Elizabeth Morehead (Tracy Cerman), Deirdre O'Connell (Barbara Young), Elizabeth Perkins (Marilyn Lovell), Ruth Reid (Betty Grissom), Debra Jo Rupp (Marilyn See), Mikki Scanlon (Pat Collins), Diana Scarwid (Joan Aldrin), Cynthia Stevenson (Jane Conrad), Lesa Thurman (Joan Rossa), Jo Beth Williams (Marge Slayton), Rita Wilson (Susan Borman), Janis Benson (Margaret Chase Smith), Peter Horton (Frank Burns), Ann Magnuson (Nurse Dee O'Hara), Doug McKeon (Joe Allen), Jay Mohr (Brett Hutchins), Kevin Pollak (Apollo Program Manager Joe Shea), John Slattery (Walter Mondale), Lane Smith (Emmett Seaborn),

Tchéky Karyo (George Melies), Tom Hanks (Jean-Luc Despont).

Joan of Arc (CBS, 1999)

Length: 4 hours
Number of Episodes: 2
Alliance Atlantis Communications
Executive Producers: Ed Gernon, Peter Sussman, Graham Flashner
Producer: Peter Bray
Director: Christian Duguay
Teleplaywriters: Ronald Parker, Michael Miller
Composer: Asher Ettinger
Production Designer: Michael Joy
Costume Designer: John Hay
Editor: Ralph Brunjes
Photographer: Pierre Gill
Cast: Leelee Sobieski (Joan D'Arc), Jacqueline Bisset (Isabelle D'Arc), Powers Boothe (Jacques D'Arc), Maury Chaykin (Robert de Baudricourt), Olympia Dukakis (Mother Babette), Neil Patrick Harris (King Charles), Jonathan Hyde (Duke of Bedford), Robert Loggia (Father Monet), Cliff Saunders (Bertrand de Poligny), Maximilian Schell (Brother John LaMaire), Peter Strauss (La Hire), Jaimz Woolvett (Philip, Duke of Burgundy), Peter O'Toole (Bishop Cauchon), Shirley MacLaine (Madame de Beaurevoir), Ted Atherton (Jean D'Estivet), Chandra Engstrom (Young Joan).

Cleopatra (ABC, 1999)

Length: 4 hours
Number of Episodes: 2
Hallmark Entertainment, Babelsberg International Film Producktion
Executive Producers: Robert Halmi, Robert Halmi Jr.
Producer: Dyson Lovell
Director: Franc Roddam
Teleplaywriters: Stephen Harrigan, Anton Diether (from the novel *Memoirs of Cleopatra* by Margaret George)
Composer: Trevor Jones
Production Designer: Martin Hitchcock
Costume Designer: Enrico Sabbatini
Editor: Peter Coulson
Photographer: David Connell
Cast: Billy Zane (Marc Antony), Timothy Dalton (Julius Caesar), Leonor Varela (Cleopatra), Rupert Graves (Octavian), Indra Ové (Charmain), Josephine Amankwah (Iris), Nadim Sawalha (Mardian), Art Malik (Olympus), John Bowe (Rufio), Sean Pertwee (Marcus Brutus), David Schofield (Casca), Bruce Payne (Cassius), Elizabeth Dermot Walsh (Octavia), Ashley Clark (King Ptolmey at 12), James Cosmo (Agrippa).

The 10th Kingdom (NBC, 2000)

Length: 10 hours
Number of Episodes: 5
Carnival Films, Production Line, Babelsberg International Film Producktion, Hallmark Entertainment
Executive Producers: Robert Halmi, Robert Halmi Jr.
Producers: Simon Moore, Brian Eastman, Jane Prowse
Directors: David Carson, Herbert Wise
Teleplaywriter: Simon Moore
Composer: Anne Dudley
Production Designers: Julian Fullalove, Rob Hinds
Costume Designer: Jill Taylor
Editors: Chris Wimble, Andrew McClelland
Photographers: Lawrence Jones, Chris Howard
Cast: John Larroquette (Tony Lewis), Kimberly Williams (Virginia Lewis), Scott Cohen (Wolf), Daniel Lapaine (Prince Wendell), Diane Wiest (The Evil Queen), Rutger Hauer (The Huntsman), Ed O'Neill (Relish the Troll King), Jeremiah Birkett (Blue Bell), Dawn Lewis (Blabberwort), Hugh O'Gorman (Burly), Camryn Manheim (Snow White), Ann-Margret (Cinderella), Timothy Bateson (The Tooth Fairy), Peter Vaughan (Wilfred Peep), Arthur Cox (The Mayor of Beantown),

James Cosmo (The Blind Woodsman), Lucy Punch (Sally Peep), Eve Pearce (The Gypsy Queen), Kim Thomson (Queen Riding Hood III), Chris Crooks (The King of the Elves).

Angels in America (HBO, 2003)

Length: 6 hours
Number of Episodes: 2
Avenue Pictures, HBO Pictures
Executive Producers: Cary Brokaw, Mike Nichols
Producer: Celia D. Costas
Director: Mike Nichols
Teleplaywriter: Tony Kushner (from his own play)
Composer: Thomas Newman
Production Designer: Stuart Wurtzel
Costume Designer: Ann Roth
Editor: John Bloom
Photographer: Stephen Goldblatt
Cast: Al Pacino (Roy Cohn), Meryl Streep (Rabbi Isidor Chemelwitz/Hannah Pitt/Ethel Rosenberg), Emma Thompson (The Angel of America/Nurse Emily/Mad Street Woman), Justin Kirk (Prior Walter/Leather Man in Central Park), Ben Shenkman (Louis Ironson), Jeffrey Wright (Belize/Mr. Lies), Patrick Wilson (Joe Pitt), Mary-Louise Parker (Harper Pitt), James Cromwell (Henry [Roy Cohn's patient Doctor]), Michael Gambon (Prior#1), Simon Callow (Prior#2).

Chapter Notes

Introduction

1. Margaret Montgomerie, "The Miniseries," in *Encyclopedia of Television*, ed. Horace Newcomb (Chicago: Chicago Dearborn Publishers, 1997), 1054.
2. For a discussion of the way in which classic myth functions in the biographical miniseries *Blonde* (CBS, 2001), based on the life of Marilyn Monroe, see John De Vito and Frank Tropea, *The Immortal Marilyn: The Depiction of an Icon* (Lanham, MD: Scarecrow Press, 2007), 68.
3. David Bianculli, *Dictionary of Teleliteracy: Television's 500 Biggest Hits, Misses and Events* (New York: Continuum, 1996), 364.
4. To our knowledge there has not yet been one book published devoted to a serious study of the development of the epic miniseries in America. The best materials we have been able to discover on this sadly neglected subject are the excellent chapters devoted to the epic miniseries *Holocaust* in two books: Jeffrey Shandler, *While America Watches: Televising the Holocaust* (New York: Oxford University Press, 1999), and Judith Doneson, *The Holocaust in American Film* (Philadelphia, PA: Jewish Publication Society, 2002).

Chapter 1

1. Robert Giddings and Keith Selby, *The Classic Serial on Television and Radio* (Houndsmills, Basingstroke, Hampshire, NY: Palgrave, 2001), 1.
2. Cited in Giddings and Selby, 11.
3. Giddings and Selby, 5.
4. Ian Watts, *The Rise of the Novel* (Berkeley: University of California Press, 1957), 44.
5. Glen Creeber, *Serial Television: Big Drama on the Small Screen* (London: British Film Institute, 2004), 19–20.
6. Jon Burlingame, *TV's Biggest Hits* (New York: Schirmer Books, 1996), 269.
7. Michael Shnayerson, *Irwin Shaw: A Life* (New York: G.P. Putnam's Sons, 1989), 334.
8. For a more detailed discussion of the ideological nature of melodrama, see Paul Willemen, "Distanciation and Douglas Sirk," *Screen* 12, no. 2 (Summer, 1971), 63–67; Geoffrey Nowell-Smith, "Minnelli and Melodrama," *Screen* 2, no. 28 (Summer, 1977), 113–118; and Jon Halliday, *Sirk on Sirk* (New York: Viking, 1972).
9. Shnayerson, 357.
10. See Thomas Elsaesser, "Tales of Sound and Fury: Observations on the Family Melodrama," *Monogram* 4 (1972), 2–15.
11. Glen Creeber, "The Miniseries," in *The Television Genre Book*, ed. Glen Creeber (London: British Film Institute, 2000), 38.
12. Camille Paglia, *Sexual Personae: Art and Decadence from Nefertiti to Emily Dickinson* (London, New Haven, CT: Yale University Press, 1990), 96–97.
13. C. Wright Mills, *The Power Elite* (New York: Oxford University Press, 1957), 4.
14. C. Wright Mills, *White Collar* (New York: Oxford University Press, 1951), XVI–XVII.
15. James R. Giles, *Irwin Shaw* (Boston: Twayne Publishers, 1983), 153.
16. Frederick R. Karl, *American Fictions: 1940–1980* (New York: Harper & Row Publishers, 1983), 302.
17. Giles, 168.
18. Shnayerson, 357.
19. See Alex North's liner notes to the 1976 *Rich Man, Poor Man* soundtrack LP, Varèse Sarabande, VSD-5423.
20. Donna McCrohan, *Prime Time, Our Time* (California: Prima Publishing & Communications, 1990), 245–246.
21. Bianculli, 262.

Chapter 2

1. Henry Bail, *Acting Jewish: Negotiating Ethnicity on the American Stage & Screen* (Ann Arbor: University of Michigan Press, 2005), 57.
2. Donald Bogle, *Primetime Blues: African Americans on Network Television* (New York: Farrar, Straus, Giroux, 2002), 243.
3. Many of the more commonly cited flaws are discussed by both Bogle and Glen Creeber, *Serial Television: Big Drama on the Small Screen* (London: British Films Institute, 2004).

4. McCrohan, 246.
5. Robert Milton Miller, *Star Myths* (Metuchen, NJ, & London: Scarecrow Press, 1983), lx.
6. Paglia, 2.
7. David L. Wolper and Quincy Troupe, *The Inside Story of TV's Roots* (New York: Warner Books, 1978), 252.
8. Wolper and Troupe, 102.
9. The sense of both thematic and narrative closure would come at a later point, however, first with the television broadcasts of the epic miniseries sequel *Roots: The Next Generations* (ABC, 1979), and next with *Queen* (CBS, 1993), starring the stunning Halle Berry as Alex Haley's remarkable paternal grandmother.
10. Sally Bedell, *Up the Tube: Primetime TV and the Silverman Years* (New York: The Viking Press, 1981), 170.
11. *Roots* went on to win an unprecedented thirty-seven Emmy Award nominations (still a record). Besides being chosen the Outstanding Dramatic Series of the 1976–77 television season, *Roots* also won Emmys for Lou Gossett Jr. (Best Actor), Edward Asner (Best Supporting Actor), Olivia Cole (Best Supporting Actress), David Green (Best Direction), Ernest Kinoy and William Blinn (Best Writing), Ned Travis (Best Editing), Quincy Jones and Gerald Fried (Best Musical Score). Other actors nominated include John Amos, LeVar Burton (in his dramatic acting debut), Ben Vereen, Leslie Uggams, Madge Sinclair, Moses Gunn, Robert Reed, Ralph Waite, Sandy Duncan, and Cicely Tyson.
12. David L. Wolper (with David Fisher), *Producer* (New York: Scribner, 2003), 237.
13. Bedell, 172.
14. Jacob Neusner, *Stranger at Home: The Holocaust, Zionism, and American Judaism* (Chicago: University of Chicago Press, 1981), 89–90.
15. Jeffrey Shandler, *While America Watches: Televising the Holocaust* (New York, Oxford: Oxford University Press, 1999), 133.
16. Martin Esslin, *The Age of Television* (San Francisco: W.K. Freeman and Company, 1982), 53–54.
17. Cited in Judith E. Doneson, *The Holocaust in American Film* (Philadelphia, New York: The Jewish Society Press, 1987), 145.
18. Jennifer Ring, *The Political Consequences of Thinking: Gender and Judaism in the Work of Hannah Arendt* (New York: State University of New York Press, 1997), 45.
19. Shandler, 161.
20. Hannah Arendt, *Eichmann in Jerusalem: A Report on the Banality of Evil* (New York: Penguin, 1963).
21. Doneson, 157.
22. *Back to the Sources: Reading the Classic Jewish Texts*, ed. Barry Holtz (New York: Touchstone Books, Simon and Schuster, 1984), 63.
23. Shandler, 161–162.
24. Lawrence Langer, "The Americanization of the Holocaust on Stage and Screen," in *From Hester Street to Hollywood*, ed. Sarah Blocke Cohen (Bloomington: Indiana University Press, 1983), 213–230.
25. Doneson, 161.
26. This "over 50 percent of the television audience" figure translated into the quite impressive viewership of 120 million people in America alone, placing *Holocaust* within hailing distance of the blockbuster *Roots*.
27. Bedell, 173.

Chapter 3

1. Edward Wagenknecht, *The Movies in the Age of Innocence* (Norman: University of Oklahoma Press, 1962), 202.
2. Edward Said, *Orientalism* (New York: Vintage Books, 1994), 58.
3. Gina Macdonald, *James Clavell: A Critical Companion* (Westport, CT: Greenwood Press, 1996).
4. "Warning," reprinted in Harold C. Gardiner, "Follow-up on Waugh," *America* 74 (1946), 536.
5. Jacqueline McDonnell, *Evelyn Waugh* (New York: St. Martin's Press, 1988), 92.
6. Robert Murray Davis, *Brideshead Revisited: The Past Redeemed* (Boston: Twayne Publishers, 1990), 43.
7. It should be pointed out that the role of Father Ralph de Bricassart is beefed up considerably in the epic miniseries, doubtlessly to accommodate the star power of leading man Richard Chamberlain.
8. Sigmund Freud, "Some Physical Consequences of the Anatomical Distinction Between the Sexes," in *Sexuality and the Psychology of Love* (New York: Touchstone Books, 1997), 178.
9. Herbert Marcuse, quoted in Martin Jay, *The Dialectical Imagination: A History of the Frankfurt School and the Institute of Social Research* (Berkeley: University of California Press, 1973), 59.
10. In a very rare latter-day acting role, Barbara Stanwyck won both the Golden Globe and Emmy Award for Best Actress for her performance in *The Thorn Birds*.
11. Sigmund Freud, *The Standard Edition of the Complete Psychological Works of Sigmund Freud* (London: Hogarth Press, 1959), vol. 9, 236–241. In his insightful essay "Family Ro-

mances," Freud outlines a common fantasy of many children — that their "real" parents are not their "true" mother and father. Those parents (or parent) are more exalted and therefore more truly deserving of the child's love and affection. The actual source of the childhood fantasy can be complex and grows out of the child's awareness and comparison of other, more privileged families. It can also arise out of the child's anger with the parents for what are perceived to be wrongful slights, or divided or insufficient love and attention. Typically, these are explained and even revenged by the child's fantasy of belonging to another family.

12. Originally, *Lonesome Dove* was developed as a feature film entitled *The Streets of Laredo*, to be directed by Peter Bogdanovich, in the early 1970s. John Wayne (Call), James Stewart (Gus), and Henry Fonda (Jake) had all been cast to play the iconic leading roles. However, when the project fell apart in developmental Hollywood Hell, McMurtry decided to refashion his screenplay into an epic novel. The book would go on to become an international bestseller and win the Pulitzer Prize for Best Fiction of 1986 for McMurtry. James Kitses and Gregg Rickman, eds., *The Western Reader* (New York: Limelight Editions, 1998), 16.

13. James Kitses and Gregg Rickman, eds.; *The Western Reader* (New York: Limelight Edition, 1998), 16.

14. John M. Reilly, *Larry McMurtry: A Critical Companion* (Westport, CT: Greenwood Press, 2000), 109.

15. Burlingame, 286.

16. Had space permitted, we would have gone on to conduct close readings of some other epic miniseries of the 1980s such as *The Manions of America* (ABC, 1981), *Masada* (ABC, 1981), *The Blue and the Gray* (CBS, 1982), *George Washington* (CBS, 1984), *North and South* (ABC, 1985), or the messed-up but still powerful and affecting *Amerika* (ABC, 1987).

Chapter 4

1. Daniel "Dan" Curtis (1927–2006) won his greatest fame and acclaim as the producer/director of the long-running cult television soap opera *Dark Shadows* (ABC, 1966–71), which would go on to air continuously in syndication for well over thirty years. Curtis is also most closely connected to a series of increasingly macabre televisual texts, some of the most notable being: *The Night Stalker* (ABC, 1972), which inspired the later series *Kolchak: The Night Stalker* (ABC, 1974–75); *Dracula* (CBS, 1974); *Trilogy of Terror* (ABC, 1975); and *Intruders* (CBS, 1992). We see ample evidence of Curtis's attraction to darkness and the macabre in the chilling evocation of the many atrocities of the Nazi Holocaust in the epic narrative of *War and Remembrance*. Indeed, the case could easily be made that his depiction of the Nazis is infinitely more frightening than anything in his horror films.

2. Laurence W. Mazzeno, *Herman Wouk* (New York: Twayne Publishers, 1994), 77.

3. Pearl Bell, "Good-Bad and Bad-Bad," in *Commentary* 66 (December 1978), 71.

4. Ruth Crego Benson, *Women in Tolstoy: The Ideal and the Erotic* (Chicago: University of Illinois Press, 1973), IX.

5. Mazzeno, 98.

6. It is interesting to point out that, despite his intense longing for the highly desirable Pamela, Pug stoically resists temptation. He consummates their relationship only *after* Rhoda has agreed to divorce him.

7. Richard Chamberlain, *Shattered Love* (New York: Regan Books, 2003), 173.

8. John Simon, *Something to Declare* (New York: Clarkson N. Potter, Inc. 1983), 252.

9. Pauline Kael, *For Keeps* (New York: Dutton, 1994), 743–744.

10. In Chapter 5 we will take up the matter of how various Brechtian effects would be employed in several other epic miniseries of the 1980s.

11. Shot in ten countries over a two-year period, the commanding *War and Remembrance* remains the most expensive and grandest single-story undertaking ever to be attempted in the history of American television. At a cost of well over $100 million (estimates run as high as $130 million), the epic miniseries includes 360 individual speaking roles. Some epic scenes feature as many as 10,000 extras at a single time.

12. So affecting is this iconic scene, Steven Spielberg pays a special visual homage to it in his masterful *Schindler's List* (1993). When Oskar Schindler (Liam Neeson) is out horseback riding with one of his many mistresses, the couple stop on a hilltop to watch from a distance the savage Nazi roundup of the Krakow Jews. Schindler is especially moved by the fate of one beautiful little girl, whose bright red overcoat is the only hint of color in the otherwise gritty black-and-white mise-en-scène. Although the child initially seems to evade the murdering grasp of the Nazis, later Schindler sees her diminutive, red overcoat-clad corpse on a cart with so many others. Thus the overcoat connects the two images, as the flower does in *War and Remembrance*.

13. In *Televisuality: Style, Crisis, and Authority in American Television* (New Brunswick, NJ: Rutgers University Press, 1995), John Thornton Caldwell writes:

The high production values that pervade each of these event status program forms (such as epic miniseries like *Shogun*, *North and South*, *Peter the Great*, *Amerika*, *The Winds of War* and *War and Remembrance*)—a factor that inevitably places style center stage—also makes financial loss an ever-present possibility.... Economic clouds across network horizons had, by 1989, cast a long shadow on the programming value of epic television events. The trades headlined the fact that ABC lost well over $20 million on *War and Remembrance*.... Cap Cities boasted it would plug the "spend-spend-spend blackhole" of the former ABC Management. Cap Cities assured the press that another mega-miniseries on the scale of *War and Remembrance* is totally out of the question because it is too risky. According to the network, not only did the epic miniseries put the network on the verge of bankruptcy, it also completely missed the network's ideal viewing audience: "The over-forty-year-olds loved it, but nobody under forty watched it" [pp. 160–161].

14. Paglia, 61.
15. Identified with many of the greatest directors of the New German Cinema of the 1870s and 1980s, some of the films Dietrich Lohmann (1943–1997) shot during his lifetime include *The American Soldier* (1970), *Effie Brest* (1974), *Germany in Autumn* (1978, all directed by Rainer Werner Fassbinder), *The Serpent's Egg* (1978, Ingmar Bergman), *Confessions of Winifred Wagner* (1975), *Our Hitler* (1980, both directed by Hans-Jürgen Syberberg), and *The Lover* (1992, Jean-Jacques Annaud).
16. Walter Benjamin, *Illuminations: Essays and Reflections*, trans. Harry Zohn (New York: Schocher, 1969), 257–258.

Chapter 5

1. When *Scenes from a Marriage* was later blown up from its original 16mm format to 35mm for showing in cinemas in the United States, Sven Nykvist said that although he had shot it as an epic miniseries for television, with a preponderance of extensive close-ups and mostly claustral interior scenes, if he had known that *Scenes from a Marriage* would end up in cinemas, he would have used more tracking shots and "moved back more to give the compositions much more space...." Cited in "Sven Nykvist, ASC, Talks about filming Ingmar Bergman's '*The Magic Flute*,' *American Cinematographer*" (August 1975), 897.

2. John Simon, *Something to Declare* (New York: Clarkson N. Potter, Inc., 1983), 193.
3. Although the mythic type of the Whore (signified by Johan's unseen mistress Pamela) never does appear on screen (then again, neither do any of the other lovers or spouses of either Johan or Marianne, for that matter), Bergman uses her as the same type of absenting presence we saw with the unseen figure of Beryl in *Brideshead Revisited*. The very invisibility of each woman eventually affords her a very dominant "presence." It should also be pointed out, although Johan perceives of himself as the mythic type of the Adventurer, he, like Rudy in *Rich Man, Poor Man*, is much closer to the type of the Slave.
4. Liv Ullmann has remarked that for her, the experience of filming *Scenes from a Marriage* was like making a documentary:

> I felt very connected to the role. It is a moment of my life when I began to be directly concerned with the Woman's Movement and by my own need for freedom insofar as I am a woman. I have been completely supported by my roles and my work and I have never been permitted to really be myself. *Scenes from a Marriage* was a stage in my attaining that consciousness. There wasn't symbolism, strangeness, neurosis; everyone could relate to it; it was you and me, and in this event it was me.

Michel Ciment, "Jouer avec Bergman: Entretien ave Liv Ullmann," *Postif* 204 (March, 1978), 36.
5. Bergman creates a neat ironic contrast with Ibsen. Rather than having the exploited woman walk out the door, it is the exploiting man who leaves.
6. Marsha Kinder, review of *Scenes from a Marriage*, *Film Quarterly* (Winter 1974–75), 53.
7. The filming of *Berlin Alexanderplatz* took place at the Bavaria Ateler (the famous "Berlin" backlot), from July 1979 to April 1980.
8. Ayn Rand, *The Voice of Reason: Essays in Objectivist Thought* (New York: Meridian, 1990), 160.
9. The Catholic Church of Germany organized an extensive letter-writing campaign in newspapers against the controversial epic miniseries. The text read in part: "This broadcast performs a terrible mockery of the resurrection of Jesus Christ, blackens the religious feelings of Christians; it is blasphemous. The broadcast should be condemned and banished." Cited in Kristin Zerger "Die TV-Series *Berlin Alexanderplatz* von Rainer Werner Fassbinder," *Spiel* 1 (1983).

10. "I Am Biberkopf" was the memorable cover story headline for *Der Spiegel*, October 13, 1980.

11. Stephen Gilbert, *The Life and Work of Dennis Potter* (Woodstock, NY: The Overlook Press, 1998), 263.

12. Peter Stead, *Dennis Potter* (Wales: The Alden Press, 1993), 112.

13. Potter has described his condition in graphic detail:

> It was like one of the plagues of Egypt! With one hundred percent psoriasis, you lose control of your body temperature. You hallucinate ... and you're in danger of dying.... You can't find a point of normal skin. Your pores, your whole face, your eyelids, everything is caked and cracked and bleeding and oozing, to such a degree that without drugs you could not possibly survive. It was physically like a visitation, and it was a crisis point ... either you give in, or you survive and create something out of the bombsite which you've become.

Cited in Graham Fuller, ed., *Potter on Potter* (London: Faber and Faber, 1993), 12–13.

14. Horst De La Croix, Richard G. Tansey, and Diane Kirkpatrick, *Gardner's Art through the Ages Volume II: Renaissance and Modern Art* (New York: Harcourt Brace Jovanovich, 1991), 667.

15. John Addison composed six flavorful pastiche songs for the score of *Ellis Island* (with lyricists Douglas Brayfield and Fred Mustard Stewart): "Elsie" performed by Peter Reigert; "Raggedy, Ragtime Man," "Knock Knock New York" performed by Melba Moore; "Lucky Star," "Why Can't We Marry Now?," and "We're Already Falling in Love" performed by Ann Jillian.

16. In the 1990s, beginning with the excellent epic miniseries *Gulliver's Travels* (NBC, 1996), Hallmark Entertainment produced a series of sumptuous and popular epic miniseries of fantasy and myth. Among these texts are the masterpieces of high fantasy: *The Odyssey* (NBC, 1997); *Merlin* (NBC, 1998); the mostly uneven *Noah's Ark* (NBC, 1999); and the mysterious *Arabian Nights* (ABC, 2000). These led up to the highly imaginative, but regrettably grossly misunderstood and underappreciated, *The 10th Kingdom* (NBC, 2000), which we discuss in Chapter 7.

17. Susan Sontag, *Against Interpretation* (New York: Dell Publishing Co., 1966), 284.

18. John Leonard, *Smoke and Mirrors: Violence, Television, and Other American Cultures* (New York: The New York Press, 1997), 78.

19. Actually, Farrah Fawcett's performance as Diane Down in *Small Sacrifices* is only one in a long line of epic miniseries depicting the disturbing archetype of the Murderous Mother, which begins in the 1980s and continues well into the New Millennium. One of the very first and arguably still one of the very best of these is Jane Seymour's performance as the character of Cathy/Kate in *John Steinbeck's "East of Eden"* (ABC, 1981). While only a lovely young girl, with a heart of solid ice, Seymour's Cathy takes sadistic pleasure in causing an entranced male teacher's suicide. Then she promptly murders her parents (Vernon Weddle and Grace Zabriskie) and burns down her family home with their bodies inside. During the course of the eight-hour epic narrative, she gets down to seducing two brothers, Adam and Charles Trask (Timothy Bottoms and Bruce Boxleitner), and eventually beguiles Adam into marrying her (while still remaining in a 1980s triangular relationship with brother Charles, who knows her for what she really is). After finding out she's pregnant, she unsuccessfully attempts to abort, but eventually gives birth to fraternal twins—Carl and Aaron (Sam Bottoms, Hart Bochner)—both of whom she disowns at birth and soon abandons forever. After shooting Adam, Cathy transforms herself into sado-masochistic prostitute Kate, makes a lucrative living for herself turning tricks. She murders Faye (Anne Baxter), the good-hearted Madam of the brothel that employs her, and takes over the place as the new Madam. She later becomes a morphine addict and has contact with her sons. While the sensitive but doomed Aaron finds it difficult to live with the polarizations of the good and evil of his parents within him, the wilier Cal learns to subdue his mother's evil and hold onto his father's strength and goodness. As for Seymour's Kate, she remains the most bewitchingly seductive and fascinating type of the Murderous Mother of the Epic Miniseries. Some of the other riveting Murderous Mothers include: Dyan Cannon in *Master of the Game* (CBS, 1984); Stefanie Powers in *At Mother's Request* (CBS, 1987), and Lee Remick in *Nutcracker: Money, Madness & Murder* (NBC, 1987) (both actresses play the same treacherous Frances Shreuder); Kelly McGillis in *In the Best of Families: Marriage, Pride and Madness* (CBS, 1994); Laura Dern in *Ruby Ridge: An American Tragedy* (CBS, 1996); and Diane Wiest in *The 10th Kingdom* (NBC, 2000).

20. *Peter the Great* ranks high on the list of the most ambitious and expensive epic miniseries ever made. It was also the first epic miniseries to be filmed in the Soviet Union at a cost of over $35 million and under particularly arduous working conditions, the

frigid Russian winter hardly being the least of these.

21. John Simon, *Private Screenings* (New York: The Macmillian Company, 1967), 204–205.

Chapter 6

1. Robert Tam, *Reflexivity in Film and Literature: From Don Quixote to Jean-Luc Godard* (Baltimore, MD: Johns Hopkins University Press, 1989).

2. The 1990s produced a small but quite striking group of epic miniseries that recall something of the Minimalist approach Ingmar Bergman took in *Scenes from a Marriage*. The group includes *World War II: When Lions Roared* (NBC, 1994), *Stephen King's "The Shining"* (ABC, 1997), and *Intensity* (FOX, 1997). In each, sequential epic narrative line and characterization, as well as form and content, are manipulated and diminished. In the first, the whole of World War II is filtered totally through the distinctive personalities of the Big Three: FDR (John Lithgow), Churchill (Bob Hoskins), and Stalin (Michael Caine). While reaching toward the possibility of minimalist experience, the epic narrative still paradoxically touches upon epic absolutes and infinitudes. In the second and third miniseries, epic narrative is minimalized through the terror of a heroic female protagonist as she wages battle against a male antagonist in a world that makes distinctions between sanity and insanity suddenly seem meaningless. *The Shining* concerns a wife (Rebecca DeMornay) in a life-and-death struggle against her demon-possessed husband (Steven Weber) in an isolated resort hotel, while *Intensity* features a young woman (Molly Parker) rescuing a young girl from a psychotic killer (John C. McGinley).

3. Adele Getty, *Goddess: Mother of Living Nature* (New York: Thames and Hudson, 1990), 5.

4. For example, between 1980 and 1999, there were approximately 15 epic miniseries broadcast annually. This amounts to 150 epic miniseries for each decade, for a total of 300 over a 20-year span. Of this number, around 50, or roughly one-third, of those broadcast during the 1980s were constructed predominately around the figure of a dynamic female protagonist. However, an examination of the epic miniseries broadcast during the 1990s reveals that 80, or more than one-half, featured a strong female protagonist.

5. Paglia, 360.

6. Cited in Paglia, 360.

7. Paglia, 521.

8. Pauline Kael, *I Lost It at the Movies* (Boston: Little, Brown and Company, 1965), 91.

9. Camille Paglia, *Vamps and Tramps* (New York: Vintage Books, 1994), 131.

10. Ken Wlaschin, *The Illustrated Encyclopedia of the World's Great Movie Stars* (New York: Bonanza Books, 1979), 223.

11. There are re-creations in *Liz: The Elizabeth Taylor Story* of the films *National Velvet* (Clarence Brown, 1944), *A Place in the Sun*, *Giant* (George Stevens, 1951, 1956), *Cat on a Hot Tin Roof* (Richard Brooks, 1958), and *Who's Afraid of Virginia Woolf?* (Mike Nichols, 1966).

12. Besides the highly problematic character of Bobbi (Michael Caine) in *Dressed to Kill*, other troubling, negative depictions of transgendered and transvestite characters include the destructive Myra Breckenridge (Raquel Welch) in *Myra Breckenridge* (Michael Sarne, 1970) and the psychotic serial killer Buffalo Bill (Ted Levine) in *Silence of the Lambs* (Jonathan Demme, 1991).

13. Edwin F. Casebeer, "The Three Genres of *The Stand*," in *The Dark Descent: Essays Defining Stephen King's Horrorscope*, ed. Tony Magistrale (Westport, Connecticut: Greenwood Press, 19), 55.

14. Ruby Dee gives stunning performances in these films: *The Jackie Robinson Story* (Alfred E. Green, 1950); *St. Louis Blues* (Allen Reisner, 1958); *A Raisin in the Sun* (Donald Petrie, 1961); *The Incident* (Larry Peerce, 1967); *Do the Right Thing*, and *Jungle Fever* (Spike Lee, 1989, 1991); and in these television productions: *I Know Why the Caged Bird Sings* (CBS, 1979); *All God's Children* (ABC, 1980); *Long Day's Journey Into Night* (PBS, 1982); *Go Tell It on the Mountain* (PBS, 1985); *Having Our Say: The Delaney Sisters' First 100 Years* (CBS, 1999); and *Their Eyes Were Watching God* (ABC, 2005).

15. Ed Harris appears in the film versions of Stephen King's *Creepshow* (George Romero, 1982) and *Needful Things* (Fraser Heston, 1993). Kathy Bates is in *Misery* (Rob Reiner, 1990), for which she was awarded the Academy Award for Best Actress, and *Dolores Claiborne* (Taylor Hackford, 1995).

16. Stephen King, *Danse Macabre* (New York: Berkley, 1982), 400.

Chapter 7

1. Susan Sontag, "Fascinating Fascism," in *Under the Sign of Saturn* (New York: Vantage Books, 1981), 91.

2. Norman Mailer, *Of a Fire on the Moon*

(Boston: Little, Brown and Company, 1970), 39.

3. Tom Wolfe, *The Right Stuff* (New York: Farrar, Straus and Giroux, 1979), 154–55.

4. Some of the more negative aspects of this late 1990s development are discussed at the beginning of this chapter.

5. Kathleen O'Steen, "Moonstruck: With the help of HBO — and $65 million — Tom Hanks re-creates mankind's giant step," *Emmy* (April, 1998), 26–30. In this article, O'Steen details the way in which Hanks and his fellow producers, Ron Howard and Brian Grazer, viewed the epic narrative structure as being an eclectic hybrid told in an unconventional manner. This allowed the large cast of characters to move in and out of the storyline freely, and as needed.

6. O'Steen, 27. O'Steen also describes how the otherworldly mise-en-scène of the landing on the Moon was created: Much of the film work for *From the Earth to the Moon* occurred at the Disney–MGM Studios in Orlando, Florida, although extensive location work was also done at the Kennedy Space Center in Florida, Edwards Air Force Base in California, and in an airport hangar in Tustin, California (where the massive moonscape set was built).

7. Bruno Bettelheim, *The Uses of Enchantment: The Meaning and Importance of Fairytales* (New York: Vantage Books, 1976).

8. Much like the famous scene of Little Red Riding Hood unexpectedly finding the Big Bad Wolf in Grandmother's bed ("What big eyes you have," etc.), the character of Wolf in *The 10th Kingdom* plays the role of the aggressive male seducer in the scene. In his attempts to seduce the naïve and virginal Virginia, he exhibits what Bettelheim believes are "the selfish, asocial, violent, potentially destructive tendencies of the id," of which Wolf, in this context, is a signifier to the max.

9. Bettelheim, 171.

10. In the scene, composer Anne Dudley's music takes on the lovely, lyrical simplicity of a child's lullaby, as in a fairly complex example of intertextuality Snow White tells Virginia the story of her life. As she speaks, Snow White touches upon all of the famous highlights of her life, encompassing her real mother's untimely death and her father's remarriage to her cruel stepmother, the dreaded Evil Queen, who first orders her stepdaughter to be killed by the hunter, and later to be put to death by the poisoned apple.

11. Bettelheim, 206–207.

12. Laura Mulvey, "Visual Pleasure and Narrative Cinema," in *Visual and Other Pleasures* (London: Macmillan, 1989), 19.

13. David Savran, "Ambivalence, Utopia, and a Queer Sort of Materialism: How *Angels in America* Reconstructs the Nation," in *Approaching the Millennium: Essays on Angels*, ed. Deborah Geis and Steven Kruger (Ann Arbor: University of Michigan Press, 1997), 13.

14. Tony Kushner, *Angels in America: A Gay Fantasia on National Themes* (New York: Theatre Communications Group, 1985), 118.

15. John Lahr, "Angels on Broadway," *New York Theatre Critics Reviews* 54, 11 (1993): 208.

16. Although *Beauty and the Beast* was only his second feature film, Jean Cocteau approached the text with much assurance as a piece of visual poetry. After casting his handsome young lover Jean Marais in the role of the hideous Beast, he proceeded to infuse the film with a wide array of metaphors and Freudian-based images. The Beauty of Josette Day not only can walk through walls, she does so in a gliding, dancer-like manner; mirrors become liquid portals transporting the characters from place to place, and flames can flicker and extinguish almost as if with a mind of their own. And because it is impossible for Beauty to consummate her intensifying love for the Beast, Cocteau depicts her resorting to sensuously fondling the hard handles of large carving knives and candlestick holders, and traveling down long, darkened womb-like corridors as a means of revealing her deep, unconscious longings.

17. Unveiled in 1873, the monumental Bethesda Fountain commemorates the purifying of the New York City water supply. While the base of the Fountain was designed by Calvert Vaux, with detail work by Jacob Wrey Mould, it is the majestic Bethesda Angel (aka "The Angel of the Waters") that is the definitive crown jewel of the work. Derived from *The Bible*, the Angel was designed by sculptor Emma Stebbins, the first woman ever to receive a commission for a major work of art in New York City. The Bethesda Angel stands an impressive eight feet high. Constructed of gilded bronze, she carries a lily in her hand, symbolic of the purity with which she blesses the powerful healing waters flowing beneath her.

Bibliography

Arendt, Hannah. *Eichmann in Jerusalem: A Report on the Banality of Evil.* New York: Penguin, 1963.

Bail, Henry. *Acting Jewish: Negotiating Ethnicity on the American Stage & Screen.* Ann Arbor: University of Michigan Press, 2005.

Bedell, Sally. *Up the Tube: Primetime TV and the Silverman Years.* New York: The Viking Press, 1981.

Bell, Pearl. "The Good-Bad and Bad-Bad." *Commentary* 66 (December, 1978).

Benjamin, Walter. *Illuminations: Essays and Reflections.* Translated by Harry John. New York: Schofer, 1969.

Benson, Ruth Crego. *Women in Tolstoy: The Ideal and the Erotic.* Chicago: University of Illinois Press, 1973.

Bettelheim, Bruno. *The Uses of Enchantment: The Meaning and Importance of Fairytales.* New York: Vantage Books, 1976.

Bianculli, David. *Dictionary of Teleliteracy: Television's 500 Biggest, Hits, Misses and Events.* New York: Continuum, 1996.

Bogle, Donald. *Primetime Blues: African Americans on Network Television.* New York: Farrar, Straus, Giroux, 2002.

Burlingame, Jon. *TV's Biggest Hits.* New York: Schirmer Books, 1996.

Caldwell, John Thornton. *Televisuality: Style, Crisis, and Authority in American Television.* New Brunswick, New Jersey: Rutgers University Press, 1995.

Casebeer, Edwin F. "The Three Genres of *The Stand*." In *The Dark Descent: Essays Defining Stephen King's Horrorscope.* Westport, CT: Greenwood Press, 1992.

Chamberlain, Richard. *Shattered Love.* New York: Regan Books, 2003.

Ciment, Michel. "Jouer avec Bergman: Entretien ave Liv Ullmann." *Postif* 204 (March, 1978).

Creeber, Glen. "The Miniseries." In *The Television Genre Book.* Edited by Glen Creeber. London: British Film Institute, 2004.

_____. *Serial Television, Big Drama on the Small Screen.* London: British Film Institute, 2004.

Davis, Robert Murray. *Brideshead Revisited: The Past Redeemed.* Boston: Twayne Publishers, 1990.

De La Croix, Horst, Richard G. Tansey, and Diane Kirkpatrick. *Gardner's Art Through the Ages Volume II: Renaissance and Modern Art.* New York: Harcourt Brace Jovanich, 1991.

Doneson, Judith. *The Holocaust in American Film.* Philadelphia, PA: Jewish Publications Society, 2002.

Elsaesser, Thomas. "Tales of Sound and Fury: Observations on the Family Melodrama." *Monogram* 4 (1972).

Esslin, Martin. *The Age of Television.* San Francisco: W.H. Freeman and Company, 1982.

Fassbinder, Rainer Werner. "I Am Biberkopf." *Der Spiegel*, October 13, 1980.

Freud, Sigmund. "Family Romances." In *The Standard Edition of the Complete Psychological Works of Sigmund Freud.* London: Hogarth Press, 1959.

_____. "Some Physical Consequences of the Anatomical Distinctions Between the Sexes." In *Sexuality and the Psychology of Love.* New York: Touchstone Books, 1997.

Gardiner, Harold C. "Follow-up on Waugh." *America* 74 (1946).

Getty, Adele. *Goddess: Mother of Living Na-*

ture. New York: Thames and Hudson, 1990.

Giddings, Robert and Keith Selby. *The Classic Serial on Television and Radio.* Houndsmills, Basingstroke, Hampshire, New York: Palgrave, 2001.

Gilbert, Stephen. *The Life and Work of Dennis Potter.* Woodstock, NY: The Overlook Press, 1998.

Giles, James R. *Irwin Shaw.* Boston: Twayne Publishers, 1985.

Holtz, Barry. *Back to the Sources: Reading the Classic Jewish Texts.* Edited by Barry Holtz. New York: Touchstone Books, Simon and Schuster, 1984.

Kael, Pauline. *For Keeps.* New York: Dutton, 1994.

_____. *I Lost It at the Movies.* Boston: Little, Brown and Company, 1965.

Karl, Frederick Robert. *American Fictions, 1940–1980: A Comprehensive History and Critical Evaluation.* New York: Harper & Row Publishers, 1983.

Kinder, Marsha. "Review of *Scenes from a Marriage.*" *Film Quarterly* (Winter, 1974–1975).

King, Stephen. *Danse Macabre.* New York: Berkeley, 1992.

Kushner, Tony. *Angels in America: A Gay Fantasia on National Themes.* New York: Theatre Communication Group, 1995.

Lahr, John. "Angels on Broadway." *New York Theatre Curtis Reviews* 54, 11 (1993).

Langer, Lawrence. "The Americanization of the Holocaust on Stage and Screen." In *From Hester Street to Hollywood: The Jewish-American Stage and Screen.* Edited by Sarah Blacher Cohen. Bloomington: Indiana University Press, 1983.

Leonard, John. *Smoke and Mirrors: Violence, Television, and Other Cultures.* New York: The New York Press, 1997.

Macdonald, Gina. *James Clavell: A Critical Companion.* Westport, CT: Greenwood Press, 1996.

Mailer, Norman. *Of a Fire of the Moon.* Boston: Little Brown and Company, 1970.

Marcuse, Herbert. Quoted in Jay Martin. *The Dialectical Imagination: A History of the Frankfurt School and the Institute of Social Reach (1923–1950).* Berkeley: University of California Press, 1973.

Mazzeno, Laurence W. *Herman Wouk.* New York: Twayne Publishers, 1999.

McCrohan, Donna. *Prime Time, Our Time: America's Life and Times Through the Prism of Television.* California: Prima & Communications, 1990.

McDonnell, Jacqueline. *Evelyn Waugh.* New York: St. Martin's Press, 1988.

Miller, Robert Milton. *Star Myths: Show Business Biographies on Film.* Metuchen, New Jersey, & London: The Scarecrow Press, 1983.

Mills, C. Wright. *The Power Elite.* New York: Oxford University Press, 1957.

_____. *White Collar.* New York: Oxford University Press, 1951.

Montgomery, Margaret. "The Miniseries." In *Encyclopedia of Television.* Edited by Horace Newcomb. Chicago: Chicago Dearborn Publishers, 1997.

Mulvey, Laura. *Visual and Other Pleasures.* Bloomington: Indiana University Press, 1989.

Neusner, Jacob. *Stranger at Home: The Holocaust, Zionism, and American Judaism.* Chicago: University of Chicago Press, 1981

North, Alex. *Rich Man, Poor Man.* Soundtrack. Varèse Sarabande, VSD-249.

Nowell-Smith, Geoffrey. "Minnelli and Melodrama." *Screen* 2, no. 28 (Summer, 1977).

Nykvist, Sven. "Sven Nykvist, ASC, Talks About filming Ingmar Bergman's *The Magic Flute.*" *American Cinematographer* (August, 1975).

O'Steen, Kathleen. "Moonstruck: With the help of HBO — and $65 million — Tom Hanks re-creates mankind's giant step." *Emmy* (April, 1998).

Paglia, Camille. *Sexual Personae: Art and Decadence from Nefertiti to Emily Dickinson.* London, New Haven: Yale University Press, 1990.

_____. *Vamps and Tramps.* New York: Vantage Books, 1994.

Rand, Ayn. *The Voice of Reason: Essays in*

Objectivist Thought. New York: Meridian, 1990.
Reilly, John M. *Larry McMurtry: A Critical Companion*. Westport, CT: Greenwood Press, 2000.
Ring, Jennifer. *The Political Consequences of Thinking: Gender and Judaism in the Work of Hannah Arendt*. New York: State University of New York Press, 1997.
Said, Edward. *Orientalism*. New York: Vantage Books, 1994.
Savran, David, "Ambivalence, Utopia, and a Queer Sort of Materialism: How *Angels in America* Reconstructs the Nation." In *Approaching the Millennium: Essays on Angels*. Edited by Deborah Geis and Steven Kruger. Ann Arbor: University of Michigan Press, 1997.
Shandler, Jeffrey. *While America Watches: Televising the Holocaust*. New York: Oxford University Press, 1999.
Shnayerson, Michael. *Irwin Shaw: A Life*. New York: G.P. Putnam's Sons, 1989.
Simon, John. *Private Screenings*. New York: The Macmillan Company, 1967.
_____. *Something to Declare*. New York: Clarkson N. Potter, Inc., 1983.
Sontag, Susan. *Against Interpretation*. New York: Dell Publishing Co., 1966.
_____. *Under the Sign of Saturn*. New York: Vantage Books, 1991.
Stead, Peter. *Dennis Potter*. Wales: The Alden Press, 1993.
Tam, Robert. *Reflexivity in Film and Literature: From Don Quixote to Jean-Luc Godard*. Baltimore, MD: Johns Hopkins University Press. 1989.
Wagenknecht, Edward. *The Movies in the Age of Innocence*. Norman: University of Oklahoma Press, 1962.
Walschin, Ken. The *Illustrated Encyclopedia of the World's Great Movie Stars*. New York: Bonanza Books, 1979.
Watt, Ian. *The Rise of the Novel: Studies in Defoe, Richardson and Fielding*. Berkeley: University of California, 1957.
Willemen, Paul. "Distanciation and Douglas Sirk." *Screen* 12, no. 2. (Summer, 1971).
Wolfe, Tom. *The Right Stuff*. New York: Farrar Strauss and Giroux, 1979.
Wolper, David L. *Producer*. New York: Lisa Drew Books, 2003.
Wolper, David L., and Quincy Troope. *The Inside Story of TV's Roots*. New York: Warner Book, 1978.

Index

Numbers in **_bold italics_** indicate pages with photographs.

Addison, John 203n
The Adventurer 3, 53, 55
Alice in Wonderland 120
Amos, John 3
Andrews, Anthony 61, ***64***
Angels in America 169–177
Ann-Margret 164, 167
Arendt, Hannah 46
Arthur, Karen 135
Asner, Edward 14, 28–29
The Avenging Angel 4–5, 112, 126,128–130

Bancroft, Anne 133
Bates, Kathy 152
Beauty and the Beast (Cocteau) 173, 205n
Bella Mafia 141
Benjamin, Walter 100
Bercovici, Eric 57
Bergen, Polly 82, 87–88
Bergman, Ingmar 102–107
Berlin Alexanderplatz 107–112
Berry, Halle 131, 200n
Bertinelli, Valerie 130
Bettelheim, Bruno 165–167, 205n
Blake, William 115
Blakely, Susan 14, ***26***, 28–29
Brecht, Bertolt (Brechtian disruptive effect) 57, 61, 93, 114, 118, 127–128
Brideshead Revisited 60–67
Brodkin, Herbert 44
Buffalo Girls 134–135
Burgon, Geoffrey 62, 66
Burton, LeVar ***31***, 35

Captains and the Kings 30, 40, 53–55
Cates, Phoebe ***121***
Chamberlain, Richard 55, ***58***, 59, 72, 89
Chomsky, Marvin J. 49–50
Christopher Columbus 124
Clavell, James 55, 57
Cleopatra 141–142
Cobert, Bob 89, 99–100
Collins, Joan 122
Correll, Charles 89
Curtis, Dan 81–82, 88, 90–92, 96–97, 201n

Darlings of the Gods 137–138
Davis, Ossie 41, 148
Dee, Ruby ***149***, 151–152, 204n
Delaney, Dana 135–136
Diana: Her True Story 138
Diller, Barry 12–13, 39, 41
Douglas, Illeana 141
Duality: Apollonian vs. Dionysian 19–22, 34, 76, 149–150; Black vs. White 34, 36; East vs. West 56, 58; Good vs. Evil 45–46, 148, 153; Jew vs. Nazi 45–48; Male vs. Female 110–111
Dukakis, Olympia 142, ***144***
Duke, Patty 55, 132–133
Duvall, Robert 73, ***74***

Ellis Island 118–119

Family Pictures 132–133
Fassbinder, Rainer Werner 107–109, 111–113
Fawcett, Farrah 122–123
Fenn, Sherilyn ***140***, 141
Fresno 123
Freud, Sigmund 68, 71, 115, 200–201n

Gambon, Michael 113–114, ***115***, 169
Gazzara, Ben 12
Gielgud, Sir John 61, 90–91, 99–100
Gish, Annabeth 135–136
Goldblatt, Stephen 171–172
Goldsmith, Jerry 13
Gould, Martin 49

Haley, Alex 31–32, 131–132
Hanks, Tom 157, 160–161
Hannon, Frances 116
Harris, Ed 152
Heine, Heinrich 93–94
Heroic Slave 23, 34–35
Hitchcock, Alfred 89, 146–147
Hobbes, Thomas 34
Hollywood Wives 122
Holocaust 42–52
Hopkins, Anthony 34
Huston, Anjelica 75, 77, 132–133, ***134***, 135

Index

Imi, Tony 132
In a Child's Name 131
Inglis, Jack 9
Irons, Jeremy 60, **64**

Jarre, Maurice 58–59
Joan of Arc 141–142
Jolie, Angelina 135–136
Jones, Quincy 36–37
Jones, Tommy Lee 73, **74**
Jordan, Richard 54

The Kennedys of Massachusetts 130–131
Kensit, Patsy 138–139
King 41–42
King, Stephen 152–153
Kinski, Nastassja 141
Kirk, Justin 169, 176

Lace 120–122
Lamprecht, Günter 108–109, **111**
Lane, Diane 74, 133
Lazar, Irving "Swifty" 13–14, 17
Lindsay-Hogg, Michael 62
Linney, Laura 142
Liz: The Elizabeth Taylor Story 139–141
Lloyd, Walt 146
Locke, John 33–34
Lohmann, Dietrich 97–98, 100, 202n
Lonesome Dove 73–80
Long, Shelley 136
Loren, Sophia 119
Love Betrayal: The Mia Farrow Story 138–139
Lowe, Rob 148, **149**

Mackie, Bob 123, 143
Mailer, Norman 157, 161
Mancini, Henry 70, 72
Manheim, Camryn 164–167
Mann, Abby 41–42
Marco, Polo 124
Marcuse, Herbert 69, 72
Mario Puzo's "The Fortunate Pilgrim" 119
Martin, Mel 137
A Matter of Justice 132–133
Mifune, Toshirô 56, 59
Miller, Nolan 122
Mills, C. Wright 21
Mitchum, Robert 82, **85**
The Moon 158–159
Moriarty, Michael 43, 46–47
Mortimer, John 61
Mulvey, Laura 167–168

Newman, Thomas 173–174, 176
Nichols, Mike 169, 171

Nolte, Nick 14, **20**, 28–29
North, Alex 28–29
Nykvist, Sven 104–107, 202n

The Oldest Living Confederate Widow Explains All 133
Onassis: The Richest Man in the World 119
Ormond, Julia 136–137
O'Toole, Annette 130

Pacino, Al 169–171, 175
Paglia, Camille 20
Pei, Edward 152–153
Persona 147
Peter the Great 124–125
Poledouris, Basil 79
Potter, Dennis 112–114, 203n
Prisoner of Zenda 9–10

QB VII 12–13
Queen 131–132

Rand, Ayn 111
Redgrave, Vanessa 125, 136, 141
Reid, Alastair 146
Rich Man, Poor Man 13–29
Riesner, Dean 16, 24
Roots 31–40, 132
Rosenthal, Laurence 125
Rousseau, Jean-Jacques 33–34

Sade, Marquise de 111–112
Said, Edward 56–58
Scenes from a Marriage 102–107
Schell, Maximilian 125
Schwarzenberger, Xaver 108–109
Schygulla, Hanna 108, 125
Scott Thomas, Serena 138
Seymour, Jane 90–91, **95**, 98, 100–101, 119, 203n
Shaw, Irwin 12–13, 17
Shimada, Yoko 56, 59
Shogun 55–60
Silverman, Fred 40
The Singing Detective 112–117
Sins 122
Small Sacrifices 122–123
Sobieski, Leelee 141
Sontag, Susan 120, 155
Stager, Martin 12–13, 39, 41
The Stand 147–153
Stanwyck, Barbara 67, 69
Storaro, Vittorio 125
Strauss, Peter 14, **26**, 28–29
Streep, Meryl 44, **46**, 169–170, 175–176
Sturridge, Charles 62
Sukowa, Barbara 108, **110**

Suspicion (Hitchcock) 147
Suzman, Janet 113, 115–116

Tales of the City 142–147
The 10th Kingdom 69–73
Thompson, Emma 169, *172*, 175–176
The Thorn Birds 67–73
Tilley, Jennifer 141
Tolstoy, Leo (*War and Peace*) 82, 88, 92
Topol 82, 85
True Women 135–136
Tyson, Cicely 31, *41*, 42

Uggams, Leslie 32
Ullmann, Liv 103, 105–106, 202n

Varela, Lenor 141
Vereen, Ben 32
Vertigo (Hitchcock) 89, 196–197
Visions of Eden (Edenic Visions) 22–23, 33–34, 50–51, 72

Walden, W.G. Snuffy 153
Ward, Rachel 67, *70*, 72
Watt, Ian 10–11
Westbury, Ken 116–117
Whalley, Joanne 113–114, *115*, 116
The Whore 3–4, 23, 35–36, 77, 130
Wiest, Diane 163, 167
The Wife 3–4, 23–24, 77
Wilson, Rita 156, 160
Winfield, Paul *41*, 42
Wolfe, Tom 157, 160
Wolper, David L. 40
Wouk, Herman 81–83
Wright, Jeffrey 169, 175

Young Catherine 136–137

Zastupnevich, Paul 120

www.ingramcontent.com/pod-product-compliance
Ingram Content Group UK Ltd.
Pitfield, Milton Keynes, MK11 3LW, UK
UKHW041959140426
5217IPUK00015B/882